CLASS, NATION & SOCIALISM

The Red Paper on Scotland 2014

Published by Glasgow Caledonian University Archives
Glasgow

First Published 2013

Edited by Pauline Bryan and Tommy Kane

British Library Cataloguing in Publication Data is available

ISBN 978-1-905-86668-7

Printed and bound in Great Britain by:
Clydeside Press, Glasgow

Typeset by Alan Mackinnon

Cover design by John Gahagan

Thanks to Carole McCallum, Glasgow Caledonian University Archives
and to John Foster who is the link between three volumes of The Red Paper on Scotland

www.redpapercollective.net

CONTENTS

AUTHORS

Stephen Boyd is Scottish Trades Union Congress (STUC) Assistant Secretary with responsibility for economic and industrial policy. He is writing here in a personal capacity.

Pauline Bryan is Editor of The Citizen, journal of the Campaign for Socialism and is Convener of the Red Paper Collective. She contributed to The Red Paper on Scotland 2005 and Scotland's Road to Socialism: Time to Choose.

Katy Clark MP was elected as the Labour MP for North Ayrshire and Arran in 2005. Prior to that she worked as a solicitor in private practice and for the union UNISON. She is involved in a wide range of anti-austerity, equality and justice campaigns.

Chik Collins teaches and researches in the School of Social Sciences at the University of the West of Scotland. He has researched and written on urban policy and community development and also on the role of language in industrial and urban struggles. More recently, he has worked on the issue of Scotland's health outcomes.

David I. Conway is Senior Lecturer/Consultant in Dental Public Health, University of Glasgow/NHS National Services Scotland and Chair of Socialist Health Association in Scotland. His research interests focus on understanding and tackling health inequalities, cancer epidemiology and children's dental health. He is writing in a personal capacity.

Matthew Crighton is chair of Friends of the Earth Scotland and of Edinburgh World Justice Festival. In the past he has been on the Executive Committee of Scottish CND, in which capacity he set up Scotland for Peace. Professionally he works in economic development and is writing in a personal capacity.

Jackson Cullinane is Regional Political Officer, Unite Scotland. He is writing in a personal capacity.

Neil Findlay MSP is Labour MSP for the Lothians. He is a former bricklayer and school teacher; he is a member of the EIS and Unite unions. Elected to the Scottish Parliament in 2011 he served on West Lothian Council for nine years prior to entering Holyrood.

John Foster is Emeritus professor, social sciences, USW. He has contributed to the Red Papers of 1975 and 2005, is joint author of The UCS Work-In, Track Record, Paying for the Piper and the New Penguin History of Scotland.

Rozanne Foyer is Senior Regional Organiser for Unite the Union in Scotland and a Member of STUC General Council. She is writing in a personal capacity.

James Gillies graduated from Stirling University with Honours (first) in sociology and social policy and is currently doing postgraduate academic research in Housing Studies while completing a full-time internship with Dunedin Canmore Housing Association.

Lynn Henderson is Scottish Secretary and National Officer for Northern Ireland Public and Commercial Services Union. She has contributed to the Scottish Road to Socialism: Time to choose and has written for the Morning Star, Guardian Public Leaders Network, Scottish Left Review and The Citizen among other publications. She is writing in a personal capacity.

Dr Muir Houston is Lecturer, University of Glasgow. He is a sociologist by training and his current research includes widening participation, adult education and learning cities and regions. In addition, he has published on the relative salience of class and sectarianism on Clydeside in Victorian Britain.

Tommy Kane has researched and written extensively on the water industry in Scotland as part of PhD research. He was a Campaigner with the Global Campaigning Alliance, 'Reclaiming Public Water Network', is a member of the Red Paper Collective and currently works as Parliamentary Researcher in the Scottish Parliament for Neil Findlay MSP.

Richard Leonard is Political Officer, GMB Scotland. He is a contributor to Scotland's Road to Socialism: Time to Choose, Is There A Scottish Road to Socialism, The Red Paper on Scotland 2005 and Scotland's of the Future.

Kevin Lindsay is Scottish Secretary, ASLEF, the train drivers' union. He joined the railway in 1987 as a traction trainee and became a driver in 1990 before he then went on to become the Scottish Secretary of ASLEF in 2001. He is a lifelong trade unionist and Labour Party member.

Stephen Low is Policy Officer for UNISON Scotland. Before becoming a trade union Official he was a journalist reporting on politics for the BBC from Holyrood and Westminster.

Alan Mackinnon is a medical practitioner and a peace movement activist. He is a former chair of Scottish CND and editor of Nuclear Free Scotland. He contributed to Red Paper on Scotland 2005.

Vince Mills is Director of the Scottish Centre for Work-Based Learning at Glasgow Caledonian University and has responsibility for the Trade Union Research unit. He was editor of The Red Paper on Scotland 2005 and writes regularly for The Citizen, Labour Briefing and the Morning Star.

Dave Moxham is the Deputy General Secretary of the STUC and has responsibility, among other matters, for developing STUC's response to the independence debate. He is writing in a personal capacity.

Gordon Munro has been Councillor for Leith in Edinburgh since 2003. He is a member of trade union Unite and the Campaign for Socialism. He is currently Vice-Convenor of the Economy Committee of City of Edinburgh Council.

David Shaw works in the Scottish Labour Support Unit with portfolio responsibility for Education, Social Justice, and Environment and Rural Affairs. He is writing in a personal capacity and his chapter does not necessarily reflect the views of the Scottish Labour Party.

Eric Shaw is Senior lecturer, University of Stirling. He is author of The Labour Party since 1945; Losing Labour's Soul? New Labour and the Blair Government 1997-2007; The Strange Death of Labour Scotland (with Gerry Hassan) and other books on the Labour Party.

Stephen Smellie is Deputy Convenor for UNISON Scotland and South Lanarkshire Branch Secretary.

Dave Watson is Head of Bargaining and Campaigns at UNISON Scotland. He is a past Chair of the Scottish Labour Party and current member of the Scottish Executive Committee. He is Secretary of the Scottish Labour Trade Union Committee and Secretary of SHA Scotland. Contributor to The Red Paper on Scotland 2005.

FOREWORD
Owen Jones

For over 30 years, the left across Britain has been ridden with crisis. The social gains won by Scottish, English and Welsh workers have been eroded, reversed and stripped away by successive governments. The consensus established by the post-war Attlee administration - of state intervention in the economy, a universal welfare state, high taxes on the rich and strong trade unions - has long been smashed. The labour movement - uniting working people across our three nations - is considerably smaller and weaker than it was a generation ago.

Despite the fact that the Tories failed to win the last election, they have managed to hijack a financial crisis and turn it into a renewed opportunity to roll back the state. What should have been the death-knell of neo-liberalism has become its greatest opportunity yet: cuts beyond anything Thatcher could have dreamt of, the privatisation of the NHS, an onslaught against comprehensive education, further reversals of what limited rights working people have, and so on.

The consequences of both the economic crisis and its Tory hijack have been devastating for working people. We're going through the biggest squeeze in living standards on record. One of the only industries booming is food banks, which half a million workers now depend on in the seventh richest country on earth. Six-and-a-half million people are now looking for full-time work, and one in six workers claimed Jobseekers Allowance between 2010 and 2012. The next generation faces being poorer than the last for the first time since the Second World War.

And yet - despite a startling crisis with little precedent for most people alive in Britain - the left has yet to go on the offensive. It is true that the inspirational activists of UK Uncut have put tax avoidance back on the agenda, showing that protest works. The Occupy movement has reminded us who caused the crisis, and who is being made to pay for it. Trade unions have organised some of the biggest protests and strikes for generations. And yet the left remains in a defensive posture, struggling to carve out a coherent alternative to an economic disaster that is unfolding in the lives of millions of working people.

That's why this book is such an important contribution to renewing a crisis-ridden left. The outcome of the current debate in Scottish politics has clear ramifications in Britain and elsewhere. It was once the case that the majority of Scots voted Unionist, then the local variation of the Tory Party, as relatively recently as the mid-1950s. The decline of religious sectarianism and the hammering of working-class communities under Thatcherism were among factors that ensured that Scottish Toryism has been confined to fringe party status.

The return of a Tory Government with an aggressive right-wing agenda in London has boosted the idea among a large section of the Scottish left that independence is the only hope for a new progressive settlement in Scotland.

The original *Red Paper on Scotland* was written at a time when the left seemed to be on the ascent, but today's reactionary political climes make this book equally necessary. The political vacuum has been easily filled by a nationalism that apes the social democratic rhetoric abandoned by the Labour leadership north and south of the border. A Scottish left that can present a coherent, convincing case would be a boost for socialists in England and Wales, too.

Whatever the outcome of the referendum, building working-class unity is an essential precondition for any left advance, which is why research detailing the attitudes shared by Scottish and Northern English workers is so crucial. Making the case for a new class politics - taking into account the shift from an industrial to largely service sector working class - is the key task of the 21st-century left.

Scotland has proud traditions: The Red Clydeside; the Independent Labour Party's (ILP) leader James Maxton; Mary Barbour and other women who led the rent strikes; the Upper Clyde Shipbuilders Work-In; the Poll Tax struggle - here are historic examples that can inspire a rejuvenated Scottish left. A crisis of capitalism has been ably used to justify a renewed onslaught against social gains won through much struggle and sacrifice. It does not have to remain like this. The old New Labour dogmatists are ideologically bankrupt. By fleshing out a coherent alternative, by debating and discussing a strategy rooted in practice, the left can drive the tide of reaction back. I hope this book plays an important role in this mission.

INTRODUCTION
Pauline Bryan and Tommy Kane

The referendum in 2014 will be important for the whole of the UK and not just for Scotland. For the first time in nearly 100 years there is the potential for a significant shake-up of the Union of Great Britain and Northern Ireland. For socialists the constitutional debate provides an opportunity to raise fundamental questions about current political and economic conditions and go on to explore political alternatives which would be beneficial for people across Scotland and the rest of the UK. Beneficial, not for the wealthy, not for the bankers and hedge fund managers, not for the MPs in Westminster or Assembly Members and MSPs but for ordinary working people whose lives are so vulnerable to the vagaries of the market whether they live in Scotland, Wales, Northern Ireland or England.

The Red Paper argues that any constitutional change must be measured against its potential to challenge the power of capitalism and bring the economy under democratic control. The purpose of achieving democratic control would be to enable a variety of forms of public ownership in order to build a sustainable and secure economy and also to redistribute wealth from the rich to the rest of the population, and geographically from areas of greater wealth to areas of need.

This approach by no means precludes support for independence, but it does mean that we have to respond to the SNP's version of independence rather than the idealised version advocated by proponents of those on the left who support independence, such as the alliance that makes up Radical Independence. Some on the left who support independence believe that once it has been achieved it will allow 'normal' politics to resume and the real fight for the future character of Scotland will commence with new left party/parties having a major role in shaping the new Scotland.

If the SNP is successful in the referendum, it is likely that it will form the first Government within an independent Scottish Parliament and introduce a written constitution. A constitution is not a set of neutral rules and regulations, but serves to mould a state in a particular way. Whatever party drafts the constitution will get to put its stamp on the future development of the country and that will be hard to alter. Given recent declarations we must assume that an SNP-led constitution will include commitments to retaining the monarchy, remaining part of the European Union and NATO, being part of a sterling zone with the consequent restrictions on economic policy, and will have a plan for inward investment based on lower corporation tax and the continuation of restrictions on trade union rights.

The Red Paper Collective, when considering any alteration to the Constitutional Arrangements for Scotland, wants to include our fellow workers in the rest of the UK. How can we leave them out of the equation? Carwyn Jones, the Leader of the Welsh Labour Party, has called for a Constitutional Convention rather than a series of piecemeal changes. He favours a federal constitution and we believe that this would offer exciting possibilities for developing a progressive agenda. This book has been written to contribute to the debate not only in Scotland, but throughout the UK and the group behind this book, the Red Paper Collective, has consulted widely through meetings and seminars. It has invited others with ideas and expertise to join the quest for understanding where power really lies and how it can be put in the hands of working people. We conclude that the answer to the problems facing people in Scotland is not to be found in a flag, a border or even a list of powers in Edinburgh and London, it is what we intend to do with these powers and for what purpose.

Home Rule: class and nation

The views of those on the left who support independence are entirely understandable as an immediate response to the intensified neo-liberal assault by Cameron and Clegg. What is there to lose, they ask? Our argument is: a great deal. The only form of constitutional change offered in the referendum is not what was traditionally demanded by the Scottish trade union and labour movement. What is on offer in this referendum would break the class unity of working people across the nations of Britain without breaking the chains of economic control that bind them. And thereby it also threatens something scarcely less important: the progressive content of Scottish national consciousness. What made Keir Hardie, Jimmy Maxton, Willie Gallacher and Mick McGahey champions of a Home Rule Scottish Parliament was the belief that it strengthened the democratic power of working people against capitalist state power at the British level. For them a Home Rule Parliament would supplement the organisational strength of labour and therefore heighten class understanding both inside Scotland and across Britain. This Red Paper on Scotland unashamedly takes this class position.

We can trace the trade union and labour movements' involvement with Home Rule back to the formation of the Labour Party, the early years of the Scottish Trades Union

Congress (STUC), the first Labour Government of 1924 and the first Scottish Home Rule Bill. Although officially the Bill had Government support, no time was made available to enable its passage through Parliament. In 1927, the STUC maintained its support for Home Rule, but rejected a call to support independence, confirming that position in 1931 when it stated that the interests of people in Scotland and the rest of the UK were identical.[1]

In 1949 the Scottish Covenant, a break away from the SNP mobilised by John MacCormick, achieved a staggering 2 million signatures, nearly half the population. The Covenant read:

> We, the people of Scotland who subscribe to this Engagement, declare our belief that reform in the constitution of our country is necessary to secure good government in accordance with our Scottish traditions and to promote the spiritual and economic welfare of our nation. We affirm that the desire for such reform is both deep and widespread through the whole community, transcending all political differences and sectional interests, and we undertake to continue united in purpose for its achievement.
> With that end in view we solemnly enter into this Covenant whereby we pledge ourselves, in all loyalty to the Crown and within the framework of the United Kingdom, to do everything in our power to secure for Scotland a Parliament with adequate legislative authority in Scottish affairs.

The momentum of collecting signatures for the Covenant was not maintained and the Attlee Government and the Secretary of State for Scotland Arthur Woodburn chose to ignore it. Moreover, its support did not translate into support for the SNP, which lost votes in the 1950 election and that same year the STUC first weakened and then abandoned its Home Rule position and support for a Scottish Parliament.[2] The STUC General Council moved a motion entitled 'The Future of Scotland' stating that:

> The trade union movement is not insensitive to the influences created by the cultural heritage and deep-seated traditions of Scotland, but submits that economic security remains the primary factor for the Scottish people and this cannot be divorced from the economic prospects of the country as a whole. Scotland's economic prosperity, it should be obvious, is inseparable from that of England and Wales and it cannot be imagined as a self-supporting entity.

An amendment moved by the Miner's Union which tried to insert a commitment to a Scottish Parliament was defeated 243 votes to 78. Historian Tom Devine believes that 'Westminster had delivered to the Scots where it mattered most, in jobs, wages and welfare'.[3] This position was confirmed in 1955 and eventually adopted by the Labour Party in 1958. At that time the issue of Home Rule and independence ceased to be central to the Scottish labour movement. The continuation, regardless of Tory governments, of a centrally controlled economy, with nationalised industries operating across the whole of Britain brought a unity of purpose to trade unions in transport, mining, energy, steel, post office and telecommunications, health, shipbuilding, etc. with joint negotiation of wages and terms and conditions across the UK in these industries.

It was not until 1968, when a motion from the Scottish National Union of Miners supporting a Scottish Parliament was moved by Mick McGahey and adopted without a vote, that the STUC once again supported a Scottish Parliament and that has continued until this day. In moving the motion, Mick McGahey made a distinction between 'healthy nationalism' and chauvinism and went on to call for a federal arrangement within the UK. The Conference report of the STUC[4] reports him saying:

> It was said that a Scottish Parliament, with its forms and powers to be decided by the Scottish electorate, would mean separatism. His colleagues and he rejected out rightly the theory of separating Scotland from a United Kingdom, nor did they accept the theory of a classless Scotland at the present stage. They had more in common with the London dockers, the Durham miners and the Sheffield engineers than they ever had had with the barons and landlord traitors of that kind in Scotland.

By 1971 the Upper Clyde Shipbuilders (UCS) Work-In provoked a recognition that Scotland's economy was not within its control. The STUC convened a Scottish Assembly which adopted the war-time partnership model of involving churches and employers' organisations, which possibly reflected the degree of crisis that was felt. However, on this occasion Jimmy Jack, the General Secretary of the STUC, called for a Scottish Parliament and predicted that it would be 'a workers' Parliament'.[5]
Within a few years the Labour Government gave approval for a referendum on a Scottish Parliament in 1979 when a majority voted in favour, but it failed to meet the last-minute stipulation of a minimum of 40 per cent of the electorate voting yes. This led to the SNP withdrawing its support for the Labour Government in Westminster and the return of the Tories led by Margaret Thatcher.

The impact of Thatcherism created an impetus for a Scottish Parliament that proved unstoppable. The Scottish Constitutional Convention and the Claim of Right for Scotland, which had the support of the STUC and the Labour Party, provided that drive but also set the framework for a Scottish Parliament. When Labour under Blair and Brown was elected in 1997 the referendum for a Scottish Parliament was a priority. The referendum was not only successful in winning 74.3 per cent of the vote for a Scottish Parliament but also 63.5 per cent in support of tax varying powers.

The Red Paper - socialist thought since the 1970s

The three editions of The Red Paper on Scotland have provided a rich contribution to socialist thinking set, as they have been, against capitalist crises and debates over

Scotland's constitutional future. The first Red Paper was edited by a young Labour Party activist, then Student Rector of Edinburgh University, but eventual New Labour architect, Gordon Brown. As Vince Mills says in the second volume, the first Red Paper 'exudes confidence in the inevitability of socialism that is today almost shocking given the retreat that socialism has experienced and Brown's own determined role in forcing that retreat in the British Labour Party'.[6]

The first Red Paper on Scotland was published in the year following the two General Elections in 1974. There was a heightened political atmosphere, reinforced by the oil crisis and subsequent rationing of power to three days a week, the miners' strikes in 1972 and 1974 and the ground-breaking UCS Work-In. In Scotland there was a falling away of support for the Scottish Conservative Party which had peaked at 36 MPs in 1955, but had been reduced to 21 in the February 1974 election, and 16 in October 1974. The SNP on the other hand was making electoral inroads, gaining 7 MPs in February and then 11 in October 1974, giving them a pivotal role in the closely balanced House of Commons, which ended when, as noted earlier, they supported a vote of no confidence in the Labour Government in 1979.

Against the turmoil of the time, the first Red Paper provided clarity of purpose and socialist thought. So much so that in reading Gordon Brown's introduction it is hard to believe that this could be the same person whose first act as Chancellor of the Exchequer in 1997 was to let go the reins of control of the economy, by making the Bank of England independent. In 1975 he referred positively to Labour Party publications that 'propose how public control of banks, insurance and pensions companies, could have a two-sided effect; creating greater social justice in the social services and providing substantial resources for industrial investment. Such a policy could be enacted without compensation and would in itself constitute a major erosion of the power of the British upper class.'

Gordon Brown may now reject his analysis of 1975 but for the Red Paper of 2013 it still resonates and arguably is more relevant now than ever. Particularly, when he suggested:

> That the social and economic problems confronting Scotland arise not from national suppression nor from London mismanagement (although we have had our share of both) but from the uneven and uncontrolled development of capitalism and the failure of successive governments to challenge and transform it. Thus we cannot hope to resolve such problems merely by recovering a lost independence or through inserting another tier of government: what is required is planned control of our economy and transformation of democracy at all levels.

The second edition of The Red Paper on Scotland, produced eight years into the New Labour Government, had one primary objective: neo-liberalism. By then this right-wing dogma not only shaped the policies and politics of Chancellor Gordon Brown and the

UK Government but in contradiction to what pro-devolutionists had assumed, also the policies and politics of the Scottish Parliament. The Lab/Lib coalition in the Scottish Parliament was not the workers' Parliament as predicted by Jimmy Jack of the STUC in 1972.

This third Red Paper on Scotland continues these themes of analysis and commitment. The limitations of Scottish Labour, now in opposition, and the SNP, now in Government, are considered through a coherent review of the state of Scotland today, but this version too draws on the long tradition of struggle in Scotland for a better way. Most importantly it looks ahead across a wide range of issues and outlines how that better way can be achieved.

Scotland like the rest of the UK has suffered under the subservience to neo-liberal orthodoxy and the consequences of the latest crisis and failure of capitalism. Massive wage deflation, unemployment and its first cousin underemployment, welfare cuts, public service cuts, pension cuts and other factors cumulatively amount to an unprecedented attack on working people. All the while the rich and the super-rich see their wealth reach record levels.[7]

It is against this backdrop that the SNP has won two successive Scottish Elections; the first in 2007 as a minority Government and the second an unprecedented outright majority, which has enabled it to call a referendum on independence in September 2014. Hard-headed arguments are required to help inform the Scottish electorate prior to the referendum. The Red Paper Collective has sought to provide a socialist analysis of that debate, which moves away from the flag waving on both Yes and No sides. We have tried to scrutinise the material reality for Scottish and English, Welsh and Northern Irish workers of any constitutional change. This approach deliberately avoids both romantic nationalism and describing a socialist Scotland when no realistic road map exists for its implementation.

Conclusion

The Red Paper Collective believes that, while the constitutional debate has enabled discussion around the future vision for Scotland, it has also detracted from important struggles in the here and now. Impatience or sometimes despair at the lack of progress has led some on the left to see independence as the key to any progress. In so doing they mistake constitutional change for social change, projecting on to an independent Scotland radical scenarios more reflective of their own desires than political or economic realities.

The Red Paper Collective argues that whatever the ultimate solution for the UK, the answer to the real problems facing us all will not be found in constitutional change, but in political change. If we can find a constitutional solution that enhances our capacity to make that political change and that meets the majority demand for greater devolution, it will allow the energies and imagination of all those concerned with a progressive future for Scotland to be put to more effective use. We could then take on the task of turning back the tide of austerity and rebuild a base for socialism in Scotland, a base that has been eroded as much by the ideological lethargy and political self-satisfaction of Scotland's Labour leadership, as it has by the bullying and blandishments of international capital. In the words of the 1975 Red Paper:

> There are as many Scottish roads to Socialism as there are predictions of Britain's economic doom - but most of them demand three things: a coherent plan for an extension of democracy and control in society and industry which sees every reform as a means to creating a socialist society; a harnessing of the forces for industrial and community self-management within a political movement; and a massive programme of education by the labour movement as a whole.

Endnotes

1. Aitken K., The Bairns o' Adam: The Story of the STUC, Polygon, 1997.
2. See note 1
3. Devine T.M., The Scottish Nation 1700-2000, Allen Lane: The Penguin Press, 1999.
4. Glasgow Caledonian University Research Collections.
5. See note 1
6. Mills V. Ed, The Red Paper on Scotland Research Collections@Glasgow Caledonian University 2005.
7. Sunday Times Rich List April 2013.

Section 1 - The Economy
Introduction

John Foster and Richard Leonard

This section examines how to redevelop Scotland's economy in the interests of the great majority of its people – those who depend for their livelihoods on their productive skills and abilities and who want a Scotland that is more equal and environmentally sustainable.

It begins by reviewing what is wrong with Scotland's economy: the erosion of its productive base, its lack of long-term investment and the very real danger that within two decades its remaining areas of productive strength will have been lost. The second chapter looks at one of the causes: the dramatic shift in ownership away from Scotland. Key decisions are increasingly geared to profit targets enforced by externally-based investors and too often result in arbitrary run-down and closure.

This frames the section's key question. A generation ago the trade union and labour movement, when faced with similar closures, was still able to create alliances that turned the political tide in favour of state intervention and public ownership. Does the potential still exist for such alliances today – and is the objective of public sector involvement still feasible in a more globalised world?

Chapters 3 and 4 look at the political obstacles: the degree to which policy structures in Scotland are dominated by the neo-liberal assumptions of the banks and finance houses and how far globalization makes such assumptions inevitable. It is argued, on the contrary, that the social base for current policies is very narrow and the great majority of smaller businesses are both disadvantaged and could be won for alternative policies. It is also argued that elsewhere in the world, particularly where growth has been fastest, public sector involvement has been critical for economic development – not just in developing nations but in countries such as Germany and France. In smaller regional economies in particular co-operative forms of ownership have been notably effective in ensuring that control is locally rooted. The final chapter examines the growing evidence that greater social equality also promotes social efficiency and longer term prospects for economic development.

From this the following conclusions are drawn. The first is the importance of economic democracy and the development of public ownership at Scottish level. Especially for smaller economies public or co-operative ownership is critical for anchoring production. The ability to promote such ownership would therefore appear to be an essential future responsibility for a Scottish Parliament. Life sciences, food processing, creative industries, some aspects of renewables engineering and most public utilities are all areas where private capital has to some extent failed.

The second conclusion is about political agency. The review of experiences elsewhere underlines the importance of explicit mass support for any advance in public ownership. In current circumstances it would seem to be the trade union movement that has to bear the crucial responsibility for building such support and creating the wider alliances that will be necessary. The SNP is not likely to supply this. Its policy links are with those sectors of business that are integrated with finance capital at British level and its commitment to the EU would ensure that such pro-big business policies became constitutionally mandatory. But neither is the Labour Party – without the support of the trade union movement.

The third conclusion is about where and how such political pressure must be directed and the constitutional forms that best match these objectives. In light of current economic structures, these can be neither purely Scottish nor purely British. The key linkages between big business and political power operate at British level – on currency, credit, banking regulation and the allocation of public subsidy to the private sector. Ownership of productive resources is also primarily held at British level – as is, correspondingly, the extraction of wealth from labour. Political independence on SNP terms would change none of this.

What is required is therefore a two-part solution. Political mobilization has to be conceived and constructed at British level – not abstractly but from its regional and national components – and directed towards ending the policy grip of big business. At the same time the power to develop accountable and democratic ownership is one that can and must be exercised at national Scottish level. In order to salvage and develop the economy a Scottish Parliament needs, at minimum, powers to:

❑   Provide state aid to strategic and socially essential industries
❑   Develop various forms of public, democratic ownership
❑   Tax and borrow on a scale that matches these responsibilities.

These powers are, however, only conceivable within wider policy structures at British level that permit:

❑   Taxation that addresses the extreme concentration of wealth both geographically and socially
❑   Fiscal and monetary policies that promote sustainable development
❑   Labour market regulation that sustains purchasing power and enhances skills and trade union rights.

Winning these objectives would begin to lay the foundations for the political economy of social progress.

WHAT'S WRONG WITH SCOTLAND'S ECONOMY?

John Foster and Richard Leonard

In many ways Scotland's economic problems are exactly the same as those for the wider British economy. The manufacturing economy has shrunk disproportionately to less than 12 per cent of GDP. The level of research and development is extremely low - lower even than Britain's as a whole.[1] It also has a disproportionately big financial sector, mainly based in Edinburgh, and now shrinking.[2] Its service sector, though large and diverse, is also contracting. Key areas, such as retail trade and utilities, are mostly in external ownership. Its historically large public sector is facing a period of unprecedented retrenchment and thereby exercising a depressing effect on the wider economy, particularly on smaller firms in the service sector. Unemployment is currently slightly higher than the British level although it has not been consistently so. On the other hand, most measures for poverty and that for life expectancy have been consistently worse than the British average, probably reflecting the prevalence of long-term unemployment, low pay in work and casualised employment, coupled with a sense of hopelessness and powerlessness.[3]

There are two major differences between the Scottish and the wider British economies. One is the existence of the very large sector based on oil and gas extraction. The value of the oil and gas extracted was equal to around 20 per cent of Scotland's GDP in 2011/12 and its share of tax revenue, within Scottish waters, amounts to around 8 per cent.[4] The dominant companies are all externally owned and have a long history of using their control over the pace of extraction and exploration as a bargaining tool to win concessions from governments. The sector is now facing fairly rapid depletion and, even using new technologies and with further investment, output is scheduled to halve well before 2030.[5]

The other major difference is the scale of Scotland's economy. It is less than a tenth of the size of Britain's as a whole and for manufacturing and some services in particular scale is important. In creative industries, for instance, Scotland possesses significant assets but their marketing has been almost entirely dependent on externally controlled networks.[6] In manufacturing there are only five areas of significant concentration left: electronics and computing (half the size it was a decade ago), defence engineering (almost entirely dependent on MoD contracts), food and drink (principally whisky), life sciences and chemical sciences.

The Scottish Government and Scottish Enterprise sector profiles highlight two problems: one is external ownership and the other is the fragmentation of the internally owned sectors. Chemical sciences, though significant in size (and operating on feedstock from local oil and gas) is entirely externally owned with ten companies controlling 90 per cent of output. research and development (R&D) is located overseas and there are few sector-wide synergies.[7] The Life Sciences sector, on the other hand, has a significant local base and is largely spun out of Scotland's research universities with some public subsidy. Yet the local enterprises are small-scale, fragmented, challenged in terms of global markets and, once patents are developed, usually subject to external takeover. In 2009 the Scottish Government listed six companies with international potential. Already by 2011 two, Axis Shield and Pro-Strakan, had been bought up by US and Japanese multinationals.[8] In food and drink, the two areas with significant export presence are spirits and fish farming. Both are largely externally owned. The Scottish Government sector profile compares the rest of the food and drink sector unfavourably with Finland, Norway and Ireland in terms of fragmented ownership, low investment in R&D and lack of coherent marketing.[9]

It is true that Scotland retains some areas of advanced engineering expertise, such as the Wood Group and Weirs, though both are now moving out of Scottish hands.[10] Scotland still also possesses a handful of globally operating companies such as Stagecoach and First Group, though again ownership is mainly external and the level of technology low.[11] It is also true that there are potential areas of expansion for the future, particularly in the greening of the Scottish economy through the supply of renewable energy and the decommissioning of North Sea oil rigs. But neither seems likely to generate self-sustaining growth unless policies are changed. Despite Scotland's very ambitious renewable targets, the focus on wind turbines has already demonstrated the limits of the current policy framework. Renewable energy generation is largely in the hands of externally owned companies and almost all equipment is imported.[12]

At the British level, the past three decades have witnessed the end of indicative planning, the dismantling of almost all state enterprises, the privatisation of utilities and the outsourcing of many public services, the enforcement of EU no 'state aid' rules and the financialisation of ownership. These three decades have also witnessed unprecedented decline in Scotland's industrial economy with manufacturing employment plunging from 650,000 to 179,000 in 2012.[13] The same period has also seen a massive loss of ownership and control from within Scotland.

It should be stressed that such external ownership in itself is not necessarily a bad thing. It can bring new technologies and access to investment capital that might not otherwise be available. Yet this is not generally what has happened in Scotland over the past 30 years. In most cases it is existing companies that have been taken over by bigger companies based elsewhere. The loss of headquarters is often followed by the rundown of local R&D and marketing capacities and far too frequently by arbitrary plant closure. More insidiously, these decades have also seen many Scottish registered PLCs falling under the control of externally based investment banks and hedge funds with very short profit horizons and little inclination to finance long-term investment in new technologies.

Hence, without significant policy change, the outlook is not good. The post-2007 recession has resulted in an intensified concentration of industrial control on a world scale and, as will be demonstrated in the next chapter, this process has been particularly marked in Scotland. Most of Scotland's external markets appear to be entering a long-term stagnation and are unlikely to be able to offset the forces of internal economic contraction. If such contraction continues, significant areas within Scotland's productive economy seem set to pass a point of no return within 20 years.

Endnotes

1. In 2011, BERD expenditure was equivalent to 0.56 per cent of GDP in Scotland compared to 1.14 per cent of GDP in the UK. Germany's was 1.9 per cent. http://www.scotland.gov.uk/Topics/Statistics/Browse/Business/RD/BERDreport11.

2. Scottish Financial Executive website puts direct employment at 100,000-, including 13 per cent of all UK banking employment and 24 per cent of all insurance employment-, and income generated at £7 billion, about 7 per cent of GDP. Fraser of Allander Quarterly for November 2012 gives the decline in Finance and Insurance employment as 114,000 in 2005 to 89,000 in 2012.

3. In 2011 life expectancy for men in Scotland was 75.9 and in England 78.6: National Audit Office, Healthcare across the UK: A comparison of the NHS in England, Scotland, Wales and Northern Ireland, 2012. Gross median weekly earnings for a full-time employee in Scotland in 2011was £488 against a UK average of £500. At the end of 2011 30.4 per cent of UK employees were in either part-time or temporary employment (www.ons.gov.uk/ons/rel/lms/labour-market.../table-emp01.xls); the proportion in Scotland was slightly higher at 30.7 per cent and was also increasing more quickly: Fraser of Allander Quarterly November 2012. See also Steptoe, A (2005) How Stress Gets Under Your Skin, Glasgow Centre for Population Health Seminar Series 2.

4. UK government oil and gas tax revenue for 2010/11 was £8.8bn and for 2011/12 £11.2bn: the value of total oil and gas output around £38bn http://og.decc.gov.uk/assets/og/ep/taxation/4579-og-revenue-table.pdf; http://www.oilandgasuk.co.uk/cmsfiles/modules/publications/pdfs/EC030.pdf. Scotland's geographical share of output at 90 per cent would be £30bn; of tax revenue £10bn. The Scottish government statistics put GDP for 2011 at £124bn without Scotland's share of offshore economic activity and £145bn including it. http://www.scotland.gov.uk/Topics/Statistics/Browse/Economy.

5. Scottish Enterprise, Spends and Trends 2012-2016, 2012.

6. http://www.scotland.gov.uk/Resource/Doc/293235/0090515.pdf: section 2.2.

7.http://www.scottish-enterprise.com/~/media/SE/Resources/Documents/Sectors/Chemical%20sciences/chemical%20sciences%20scotland%20strategy%20formula%20success.pdf.

8. Scottish Government, Life Sciences Key Sector Report, November 2009 identified 620 organisations employing 31,500 people and, in 2006, contributing £1.3b GVA to the Scottish economy. It listed six

companies which in 2009 it believed had the potential to become 'major international companies'. The report mentions lack of critical mass and the shortage of long-term funding as continuing challenges.

9. Scottish Government, Food and Drink Key Sector Report, 2009.

10. The Wood Group 2011 Annual Report shows that the Wood family has significantly reduced its share of ownership- with BlackRock holding 16.9 per cent, Schroder 4.5 per cent and Legal and General 3.1 per cent; Weir Group has 20 investment companies together holding over 40 per cent of the shares - the top five, holding over 20 per cent, are all non-Scottish: Legal and General, Axa, Capital World, M&G and BlackRock (2012 Annual Report).

11. First Group has nine investment banks owning over 40 per cent of its shares (the top four with 20 per cent are Majedie, BlackRock, Capital Research and Lloyds). It is heavily in debt with loans of £1.9 billion on capitalised assets of £925m. Stagecoach has a smaller debt burden (£523m) and five investment companies holding 30 per cent of its shares (one is Scots, Standard Life, two US, one Dutch and one UK). Company Annual Reports for 2012.

12. This is examined further in Section 3 Chapter 3.

13. Scottish Corporate Statistics March 2012, http://www.scotland.gov.uk/Topics/Statistics/Browse/Business/Corporate/table3sic07. The Scottish Enterprise website gives a lower figure of 172,000 for manufacturing.

SECTION 1
Chapter 2

WHO OWNS AND CONTROLS SCOTLAND'S ECONOMY?

Richard Leonard

The last decade has seen a startling change in the ownership of the commanding heights of the Scottish economy. The Scottish Government's own corporate statistics chart this well. Nowhere is this shift in external ownership as pronounced as it is in the manufacturing base as measured by employment and turnover. Tables 1 to 3 present the evidence for manufacturing enterprises employing more than 250 people.[1]

Focusing on the ownership and control of these larger-scale enterprises across the economy is justified because, although they only constitute around 1.4 per cent of the total number of registered companies in Scotland, by 2012 they accounted for 50.5 per cent of all private sector employment and 63.5 per cent of all private sector turnover. Even this is an underestimate because turnover for the highly concentrated financial services sector in Scotland is not available on a comparable basis. There are 89,750 people working in financial, insurance and business services generating £17 billion gross value added. So as the figures in Tables 1 to 6 illustrate, there has been a significant denuding of Scottish ownership with over three-quarters (76 per cent) of the turnover of large-scale enterprises inside Scotland for the first time generated for corporations owned and controlled outside Scotland (Table 6) and as little as 14.5 per cent of turnover in larger manufacturing plants under Scottish ownership and control (Table 3).

That collapse in indigenous manufacturing is highlighted in Table 1 which while revealing a drop of 11 per cent in the number of overseas-owned large manufacturing enterprises over the last decade, it more tellingly shows a crash of 64 per cent in the number of rest of UK owned firms open in Scotland and a 65 per cent wipe out of Scottish-owned manufacturing firms in the Scottish economy. While Tables 2 and 3 show marginally less of a crash when measured by turnover and employment, they uncover a massive shift in Scotland's manufacturing base from Scottish and rest of UK ownership to overseas ownership. Even more striking is the shift across the whole economy to overseas ownership over the last ten years demonstrated in Tables 4, 5 and 6 which show that the share of large-scale enterprises in overseas ownership rose by 40 per cent, and the share when measured by employment and turnover rose by 42 and

TABLE 1. Manufacturing (employee size band 250+) [2]
Total no. of enterprises by country of ownership

	Scotland	UK (excluding Scotland)	Abroad	Total
2002	100	180	140	420
2012	55	65	125	245

TABLE 2. Manufacturing (employee size band 250+)
Percentage of employment by country of ownership

	Scotland	UK (excluding Scotland)	Abroad
2002	39.5%	30%	30.5%
2012	30%	22%	48%

TABLE 3. Manufacturing (employee size band 250+)
Percentage of turnover by country of ownership

	Scotland	UK (excluding Scotland)	Abroad
2002	29.5%	32%	38.5%
2012	14.5%	17%	68.5%

TABLE 4. All registered enterprises all sectors (employee size band 250+)
Total no. of enterprises by country of ownership

	Scotland	UK (excluding Scotland)	Abroad	Total
2002	465	1,315	515	2,295
2012	395	995	865	2,255*

*rounded up

45 per cent respectively. In extreme, were this speed of change to continue at this pace by the end of the next ten years, there would be virtually no large-scale firms left in Scottish ownership.

TABLE 5. All registered enterprises all sectors (employee size band 250+)
Percentage of employment by country of ownership

	Scotland	UK (excluding Scotland)	Abroad
2002	46%	38%	16%
2012	36%	36%	28%

TABLE 6. All registered enterprises all sectors (employee size band 250+)
Percentage of turnover by country of ownership

	Scotland	UK (excluding Scotland)	Abroad
2002	30.5%	43.5%	26%
2012	24%	29%	47%

The SNP, while appealing for political sovereignty, has presided in Government over an historic loss in economic sovereignty. There has been no industrial strategy and no serious challenge by either the SNP or the previous administration to this shift in ownership which, by any measure, be it turnover, employment, even the number of enterprises, is remarkable.

Nor is this all. A detailed analysis of the share-ownership of the biggest firms in the Scottish economy provides further evidence of this loss of economic sovereignty.

Each year the Scottish Business Insider publishes its listing of the Top 500 companies in Scotland. The ranking is based on a measure of annual turnover and pre-tax profit. In January 2013 the new listing showed a Top 20 dominated by wholly-owned subsidiaries of foreign multinationals and London Stock Exchange quoted corporations. As a result, even those companies, which on the face of it appear to be Scottish-owned institutions, turn out to be joint stock companies with little of their stock owned or controlled from Scotland.

Number one in the Insider's Top 20 currently is Standard Life, a financial services institution which was demutualised in 2006 and is now listed on the London Stock Exchange, with significant shareholdings by Jersey-registered but New-York-owned asset management company BlackRock, Merrill Lynch and the London-based and FTSE 100 member Legal & General group among others.

Table 7. Financial companies operating in Scotland 2012

	Scottish Companies (Scottish Partner or mutually owned)	Scottish Companies (substantial external institutional shareholders)	UK Holding Companies	The 'Big Two' 2010 British Govt	Overseas Holding Companies
Banks		Standard Life Bank	HSBC Bank RBOS/Lloyds TSB Barclays bank Tesco Retail Bank Scottish Widows bank Virgin Money Sainsbury's Bank	HBOS/Lloyds RBOS group Intelligent Finance	Clydesdale Bank National Australia Group Alliance & Leicester
Banking Services					Morgan Stanley State Street Bank J P Morgan Bank of New York
Insurance Companies			Norwich Union Co-operative Group Royal & Sun Alliance	Direct Line Ins Esure Clerical Medical HBOS/Lloyds	Axa Insurance Zurich Personal Insurance Allianz Cornhill Kwik Fit Insurance
Life Assurance		Standard Life	Scottish Widows Invest Prudential (Scottish Amic) Royal London Group		Aegon UK Abbey National Scotland
Fund Managers	Baillie Gifford & Co SVM Asset Management Martin Currie	Standard Life Investments Aberdeen Asset Management Alliance Trust Scottish Investment Trust Glasgow Investment Managers	Scottish Widows Investment Partnership	Adam & Co Investment Management	Aegon Asset Management Franklin Templeton First State Investment Managers BlackRock International Newton Investment Management Walter Scott & Partners Abbey National Asset Managers Artemis Unit Trust Managers ISIS Asset Management - F&C Britannic Asset Management

Number two, Total Upstream UK, is a wholly-owned subsidiary of the French transnational oil corporation. Scottish Widows in third place is a wholly-owned subsidiary of the Lloyds Banking group. The energy utility Scottish & Southern Energy (SSE) is fourth. Its constituent parts were in public ownership until 1991 and now it is London Stock Exchange listed and records substantial shareholdings by Los Angeles headquartered Capital Research & Management Company and the Legal and General Group Plc. Fifth placed Chevron is a wholly-owned US subsidiary operating in the North Sea. Others in the Insider's Top Ten, First Group, the Weir Group, Stagecoach and Aggreko, all list major institutional investors holding major share stakes like Prudential plc., Capital Research & Management, Legal and General and BlackRock.

Between ten and twenty in the Insider's ranking are overseas-owned North Sea oil and gas exploration corporations with headquarters in North America, the UAE and the Korean Republic as well as Scottish Water which is publicly owned and the Tesco Bank which is British owned. There are some Scottish family controlled firms: William Grant & Sons in sixteenth place and the John Wood Group in fifteenth place, but the latter is now listed on the London Stock Exchange and family influence is being diluted. Aberdeen Asset Management, which had as much as 25 per cent of its shares owned by the Credit Suisse Group in 2009, is still dependent on a 19 per cent shareholding in the hands of another overseas institution, Japan's largest bank Mitsubishi UFJ Trust & Banking, which began to acquire shares in the company in 2008.

Turning to the Scottish financial sector as a whole the same trends can be identified. Here, the increase in external control has been made far more dramatic by the collapse of the two leviathans of Scottish banking, the Royal Bank and the Bank of Scotland. The first is now under state ownership (although facing privatisation) and the second is controlled by Lloyds Bank, though again with a substantial measure of state oversight. Along with these banks went a swathe of subsidiary companies such as Adam and Co Investment Management, Intelligent Finance, Esure and Direct Line Insurance. As already noted, the demutualisation of Standard Life removed the last major Scottish assurance company (together with Standard Life Investments) from Scottish control. In fund management only three significant independent Scottish partnerships remain: Baillie Gifford, SVM and Martin Currie. All others, as listed in Table 7, are either entirely or mainly owned by financial institutions from outside Scotland. Even in the sphere of Scottish registered investment trusts, long a preserve of Scottish rentier capital, the dominant investors are also now mainly external.

It is appropriate to end this section with a brief case study of one of the consequences of external ownership: sudden and arbitrary plant closure. Halls of Broxburn provides one example of many. It closed its doors in early 2013. Established in the 1930s it was Broxburn's major employer. Its 1,700 workers produced meat products, principally sausages and haggis. The firm provided a market for dozens of farms in central Scotland and for the suppliers of packaging materials. It was bought in 2005 by the Dutch company Vion, one of the biggest European meat product producers. This ownership lasted only seven years.

In 2012, Vion announced its intention to re-organise its business to concentrate production in Germany and the Netherlands and its decision to close Broxburn. The Scottish Government set up a task force to find a buyer. Negotiations took place with a number of possible buyers, but none was successful. There were claims that Vion, as a major international supplier of pork products, did not want another producer to take over. One unsuccessful bidder threatened legal action. Eventually only the brand name was sold.

In January 2013, a Food Bank was set up in Broxburn to meet the needs of families struggling with debt and mortgage commitments. Over the previous months, as successive waves of workers were laid off, shops along the main street started to close. On 6 February 2013 the factory doors shut for the last time.

Unfortunately, this story has been repeated many times over. As we saw earlier, 185 of Scotland's larger manufacturing plants have been lost since 2002, well over a third of the total.

Endnotes

1. This builds on the research originally conducted in 2004/5 by Sandy Baird, Richard Leonard and John Foster and published in the Fraser of Allander Quarterly Economic Commentary November 2004 and Scottish Affairs, Winter 2006/7 and, with parallel statistics for 2010, in the Scottish Left Review, Issue 64, 2011.

2. 2012 figs are from Table 3: Number of registered enterprises and their total Scottish employment and turnover by sector and country of ownership March 2012 from www.scotland.gov.uk Businesses in Scotland website; 2002 figures are from Table 3: Number of registered enterprises and their total Scottish employment and turnover by sector and country of ownership November 2002 from Scottish Executive ONS 2003 now on www.scotland.gov.uk Businesses in Scotland website.

Chapter 3

ECONOMIC POLICY, CLASS ALLIANCES AND POLITICAL INFLUENCE IN SCOTLAND
John Foster

Forty years ago industrial closures were successfully resisted. In the most celebrated instance, when 8,000 shipbuilding workers occupied their yards on the Upper Clyde, Edward Heath's Conservative Government was compelled to reverse its plans and instead to embark on an active programme of regional investment. In achieving this result the Work-In itself was the crucial lever. But it was a lever that was deployed strategically. It was used by the stewards and the Scottish Trades Union Congress (STUC) to develop a broader alliance, principally with small and medium business, which broke the then dominant grip of the Conservative Party in Scottish politics. Its success depended in large measure on an understanding of the conflicts of interest that existed within Scottish capital.

The traditional industrial elite, and in this case specifically the Lithgows and Yarrows, wanted to reverse the post-war economic settlement, end state ownership of industry, abandon full employment and concentrate private production into a few dominant monopoly units. Small and medium manufacturers and suppliers, and even more local shopkeepers and traders, did not. They could see the consequences for their own businesses. The STUC and the wider trade union movement were able to mobilise sufficient support through convening its Public Inquiry, involving other sectors of business, and then the 1972 Scottish Assembly to win over local Chambers of Commerce, split the Scottish Conservative Party and force the Government into retreat. Within five years, the initial resistance of 1971 had translated itself into the full nationalisation of all shipbuilding and aerospace under a Labour Government.

This achievement, only 40 years ago, should remind us of the importance of understanding the changing structure of capital ownership and the conflicts of interest that result.

The Red Paper of 1975 used the research of John Firn, John Scott and Michael Hughes to detail the situation as it was then. Scott and Hughes found a high level of overlap between the ownership of large-scale industry and that of the Scottish banks, insurance companies and investment trusts. The same two or three dozen families that had dominated the Scottish economy in the 1920s still did so in the early 1970s. The owners of major Scottish companies in engineering, brewing, textiles and chemicals were also directors of the dominant financial institutions. They led policy bodies such as the Scottish Council for Development and Industry and held positions of influence within the Conservative Party.

But by the 1970s Scottish capital faced much more powerful economic and political challenges. Post-war regional policy had brought in a major influx of US branch plants which had poached their labour and forced up wages. Nationalisation had taken coal, power, transport and temporarily steel out of their control. For three decades small and medium businesses, and Scotland's large professional and scientific workforce, had experienced the benefits of an active regional policy and the wider prosperity deriving from full employment. This is what the Lithgows, Weirs, Coats, Colvilles and Yarrows wanted to reverse. Along with allies elsewhere, they were still powerful enough to use their influence with the incoming Conservative Government of 1970 to adopt policies that would do so.

Their defeat, along with the wider economic changes of the 1970s and especially the development of North Sea oil, saw the traditional owners of Scotland's capital shift their holdings out of large-scale industry and fully into the financial sector.

The 2005 Red Paper detailed the situation as it was 30 years later. The link between Scottish capital and industry had been almost entirely broken. Large Scottish-owned firms were the exception and the great bulk externally owned. The old dynastic families, in so far as they were still around, had moved into finance - most, it appeared, outside Scotland. Only one or two survived in distilling and publishing.

At the same time a number of new Scottish-owned firms had emerged, though of a different kind. On the one hand, there were new family firms in construction, hotels and oil services that had grown quickly in the expansionary climate of the previous 30 years. On the other, there were the giant privatised utilities in transport, telecommunications and energy. These had emerged from the Conservative privatisations of the 1980s and 1990s, with the Edinburgh financial sector acting as intermediaries to raise the requisite finance from investment banks based in London or New York. Most, especially in energy, were fairly quickly taken over by bigger firms based elsewhere. One or two, like First Group, Stagecoach and Scottish & Southern Energy (SSE), remained. It was around these newer firms, a selection of smaller banks and investment trusts and to some extent RBS and Standard Life, that some approximation of a Scottish business elite existed.[1]

The problem for its members, the Grossarts, Souters, Goodwins, Gilberts and Matthewsons, was that they lacked financial muscle and had no more than a toehold in industry. The takeover of the Scottish insurance companies over the previous 30 years had seen the great bulk of local funds pass out of Scottish control. In industry, most chief executives were accountants operating to the instructions of boards representing external investment banks. The dense inter-linkage between companies through locally based multiple directors that existed in the 1970s was a distant memory. In so far as they could deploy finance, it was on terms set elsewhere. Commentators noted the absence of any coherent business-based discussion of industrial strategy of the type still in evidence 30 years before.[2]

What the Edinburgh financiers did produce was the remarkable document published in 2004 by the Royal Bank, 'Wealth Creation in Scotland'. This was presented as a blueprint for Scottish economic growth and, because of its provenance, enjoyed considerable influence with Government and policymakers.

It was not, however, an industrial strategy. In essence it was about realising capital through privatisation and exporting it. It claimed that 56 per cent Scotland's GDP was generated by a relatively small handful of companies that had become 'global players'. These were almost entirely banks and service companies in transport and energy that had been privatised over the previous two decades and used these assets to buy up franchises overseas. On this basis, 'Wealth Creation in Scotland' argued for more privatisation in education and health as the basis for growing new global companies.[3] These arguments exercised considerable influence over the content of the New Labour Scottish Government's 2004 policy document, 'Smart, Successful Scotland'. But, as was soon demonstrated, it was a strategy built upon air. In most cases these overseas operations proved unsustainable. In the case of the Royal Bank, they turned lethal.

As a strategy it reflected the weak position of those who managed the remaining Scottish financial institutions. The Edinburgh elite made their money principally through managing other people's finances and from mergers and acquisitions on behalf of external firms. Their externally derived investment perspectives were increasingly short-term and their economic assumptions relentlessly neo-liberal.

Yet, despite the disasters of 2008, these same policy perspectives remain dominant today.[4] The SNP Government's Council of Economic Advisers is made up of the same people and their academic fellow travellers. Their main proposals for economic growth depend on lowering taxation on 'high net worth individuals' and reducing corporation tax to attract companies from elsewhere, which, in current circumstances, is likely to result not in new investment but the takeover of Scotland's few remaining independent companies. The SNP's recent promotion of both the sterling area membership and the EU reveals the degree to which the party has now travelled down this road. Scotland still lacks any active industrial strategy. Closures continue. Ownership and control is rapidly slipping away.

Changing realities

This brings us to our central question: do the forces exist that could comprise the same sort of alliance that existed in the 1970s?

It is at the level of local communities and as suppliers and subcontractors that Scottish-owned firms continue. There are upwards of 80,000 firms with a range of employees between 2 and 250. They are mainly in services: 12,000 in retail (including garages and motor sales), 11,000 in accommodation and catering, 10,000 in professional and scientific services, 5,000 in health and social care and 3,000 each in arts and entertainment and IT. There are 12,000 small construction firms, 7,000 in farming and fisheries and 5,800 remaining in manufacturing.[5] Many are now marginal and struggling. Many more than in the past are suppliers to a single larger firm and hence vulnerable to changes at that level. Very few export directly.

Politically, it is also at this level, and among salaried workers, locally based accountants and lawyers, small construction firms and shopkeepers, that the SNP derives its main membership. The recent research by Mitchell, Bennie and Johns defines the party's membership profile as disproportionately strong in rural communities and small towns, significantly older than Labour's, much more male and drawn from the small business and salaried strata. In terms of motivation there is a positive identification with the SNP's 'Scottishness' and to a somewhat lesser extent with independence. A significant number see Scottish communities and culture being 'swallowed up' by external economic forces.[6]

These feelings do indeed correspond closely to the changing realities of economic control which we have examined. But they do not correspond at all with the economic policies currently adopted by the SNP.

So how far could a new alliance be built between these forces and the trade union and labour movement? As we have noted, in the 1970s it was the ability of the trade union movement to articulate concerns about regional policy and deindustrialisation shared by small and medium business which played a major part in building the first movement for a Scottish Parliament. It is what also led to the demise of the Tory Party in Scotland as that party became identified with the conflicting interests of big business.

Up to the present there have been only limited attempts to test this potential. The STUC's Better Way campaign certainly puts this alternative across but it has not yet won wider political currency. All major political parties remain wedded to neo-liberal assumptions as do the media and establishment commentators. While there may be some slight indications of change - the leader of the Labour Party has recently spoken of the need for a renewal of industrial policy - the overall arguments in favour of a reassertion of economic democracy have still to be won. Too often any attempt to do so is met by claims that the forces of economic globalisation now make any recovery of democratic economic control impossible. Yet it is precisely when we look outside Britain to the rest of the world that we find a quite contrary reality.

Endnotes

1. Baird, S., Foster, J. and Leonard, R., Scottish Capital - is it still in control in the 21st Century?, Scottish Affairs, 2007 provides the most developed version of this analysis.

2. For instance Frank Blin in evidence to the Scottish Parliament Enterprise and Culture Committee (2005). Official Report 31 May 2005. col. 1945.

3. A critique was provided by Brian Ashcroft, Outlook and Appraisal, Quarterly Economic Commentary, Glasgow: Fraser of Allander Institute August 2004, and by Baird, S., Foster, J. and Leonard, R., Ownership of Companies in Scotland, Quarterly Economic Commentary, November 2004.

4. Davidson, N., McCafferty, P. and Miller, D., Neo-Liberal Scotland: Class and society in a stateless nation, 2010, Newcastle Upon Tyne: Cambridge Scholars Publishing, describe these policies but fail to provide any concrete analysis of ownership and control.

5. http://www.scotland.gov.uk/Resource/0038/00389595.pdf (the latest figures are for 2010).

6. Mitchell, J., Bennie, L. and Johns, R., The Scottish National Party: Transition to Power, 2011.

LEARNING FROM THE REST OF THE WORLD

John Foster and Richard Leonard

Since the crisis of 2008 it is by and large those economies with a measure of state control and active industrial policies that appear to have survived best. The 2012 United Nation's Trade and Development Report put the position very plainly. It contrasts the failure of economic recovery in Europe and the US with continuing growth in a number of developing countries where:

> targeted fiscal and industrial policies ... helped to create good-quality jobs outside the commodities sector. Higher fiscal spending created jobs directly in the public and services sectors, and indirectly in occupations related to infrastructure development and in manufacturing industry.... China was able to absorb a dramatic fall in its current-account surplus with only a small reduction of its overall growth expectation and without restraining real wage growth. The contrast with Germany, which could not avoid economic stagnation despite its huge surplus, is striking.

The report strongly criticises financial deregulation and the abandonment of active industrial policies in the major Western economies over the past two decades:

> Emphasis on the maximisation of shareholder value has led managers to focus on short-term profitability and a higher stock market valuation of their companies. This approach has changed the way companies have been responding to competitive pressures under conditions of high unemployment. Instead of adopting a long-term perspective and trying to further upgrade their production technology and the product composition of output through productivity-enhancing investment and innovation, they have increasingly relied on offshoring production activities to low-wage locations in developing and transition economies, and on seeking to reduce domestic unit labour costs through wage compression.

The resulting pressure for 'structural reform', focused on reducing real incomes and weakening labour's collective bargaining strength, has been cutting demand, reducing the scope for productive investment and thereby weakening any global recovery. Worse still, the UN report describes the EU's drive to 'export its way out of crisis' as placing an 'enormous drag on the global economy'.

By contrast, the report highlights the role of countries with active policies of industrial intervention, capital management and income redistribution. It is these countries which have, so far, been responsible for maintaining world demand:

> Several countries have been responding to the deteriorating external environment with contra-cyclical policies including higher public spending and a more accommodative monetary stance. They have been profiting from the policy space made possible by higher public revenues and active financial policies, including the management of foreign capital flows. As a result investment rates are on the rise and unemployment fallen to its lowest level in decades.[1]

The report notes that China, where the economy has continued to grow at over 7 per cent for the past five years, retains a largely state-controlled banking system and that state-owned national champions have led technological progress and that its utilities are mainly provided by either central or provincial state governments. While China also has a large private sector and income inequality has become extreme over the past two decades, the Chinese Government has retained sufficient leverage to boost internal consumer demand by strongly redistributionist policies, both geographically and socially, and by strengthening trade union rights. Real wages have risen by well over 50 per cent since 2005.[2] Countries in South America, such as Brazil, Bolivia, Argentina and Venezuela, have also maintained relatively high growth rates. Here also there have been significant levels of state intervention, attempts at redistributionist social policies and the development of various forms of public and co-operative ownership.

Although these countries may yet be adversely affected by the policies pursued by the EU and the US, their relative success so far has reawakened interest in policies based on public ownership. A range of recent studies have examined the conditions in which state-owned enterprises have been able to sustain cumulative growth and expand productive capacity. The work of Musacchio and Lazzarini at the Harvard Business School has focused on the long-term success of state-owned companies in a variety of contexts.[3] Mariana Muzzacato has demonstrated the successful track record state-funded and directed innovation strategies in the development of new products and provides concrete suggestions for the implementation of such policies in Britain.[4] The Centre for Research into Economic and Social Change (CRESC) has also put forward a series of proposals for public sector intervention to overcome monopolistic practices in the retail sector.[5]

Failing competitiveness in Britain

Conversely, recent reports have underlined the sheer inefficiency and levels of market failure plaguing Britain's private sector, particularly in the provision of infrastructure. The '2012 McNulty report' found that state subsidies for rail transport had risen fourfold since privatisation. Fares, on the other hand, were a third higher than those on largely state-owned railways in Europe which operate with much lower subsidies. In Britain itself the re-nationalised East Coast Line generated profits of well over £600m between 2009 and 2013. These profits were used by the Government to subsidise the loss-making privatised lines. The record of the privatised energy companies has been little better. The 2012 Ofgem report, 'Gas: Security of Supply', spoke of the profound consequences arising from 'market failure' in the industry, a year after the House of Commons report on UK energy supply issued very similar warnings. More generally, the years since 2008 have seen a wider and even more dangerous collapse in business investment. Over the five years to 2012 the annual rate fell below 15 per cent of GDP. This is far lower than that in any other OECD country. It is also unprecedented in Britain's own economic history. The long-term consequences for international competitiveness are likely to be profound.

It could be objected that the success of state-led development in countries such as Brazil and China depended on both their size and their potential for consumer market growth within what were very underdeveloped economies. This was undoubtedly a factor. Yet, certainly in China, much of the public sector involvement was organised and targeted much more locally at provincial government level. Commercial car production provides an instructive example.[6] A late starter in China, state policy initially focused on bringing in large external companies within joint partnership agreements with Chinese producers. Somewhat later this was supplemented by simple direct investment by external producers to boost the development of a mass market - though there was considerable dissatisfaction at the failure to utilise local suppliers. Then in the late 1990s there was the beginning of a policy switch. Some provincial governments gave support to solely indigenous firms, some private, the biggest publicly owned, moving into car production to produce low-cost models based on local supply chains. Their success in both domestic and international markets then saw a shift in central policy to back the creation of indigenous state-owned national champions.[7]

In South America where public enterprise has historically played a significant developmental role, it generally did so to sustain industrialisation projects led by domestic capital - even though in recent periods nationalisation has also become a tool for more socialist policies.[8] Petrobras in Brazil is an example of both. Initially representative of a cohort of state-owned companies playing a developmental role in the 1960s and 1970s, it has over the past decade become a central instrument for state policies aimed at socially redistributive development. Today it is both the world leader in deep water extraction technology and a key player in agrarian development using green technologies for renewable energy. Elsewhere in South America, in Venezuela,

Argentina and Bolivia, a variety of publicly owned and co-operative enterprises have been central to maintaining the pace of economic growth - particularly in conditions of international crisis and capital famine.[9]

Southern Africa has experienced far more uneven progress. Here size has been important. South Africa has been able to retain and develop its very substantial state sector and use it to fund some level of redistribution. The much smaller Mozambique was temporarily forced, in order to meet IMF governance requirements, to dismantle its publicly owned supply chains for commercial food production - with local communities excluded from markets and the wider economy damaged. This experience has resulted in a return to public sector ownership of infrastructure.[10]

Overall, while the developing world has certainly seen its share of inefficient state enterprises, the balance of opinion currently upholds their role as tools for development whose effectiveness has been amply demonstrated during the current crisis. This reassessment is reflected in the inclusion of a section on industrial policy in the '2012 United Nation's Conference on Trade and Development (UNCTAD) World Development report'. It is also increasingly reflected in policy changes in the developed world.

The United States itself has recently shown the effectiveness of such intervention. Since 2007, growth, though low, has been resumed on the basis of expansionist, semi-Keynesian monetary policies and a significant level of state intervention in manufacturing. The most notable was the $24 billion bailout of the motor industry. Even bigger state subsidies have been channelled through the defence budget. In housing, 90 per cent of all US mortgages are now provided by state-owned or subsidised providers.[11]

By contrast, the EU has applied tighter monetary policies, sought to reduce government borrowing in a 'pro-cyclical' (or anti-Keynesian) manner and maintained its ban on state aid for industry. Under its Stability and Growth Pact the key economic regulator remains the traditional 'free market' or neo-liberal one: the use of unemployment, notionally at least, to reduce labour costs and thereby to enhance profit incentives for reinvestment. The result has been a drastic contraction in the weaker economies which has now spread to the entire eurozone.

Even in the EU, however, we find that the globally competitive sectors, especially in Germany and France, have themselves been closely dependent on public sector support. Germany's dynamic manufacturing economy draws its strength from the regional concentrations of inter-related large and small firms whose stability and long-term investment programmes have been sustained by the publicly owned regional Landesbanks. In the past the role of these banks in supplying relatively low-cost and stable credit was supplemented by state-owned utilities providing cheap power and transport.[12] Today, Lande bank finance still remains important and the German determination to defend its regional banking system is closely associated with an understanding of this role and the threat otherwise posed by Anglo-US investment banks and hedge funds. Ideologically this structure of state support rests on assumptions which, while not socialist, reflect the 19th-century German understanding of the developmental role of the state - reinforced immediately after 1945 by the Concordat established between capital and labour in a period when West German capital was still fearful of comparisons being drawn with the socialist states of Eastern Europe.[13]

In France's case its pre-eminence in transport and energy utilities and certain aspects of engineering, aerospace and oil and gas production still rests on the existence of national champions which enjoy significant state support and in some cases are still fully or partly state owned. Here again, the banking system in France's case is highly centralised, and has been important in strategic financing. So also has the continuing commitment at governmental level to ensure the exemption of France's state-led firms from EU prohibitions. This strategic direction interlocks private business dynasties with state and governmental structures - and politically rests on a long-term popular commitment to public ownership which dates back to the Liberation and before.[14] The outcome has been internationally competitive state companies, 'champions capable of competing with global market rivals' as the current Director of IMF, Christine Lagarde, put it in her Foreword to the 2010 report of the Agence des participations de l'etat.

Other examples of successful public sector involvement could be provided from Norway or Finland, or from the former Yugoslavian states of Croatia and Bosnia Herzegovina where the people retain minority and majority stakes in strategic industries and companies. So it is clear that public ownership cannot be dismissed on purely doctrinaire grounds. Even those in the EU who use such arguments often come from countries whose economic success actually depends on state support.

The single market v intervention

By contrast, it has been Britain, of all the major economies the one with the weakest productive base, which has been foremost in pushing for a rigid implementation of EU single market regulation and an end of any form of state intervention. It has done so largely to serve the interests of the financial institutions that dominate its (and Scotland's) economy and which use Britain's financial centres, London and Edinburgh, to control over 60 per cent of the EU's financial services. The creation of the single market itself, dating from the 1986 Single European Act, was largely initiated by Britain and was closely related to the 'big bang' deregulation of British and American financial markets and the redevelopment of the City of London as the base for US banks in Europe.[15] Since then British governments have sought to remove all impediments to their access to financial markets and increasingly, for US investment companies, the ownership of productive assets as well. The main current concern of the British Government is to maintain this single market access in face of the eurozone's transition to banking and fiscal union.

It has been as a result of these preoccupations, and the abandonment of all attempts at industrial policy, that Britain has seen the disproportionate decline of its productive economy at the same time as the expansion of its financial sector, a course which, though immensely profitable to a small minority, would seem to be economically and politically unsustainable.[16]

Could Britain (or Scotland) therefore switch to more interventionist policies? There are clearly international obstacles: the contrary positions taken by the EU and the WTO, though in the case of the WTO these often prove much less severe.[17] There are also the economic ones: for example, being able to develop a critical mass of productive power in particular fields that can compete internationally. But almost certainly the biggest single requirement is not economic but political: winning a popular understanding that democratic state intervention is both possible and necessary and as a result changing the current balance of political forces. Currently all political parties, Conservative, Labour and the SNP, base their policies on the neo-liberal economics prescribed by the dominant financial institutions. These positions also dominate academic discussion.[18] Realistically, it is only the trade union movement that has the size and influence to re-develop a broad understanding of the disastrous consequences of the existing course and re-winning a commitment to the necessity for democratic control and public ownership.[19] This will require, as argued elsewhere is this volume, a redevelopment of class politics at British and Scottish level that focuses on the issue of state power and who deploys it. As we have seen, however, there are examples to use. A range of developing economies have already shown the effectiveness of varying forms of public ownership, and it was precisely such policies that saved the world from economic disaster when growth in Japan, the US and Europe collapsed.

With more particular relevance to smaller economies such as Scotland, it is also important to stress the potential role of the co-operative sector in ensuring that productive resources are developed in a locally rooted and accountable way.

Localised and co-operatively organised interventions have enabled particular regions within Europe to resist the worst effects of the crisis - though not in Scotland. It is not without irony that the home of the Fenwick weavers and of Robert Owen boasts today one of the smallest number of worker co-operative businesses in Europe. When it was launched in 2006 Co-operative Development Scotland estimated that there were just 34 workers co-ops in Scotland with a turnover of £21.5 million employing 273 people. Today Co-operatives UK estimate there are 32 'live' workers co-operatives in Scotland with a turnover of around £30 million, but no data on the number of workers involved.

Perhaps the most successful international comparator is the Mondragon Co-operative Corporation in the Basque country of Spain which is comprised of 258 co-operative enterprises and other bodies and employs over 83,000 people. The Corporation as a whole and individual enterprises are democratically run. Because labour is in control of capital, rather than vice versa, the co-operatives have proved resilient not just in the current Spanish economic slump but for the last 50 years. Job retention and creation are paramount and so people are explicitly put before profit, with surpluses reinvested in the enterprise rather than leaked out to speculators and shareholders with no stake other than a short-term financial one in the business. A hallmark of Mondragon is the principle of wage solidarity too, so that the highest paid person can only at most be paid six times that of the lowest paid worker.

Legislation to support co-operatives has proved valuable in continental Europe but is sadly lacking in the UK. The Industrial Common Ownership Act introduced by the 1974 Labour Government lapsed in 1981. Co-operative Development Scotland while representing a welcome move when established by the Labour/Liberal Democrat coalition in 2005/6 still unfortunately has no statutory powers at its disposal, no separate investment facility and indeed is not even itself entrenched in law. By contrast Mondragon has its own investment bank (the Caja Laboral Popular) providing patient capital to co-operatives.

Italy, under the Marcora Law introduced in 1985, has both funding powers and the ability to target support when nine or more workers are facing redundancy as a result of bankruptcy, business sale or offshoring the legal right to bid to buy out the business, with a matching state investment of up to three times the workers' own investment. In part as a result of this in Emilia Romagna in northern Italy alone 80,000 workers are in producer co-operatives in which they have a stake, and ten times that number work in co-ops across Italy as a whole.

In Scotland the introduction of legislative, investment and technical assistance could make a big difference. For a start it would be one way of stemming the loss of local ownership and even reversing it. It would place enterprises outside the Stock Exchange loop, whether in London, Paris, New York or Frankfurt. It would represent a redistribution of power and establish greater democracy in the economy and so bring with it far greater employment security. As a recent BBC report revealed while in the midst of Spain's depression unemployment in the country as a whole is running at 25 per cent, in the province of Guipuzcoa which includes Mondragon it is less than half that number. The Mondragon Co-operative Corporation itself has downsized by less than 2 per cent (85,066 workers in 2009 to 83,859 on 2010) with no redundancies, simply redeployment of workers from the less to the more successful parts of the Corporation.

To conclude, the neo-liberal policies still prescribed by financiers in Edinburgh and their counterparts in London are increasingly being exposed as fundamentally flawed. Globally they have led to economic crisis. In Britain and Scotland they have resulted in a level of deindustrialisation which now threatens the wider economy. In current circumstances where financialised capital markets dominate corporate ownership there is mounting evidence that private enterprise performs less well than public and co-operative ownership. Internationally, economic opinion is shifting decisively. State intervention and active industrial policies are viewed as essential for the maintenance of sustainable economic development.

Endnotes

1. UNCTAD, World Trade and Development Report, 2012.
2. Banister, J., China's Employment and Compensation Costs in Manufacturing, Monthly Labor Review (Washington DC), March 2011.
3. Musacchio, A. and Lazzarini, S., Leviathans in Business: Varieties of State Capitalism and the Implications for Economic Performance, Harvard Business School Working Paper, 12-108, July 2012; Fureeni, D. and Zdzjenika, A., Banking Crisis and Short and Medium Term Output Losses in Emerging and Developing Countries: the Role of Policy and Structural Variables, World Development, Vol. 40, Issue 12, December 2012; Ayca Akareay Gurbuz, Comparing Trajectories of Structural Change, Cambridge Journal of Economics, Vol. 35, Issue 6, 2011.
4. Mazzucato, M., The Entrepreneurial State, Demos, 2011.
5. Bowman, A., Froud, J., Johal, S., Law, J., Leaver, A. and Williams, K., Bringing Home the Bacon: from trader mentalities to industrial policy, CRESC Public Interest Report, June 2012.
6. Wan-Wen Chu, How the Chinese Government Promoted a Global Automobile Industry, Industrial and Corporate Change, Vol. 290, issue 5, 2011.
7. Elsewhere, particularly in strategic areas such as oil, atomic energy, steel, telecommunications and aerospace, the policy of developing state-owned national champions had long been established. Nolan, P., Indigenous Large Firms in China's Economic Reform. London: Contemporary China Institute, School of Oriental and African Studies, University of London. 1998; Nolan, P., China and the global economy: national champions, industrial policy and the big business revolution, Houndsmill: Palgrave, 2001. More recently there have been examples of attempts to initiate new industries based on research and development focused locally around universities. In nano-technology massive resources have been pumped into public sector, university-based research to give China the second highest international profile for patented innovations - although so far with disappointing levels of commercial application. Policy is now shifting to greater state sector involvement in their development. Can Huang and Yilin Wu, State-led Technological Development: a Case of Chinese Nanotechnology Development, World Development, Vol. 40, Issue 6, 2012. Ha-Jung Chang, The East Asian Development Experience, Zed, 2006, stresses the importance of state intervention and industrial policy elsewhere in East Asia.
8. Trebat, T., Brazil's State Owned Enterprises, Cambridge Latin American Studies, 45, 1983; Musacchio and Lazzarini, Leviathans in Business, as cited. Peres, W., Industrial Policies in Latin America, UN University Working Paper, 2011/48 examines the return of sectoral industrial policy over the past decade. The UN World Investment Report, 2012, notes the increasing use of industrial policy in South America 'to build productive capacities and boost the manufacturing sectors' and the probability of FDI 'barrier hopping' by external FDI to secure entry to these markets.
9. Bolivia has nationalised all hydrocarbon production, tin and zinc mining, all telecommunications and, on the grounds that that they were failing to invest in adequate supply, all the major foreign owned electricity companies (Financial Times 31 December 2012). Bolivia left the WTO in 2007. Argentina nationalised its biggest oil producer, owned by the Spanish company Repsol, in April 2012 in face of declining output and investment. It nationalised pension funds in 2008. A range of 'recovered companies' were taken over by their workers during the 2001/2 crisis. Since default in 2002, Argentina has seen a 90 per cent increase in GDP.
10. Hanlon, J., Governance as 'Kicking Away the Ladder', New Political Economy, Vol. 17, Issue 5, 2012.
11. Pickard, J., Property of the State, Financial Times, 21 April 2013.
12. Hall, P. and Soskice, D. (ed.), Varieties of Capitalism: The Institutional Foundations of Comparative Advantage, Oxford, 2001; Barca, F. and Becht, M., The Control of Corporate Europe, Oxford, 2001; and Amable, B. The Diversity of Modern Capitalism, Oxford, 2003 provide the original texts. Lane, C. and Wood, G., Capitalist Diversity and Diversity within Capitalism, Economy and Society, Vol. 38, Issue 4, 2009 review some of the more recent literature.

13. Bonefeld, W., Freedom and the Strong State: on German Ordo-liberalism, New Political Economy, Vol. 17, Issue 5, 2012.

14. Clift, B., Comparative Capitalism, Ideational Political Economy and French Post-Derigiste Responses to Global Political Crisis, New Political Economy, Vol. 17, Issue 5, 2012.

15. Roberts, R. and Kynaston, D., City State, 2002 examines the structural transformation following deregulation; Gowans, P., Crisis in the Heartland, New Left Review, 55, January 2009 the resulting crisis - as do Blankenberg, S. and Palma, J.G., The Global Financial Crisis, Cambridge Journal of Economics, 33, 4, 2009.

16. Turner, A., The Crisis, Conventional Economic Wisdom and Public Policy, Industrial and Corporate Change, October 2010, 19, 5.

17. The post-crisis period has seen an increasing tendency by governments to find ways of bypassing WTO regulations short of outright tariff protection - including infrastructural subsidy, export credits, 'countervailing duties' and 'special' industrial support (such as that for the US motor industry). All have proved legally difficult to challenge: Beattie, A., Tricks of the Trade law, Financial Times, 29 October 2012. It is also the case that the entry to the WTO of the BRICS countries, China, Brazil, Russia and India, as well as countries like Argentina that have been redeveloping their state sectors, has led to increasing challenges to the self-serving free trade doctrines of the dominant economies. It should also be noted that, unlike the EU, the WTO does not itself initiate legal actions to enforce regulations but depends on the far more problematic initiatives by individual member states to do so: Strange, G., China's post-Listian rise: beyond radical globalisation theory, New Political Economy, Vol. 16, Issue 5, 2011.

18. Turner, A., The Crisis, Conventional Economic Wisdom and Public Policy, Industrial and Corporate Change, 19, 5, 2010, notes how far academic economists have accepted the conventional wisdom of the corporate sector.

19. It should be noted that the grip of neo-liberal ideas within the Labour Party was significantly aided by the manipulation of the concept of globalisation by ideologues such as Lord Giddens (The Third Way, 1998 and The Runaway World, 1999) and Lord Mandelson (Global Europe, 2006) using the proposition that no nation state could or should seek to interfere with global markets. A more balanced assessment of globalisation is provided by Hirst, P. and Thompson, G., Globalisation in Question, 2009 edition; Stiglitz, J., Globalisation and its Discontents, 2002; and Krugman, P., The Return of Depression Economics and the Crisis of 2008, 2008.

EQUAL MEANS BETTER
Muir Houston

A s we have seen in preceding sections, the mainstream polity and media are dominated by neo-liberal assumptions in which austerity is presented as the only response to the current crisis. This has resulted in a concerted attack on the working classes of many of the advanced economies, attacks on the public provision of health, welfare and education services while demonising those on any form of state benefit.[1]

The purpose of this section is to say something about contemporary inequality at both the UK and Scottish levels. In order to understand the scale and scope of current inequalities, we must first define what we mean by inequality and situate it within the particular historical context in which it has developed. This will allow us to understand how and in what ways divisive neo-liberal economic and social policies[2] have been used to fuel the increasing disparities in income and wealth between those at the top and those at the bottom of UK and Scottish society particularly in the past decade.[3]

Most people will be aware of the concept of inequality expressed in terms of income and/or in wealth and will be familiar with comparisons of the share of national income or wealth between for example the top 10 per cent and the bottom 10 per cent. Historical data supports the claim that the post-war settlement, or the tripartite consensus between capital, labour and the state in 1945 led to a sharp fall in UK income inequality up till the mid-1970s.[4] This resulted from the creation of the welfare state, conditions of full employment, taxation of higher earners, rising wages for the working class and improvements in universal education.

However, since the mid-70s, there has been a sharp increase in income inequality especially as a result of the increased share taken by the top 1 per cent. This was associated with the expansion of the financial sector and extremely high salaries and bonuses; the privatisation of public and state assets and deregulation again especially in the financial sector; the huge rise in asset prices especially in the unsustainable bubble in the UK housing market; huge disparities in wages; cuts in higher rates of income tax and a shift from direct to indirect taxation more generally.[5] Indeed, according to The

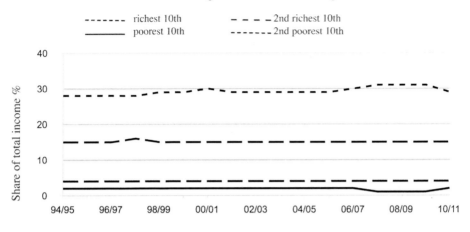

Figure 1. Source: adapted from www.poverty.org.uk/uk/s09/c.png

Poverty Site,[6] the Gini Coefficient measure of income inequality is now higher than at any time in the last 30 years.[7] What all this means for Scotland is expressed clearly in the graph in Figure 1. Unsurprisingly, the most extreme effects of income inequality are noted at both ends of the spectrum. While in a context of rising prices in terms of housing, food, fuel and utilities, the only group with noticeable gains in their share of income was in the top 10 per cent. Vast inequalities also exist in relation to land ownership in Scotland[8] and while information is incomplete, it is suggested that of the rural land (nearly 19 million acres), 83.1 per cent is in private hands, and 60 per cent of this is owned by just 969 people, giving it the most concentrated land ownership pattern in Europe.[9] It should also be noted that this rural land often attracts large subsidies and other payments which for Scotland in 2004 amounted to £115 million to the hundred largest beneficiaries.

However, it is not simply about income and or wealth or even ownership of land. An important contribution to debates on inequality was the publication in 2009 of The Spirit Level: Why more equal societies almost always do better by Richard Wilkinson and Kate Pickett. Their study was based on a long period of research initially concentrated on trying to understand the big differences in life expectancy between different social groups. Their main focus was on why do people lower down the social ladder suffer greater levels of ill health: 'Richer people tend, on average, to be healthier and happier than poorer people in the same society'.[10]

What made their study possible were developments in data collection and comparability at the international level. This allowed not only comparisons of income inequality and its effects on health issues but could also be applied to look at the relationship between income distribution and other social problems. They note that while in poorer countries life expectancy rises sharply during the early stages of development, as affluence increases the rate of improvement is subject to diminishing returns. The same is true of happiness or well-being.[11]

Their next step was to investigate whether levels of inequality in a society made any difference to the levels of health and social problems and noted that the UK, Singapore, Portugal and the USA are among the most unequal. For example, while in Japan and the Scandinavian countries the richest 20 per cent are less than four times as rich as the poorest 20 per cent, in the UK the richest 20 per cent are more than seven times as rich as the poorest 20 per cent.[12] It soon became apparent that almost all social problems that are more common at the bottom of the social ladder are additionally more prevalent in more unequal societies as a whole. Hence they decided to focus on a list of social and health-related issues for which reliable data were available and created an index of health and social problems.[13] The higher the score on any measure, the worse things are.

So how does the UK compare on a range of the problems identified by Wilkinson and Pickett? In relation to trust (most people can be trusted) in the UK, less than 30 per cent agreed with the statement in contrast to the more equal Scandinavian societies where the levels of trust were over 60 per cent. They suggest that this lack of trust in more unequal societies can also be related to an increasing uneasiness and fear of 'others' reflected in the increase of gated communities and a more atomistic rather than collective existence. When the status of women and their role in society is examined, inequality again plays a role with more unequal societies tending to have fewer women who hold political office. Women also earn less and have lower status.[14]

They note that part of the problem is that neo-liberalism sees atomistic individuals rather than collectives as important and that the grand narratives of a better society or a better world have long disappeared from public rhetoric - resulting in what they suggested may be seen as (until the 2008 crash at least) material success alongside social failure.

However, while levels of trust and social relations are relatively intangible, the other problems which the Spirit Level addresses are far more tangible and familiar to anyone with a passing acquaintance with the health and social problems prevalent in the UK and Scotland. For example, specifically in relation to the consumption of alcohol and drugs, the levels of inequality may go some way in explaining why the UK and Scotland in particular tend to head league tables of consumption. It also may help explain the high levels of mental health problems among adults (one in five in the UK) with increasing numbers of children being diagnosed with mental health problems and over a quarter of survey respondents regularly feeling depressed often as a result of family breakdown.[15]

They also noted that stress often brought on by adverse experiences and circumstances, at all levels in society, is higher in more unequal societies and link this to a number of biological effects of chronic stress including: impaired memory and increased risk of depression; deteriorated immune system; higher risk of cardiovascular disease; high hormone levels and increased risk of fertility problems and miscarriage.[16]

A familiar problem in Scotland, the rest of the UK and the developed world in general is the increasing levels of obesity with two-thirds of UK adults overweight and more than a fifth classified as obese. This adds increased risk of: hypertension, type II diabetes, gall bladder disease and some cancers. Worryingly they report that levels of child obesity are so serious that it is expected to lead to reversals in life expectancy trends for the first time since the 19th century.[17] Moreover, the effects of obesity can have serious effects on social and emotional well-being and it is not hard to see how this links with stress and mental health issues highlighted above. It is no surprise to learn that for both adults and children, levels of obesity are inversely correlated with equality or, the greater the levels of inequality, the higher the levels of obesity.

The effects of class on educational attainment are well known and there is no need to repeat them here. It has been suggested that by the age of three those from deprived backgrounds are already starting to fall behind in terms of cognitive development and that many will never make up the lost ground,[18] often condemning them to an uncertain future in what Standing has termed the precariat.[19] Interestingly, the UK still performs relatively well in terms of achievement against some other unequal societies but given the educational advantage that income and wealth can leverage, less inequality would probably go a long way in raising the attainment of the poorest in our society not least by perhaps ameliorating some of the social and health issues outlined above.

They also note that some gender effects, the possibility of being a victim of violence for males or of teenage pregnancy for females (only the US has higher rates than the UK) are increased in unequal societies and also more likely the lower down the social gradient in that society you are. Related to issues of male violence is prison rates and again more unequal societies incarcerate more people, which also has race and class aspects with higher rates of incarceration leading to the paradox in the UK of a rising prison population while crime rates are falling.

Issues of gender inequality encompass an entire spectrum of barriers which remain as stubbornly present in Scottish society as they do in England. In terms of formal legal rights the last two decades have seen some progress. Female representation in the Scottish Parliament is significantly higher than that in Westminster at 37 per cent. Access to justice in cases of domestic abuse and violence has been improved through both legislation and provision.[20] The public sector was also able to record a very slight reduction in the gender pay gap in the year to May 2013 as well as some improvement in levels of public disclosure.[21]

Yet women remain disproportionately in low paid, part-time and temporary work and hence also disproportionately exposed to the impact of economic crisis itself and to the British Government's drive to cut welfare spending. The number of Scottish women in full-time employment fell from 708,000 in 2009 to 661,000 in 2012 while the number in part-time work rose from 495,000 to 515,000.[22] Women are therefore particularly vulnerable to the cuts in tax credits as well as having to contend with the problems of familial poverty and in particular with child poverty. Here Scotland's statistics are truly bad: in Dundee, 26 per cent of children were living in poverty in 2012; in Glasgow 33 per cent.[23] The Institute of Fiscal Studies estimates that this number will further increase by a quarter by 2020 - largely as a result of the increase in housing costs.[24] Already in 2012 Save the Children reported a quarter of parents saying they skipped meals in order to provide food for children while a sixth of children were described as going to bed hungry.[25]

As elsewhere, the apparently progressive character of Scottish society is belied by the reality of low pay, stress, insecurity and downright poverty for a very significant section of the population and particularly for women. Figures from the Improvement Service in May 2013 revealed that the austerity cuts in local government are pressing hard on services on which women are particularly reliant: home care, school provision and nurseries where costs were already higher than those in England.[26] And this is before the impact of Welfare Reform which is scheduled to hit hardest on the poorest areas.[27]

The rawness of the Scottish working-class experience is further exposed when we look at figures for mortality and what is sometimes called the Scottish or Clydeside anomaly.[28] There is still today a widespread assumption that Scottish society is somehow more 'social democratic' and caring than that in other parts of Britain. This does not fit easily with what we know about the statistics for mortality and particularly for early deaths among males. When mortality rates improved fairly rapidly across Western Europe after 1950, Scotland's lagged. Over the period from 1950 to 1980 the differential was relatively modest. Since 1980 it has increased. Even when allowance is made for income levels, unemployment, poverty and poor housing, the anomaly still stands. A parallel anomaly also exists for industrial accidents and deaths, even when allowance is made for the greater incidence of accident-prone industries.[29]

The most favoured explanation of higher levels of industrial accidents is the difference in 'working practices' and specifically in more authoritarian forms of management, particularly in industries where unionisation is weak. In construction 97 per cent of fatalities between 1960 and the late 1990s in the West of Scotland occurred in workplaces without union recognition.[30] Such authoritarian management has a long history in Scotland and appears to have reasserted itself as union membership declined in the 1980s and 1990s. The result has not just been worse industrial accident statistics but higher levels of occupational stress and consequential impacts on smoking and alcohol consumption.[31] Inequalities of wealth are matched by gross inequalities of power - with particularly serious consequences in a society with a casualised and precarious workforce.

Finally, it is important to note that inequality also impacts on economic development. While there are not the same tight correlations between equality and economic growth as there are for health and well-being, there are certainly clear links with developmental potential. The 2012 OECD report 'Going for Growth' highlights a number of areas that are critical for economic development - mainly relating to the labour market and scientific potential.[32] The report finds that greater income inequality directly impairs a society's ability to create a pool of highly educated graduates and postgraduates and that high income inequality also reduces the overall quality of the labour force. Conversely, trade union recognition and collective bargaining are seen positively as enhancing security and reducing differentials, particularly those based on gender.[33]

More generally, it is also the case that growing income inequality played a central role in precipitating the economic and financial crisis that has virtually halted growth in most of the G7 economies since 2007. The use of credit to sustain purchasing power in the face of slowing real wage growth, and in the US in the face of its absolute decline, was directly related to speculation in debt that precipitated the financial crash. Subsequently the scale of corporate and private debt has been a major factor in prolonging the crisis.[34] 'The 2012 UN report on Trade and Development' puts this very clearly:

> Insufficient growth of average real wages, coupled with inappropriate tax reforms, constitute the root causes of rising inequality in most countries, but they have not led to the promised outcomes of faster growth and lower unemployment. This is because any policy approach that dismisses the important contribution of income distribution to demand growth and employment creation is destined to fail. A shift in income distribution to high income groups with a higher savings rate implies falling demand for the goods produced by companies. When productivity grows without a commensurate increase in wages, demand will eventually fall short of the production potential, thereby reducing capacity utilization and profits. This in turn will typically lead to cuts - and not to an increase - in investments.

It may therefore be concluded that if Scotland is ever to achieve the type of society demanded by Keir Hardie and the early socialists, the challenge of inequality has to be addressed. Scotland is today one of the most unequal societies in Europe. This inequality has been worsening over the past generation and looks set to intensify further over the next decade. In terms of income itself the levels of inequality may be slightly less than those in England - largely because of the concentration of extreme wealth in and around the City of London. But in terms of health and well-being inequalities would seem to be worse and related to both management practices and the greater prevalence of casualised and insecure employment. No less than the rundown in industrial investment detailed in the previous chapters, the impoverishment of Scotland's people also endangers our country's future.

Endnotes

1. Wiggan, J., Telling stories of 21st century welfare: The UK Coalition government and the neo-liberal discourse of worklessness and dependency, Critical Social Policy, 32, 2012.

2. Wiggan, J., Something Old and Blue, or Red, Bold and New? Welfare Reform and the Coalition Government, in C. Holden, M. Kilkey and G. Ramia (eds.) Social Policy Review 23, Bristol: Policy Press, 2011.

3. Centeno, M.A. and Cohen, J.N., The Arc of Neo-liberalism, Annu. Rev. Sociol., 2012. The main exceptions are the richest tenth which has a somewhat smaller share of the total income in Scotland than in Great Britain as a whole (29 per cent compared to 31 per cent) and the poorest tenth (2 per cent compared to 1.2 per cent). See the UK indicator on income inequality. Because of these differences, income inequality in Scotland is somewhat lower than in Great Britain as a whole. The Poverty Site (www.poverty.org.uk) http://www.poverty.org.uk/s09/e.pdf.

4. Data extracted from World's Top Incomes Database (http://topincomes.g-mond.parisschoolofeconomics.eu/#Database.

5. See note 4.

6. www.poverty.org.uk.

7. http://en.wikipedia.org/wiki/Gini_coefficient.

8. http://reidfoundation.org/wp-content/uploads/2012/10/QuicknoteLand.pdf.

9. Wightman, A., Scotland: Land and Power - the Agenda for Land Reform, Luath Press, 1999.

10. Wilkinson, R. and Pickett, K., The Spirit Level: Why more equal societies almost always do better, 2009.

11. Layard, R., Happiness, London: Allen Lane, 2005.

12. Wilkinson, R. and Pickett, K., Spirit Level. (The figures are for household income, after taxes and benefits, adjusted for the number of people in each household.)

13. The list included: level of trust, mental illness (including drug and alcohol addiction), life expectancy and infant mortality, obesity, children's educational performance, teenage births, homicides, imprisonment rates, social mobility. See note 12.

14. Three of the measures are: women's political participation, women's employment and earnings, and women's social and economic autonomy. See note 12.

15. The Good Childhood Inquiry. Evidence Summary 5 - Health, London: Children's Society, 2008.

16. Sapolsky, R., Sick of poverty, Scientific American (2005) 293 (6).

17. Olshansky, S.J., Passaro, D.J., Hershow, R.C., Layden, J., Carnes, B.A., Brody, J., Hayflick, L., Butler, R.N., Allison, D.B. and Ludwig, S.D., A potential decline in life expectancy in the United States in the 21st century, New England Journal of Medicine (2005) 352 (11).

18. Feinstein, L. (2003) "Very Early: How early can we predict future educational achievement?" Centerpiece, http://cep.lse.ac.uk/centrepiece/v08i2/feinstein.pdf

19. Standing, G., The Precariat: the new dangerous class, London: Bloomsbury, 2011.

20. Scottish Human Rights Commission, Submission on the Seventh Periodic Report of the United Kingdom, to the United Nations Committee on the Elimination of All Forms of Discrimination against Women, 8 July 2013.

21. Gender Pay Gaps: report from Wladyslaw Mejka and Spice Report to Equal Opportunities Committee, 13 June 2013: Scottish.parliament.uk/S4_EqualOpportunitiesCommittee/13_June_papers.pdf.

22. WISE Briefing Sheet January 2013 (Glasgow Caledonian University).

23. The Herald, 18 February 2013, citing the report by End Child Poverty.

24. Institute of Fiscal Studies cited by The Herald 8 May 2013.

25. The Herald, 5 September 2012, citing research by Save the Children.

26. The Herald, 19 May 2013, reporting survey by the Scottish Improvement Service; on child care costs SHRC UN submission 8 July 2013.

27. Beatty, C. and Fothergill, S., Hitting the Poorest Places Hardest, Sheffield Hallam University, Centre for Regional and Social Research, April 2013.

28. Collins, C. et al., Accounting for Scotland's Excess Mortality: A Synthesis, Glasgow Centre for Population Studies, April 2011.

29. National Audit Office, The Health and Safety Executive's Work in Scotland, Memorandum for the Scottish Affairs Committee, February 2011; Beck, M. and Woolfson, C., Accidents at Work: the Scottish Anomaly, Occupational Safety and Health, Vol. 29/12, 1999; Johnston, R. and McIvor, A., The Scottish Anomaly:

Occupational Health and Occupational Medicine since 1945. http://www.rcpsg.ac.uk/Triennial_Conference_ November_2008/Presentations.

30. Sutherland, E., A Political-Economy of Safety and Health in the British Construction Industry with Special Reference to Fatal Injuries in the West of Scotland, PhD dissertation, University of Paisley,1999; Sutherland, E., Modes of Exploitation and Safety in the British Construction Industry, Radical Statistics, Vol. 69, 1998.

31. The impact of long hours and workplace stress is examined by Kivimaki, M. et al., Using Additional Information on Working Hours to Predict Coronary Heart Disease - a cohort study, Annals of Internal Medicine, April 4, 2011, vol. 154, no. 7.

32. OECD, Going for Growth, Paris, 2012, chapter 5, Reducing income inequality while boosting growth'.

33. Panic, M., Does Europe need neo-liberal reforms?, Cambridge Journal of Economics, Vol. 31, 1, January 2007.

34. Montgomerie, J., Middle Class Indebtedness and Financialisation, New Political Economy, Vol. 14, 1 March 2009; Tridico, P., Financial Crisis and global imbalances: its labour market origins and aftermath, Cambridge Journal of Economics, Vol. 367, 1, 2012.

SECTION 2 - DEMOCRATIC GOVERNMENT
Introduction

Neil Findlay

his section considers aspects of the provision of services by local government, the Scottish Government and the Westminster Government and explores areas of potential conflict and co-operation. Powers are often jealously guarded and sometimes devolved only grudgingly to other layers of government. The particular areas considered in the following chapters are local government, including its relationship with the Scottish Government and Westminster, health and particularly its overlap with local government, welfare provision and its spread across all three areas of government and lastly the role of the civil service in Scotland and its relationship with both Westminster and Holyrood.

At different times in history the significant areas of struggle have occurred at different levels of government. In the 1970s and 1980s political conflict was not only at a national level, but there were also major battles in local government that were to have a lasting impact on how councils and council services developed for years ahead. These victories, however, came at a price. In the early 1970s the prolonged battle between Clay Cross Council and the Heath Government over council house rents became a cause celebre, but ultimately the Council was taken over by administrators. The defiance of Thatcher's Government by the Greater London Council, under the leadership of Ken Livingstone and John McDonnell, resulted in its eventual abolition. In Lambeth and Liverpool the councillors' defence of their cities ended in defeat with councillors surcharged and expelled from the Labour Party. While here in Scotland the powerful Regional Councils were able to challenge Westminster, and as described in a later chapter, Strathclyde Region used a referendum to overturn Government policy on water privatisation. The Tory's response was to scrap the regions and give their functions to 32 smaller, less powerful local authorities. These examples, alongside so many others, show how local government could be, and often was, an important vehicle in the defence of public services and the promotion and development of progressive social change.

The erosion of local democracy is alive and well today as shown by the constraints on local government by the Scottish Government. Currently local government taxation and spending is shackled by a centrally directed council tax freeze that denies council's finance if they fail to implement the freeze. The 2007 Concordat struck between the

SNP and the Convention of Scottish Local Authorities (COSLA) sought to build a stable relationship between central and local government. The fact that it remained in place throughout that period of government and was bolstered by single outcome agreements is evidence that this was a relatively successful tactic for maintaining a level of harmony between the two levels of government.

This harmony is being challenged. Since 2011 and the return of a majority SNP Government pressures on local government have intensified with councils shouldering significant cuts with all the consequences that this entails. Between 2011 and 2012 and 2014 and 2015, Scotland's councils will see a 5.8 per cent real term cut. The obvious way for councils to balance their budgets is through reducing staff numbers. And since 2010 there has been a 6.4 per cent reduction equating to 25,800 people or 14,000 full-time equivalent posts. Indeed the number of people employed by local authorities is at its lowest level since 1999.

These losses, however, are not solely down to redundancy and should be caveated by the fact many have had their employment transferred to Arms' Length External Organisations (ALEOs). The figures are not broken down but significant job losses have happened and of course ALEOs are a sign of the sub-contracting culture that now exists in local authorities. Meanwhile the staff left behind have had their wages frozen while services are cut.

It is striking that while we are discussing constitutional change, the role of local government is rarely discussed. These following chapters show that local services are much in need of reform, but it must be a reform that reinvigorates local democracy and helps develop the progressive social change that, as the authors observe, historically local government has been so good at.

The authors in this section have done us all a great service in exploring how greater democracy within government at every level brings benefits. Public health is not simply a function of the NHS: at its core are good local public services. Scottish civil servants in Job Centres, working with the Border Agency, the Health & Safety Executive, employment tribunals and elsewhere are often in the front line of managing the fall-out from UK and Scottish Government policies and have been subjected to the same marketisation of their roles as in local government. The provision of welfare has never been as controversial. Rather than allowing the Tories to dictate the terms of the debate, progressive politicians at local, Scottish and UK levels should challenge the perspective that says we must cut and that the only decisions are what to cut. They must, instead, restate the arguments for the welfare state that were won in the last century. These are the issues that we must consider in the referendum debate and the following chapters help draw the debate back into the areas that touch the lives of the vast majority of our citizens.

Indeed, to date the constitutional debate has been almost completely devoid of discussion about the re-democratisation and re-empowerment of local government. The Red Paper Collective believes in the principles of subsidiarity and local democratic decision-making, but these have, up until now, been rarely mentioned during the referendum campaign. Credit should be given to the Labour Party's Devolution Commission, which has included local government as a key element of its work.

Public services are an essential civilising force in our society. Within that, local authorities are a crucial mechanism for delivering democratic service at a local level and their future and that of public services will help determine our social and economic well-being. Local government could once again be a driver of social progress.

A CRITIQUE AND VISION FOR LOCAL GOVERNMENT

Vince Mills, Gordon Munro & Stephen Smellie

L ocal government built the infrastructure for modern urban living. It created education and social care services and addressed the big issue of preventative health care, poverty, housing and welfare. Local authorities were once powerful centres of change, capable of identifying need and taking radical measures, yet were democratically accountable to an engaged electorate. They contributed to huge changes in society, mostly to the benefit of working-class people effectively ensuring the delivery of the local welfare state. That was until 1979 and the Thatcherite counter-revolution which, it should be said, built on the attack on local spending during the last years of the Labour Callaghan Government.

Marketisation

There has, however, always been a tension between the democratic accountability of local government and the desire by capitalism at a local and national level to exploit it for profit. In the late 1950s Harvey and Hood as quoted by Latham[1] made this observation:

> The capitalist class in Britain has been extremely successful in adapting the traditional system of local government so as to retain the appearance of democratic control of social services, by the people, while in practice maintaining firm direction behind the scenes.

The attack on local democracy under the Thatcher Government of 1979 was intensified by the Blair Government. Blair's approach to local government was part of the ongoing neo-liberal project, which, at the behest of corporate capital, required the dilution of democratic control to allow it access to public assets and 'markets', some of which will be discussed below.

In recent years successive Scottish governments have seen councils as mere instruments to deliver government priorities either through ring-fencing funds or the council tax freeze and the Concordat. Numerous functions and powers have been removed including Further Education, water, careers, housing, police and fire. Councils have become responsible for service delivery with a restricted range of powers. The removal of non-domestic rates and the freezing of council tax constrains the ability of councils to raise funds, which is mainly restricted to charges for care services, leisure and funerals.

What was once seen as terrain for promoting progressive politics through a form of local social ownership and the local delivery of universal services is now the site of some of the most successful neo-liberal interventions in the post-1945 welfare state.

Under the pretext of 'modernising', local government was to be more strategic and business like, in the literal sense of that term, running local government through cabinet as opposed to full council and committee. It was premised on the assumption that the committee system was too slow and politically inchoate. Its very accountability had led to it becoming over-bureaucratic and it is in that accountability that we have experienced a quiet, top-down revolution. Under the guise of being more responsive to council tax payers and giving a more participative role to the wider community, including, of course the business community, democratic accountability has been circumvented.

A report[2] based on studies of local authorities in New Zealand and Scotland, sponsored by the Institute of Chartered Accountants of Scotland, gives a gushing account of the changes that have taken place in local government. They describe 'The major result, in terms of managerial and organisational changes, was that of a move away from old-style bureaucratic management to a more responsive style of management...' And how this resulted in:

❑ A shift from service providers to being enablers, by outsourcing/contracting services;
❑ A move away from a set of values which were internal, and driven by professional interests within local authorities, rather than the needs of the citizen as 'customer';
❑ A rejection of short-termism and a desire to take a more strategic perspective on the activities of the local authority; and
❑ The promotion of a corporate philosophy and perspective rather than narrow, sectional interests.

They could have added a further bullet point: an increasingly apolitical stance by all but a small minority of councillors. Most, regardless of party, have imbibed the ideological demands of neo-liberal thinking. Councillors have been helped to this position by a series of legislative changes designed to transform local authorities into what Elaine Kamarck[3] calls a 'performance managed bureaucracy'. According to Kamarck this is characterised by public sector organisations where: budget rules, personnel rules and procurement rules etc. are traded off for flexibility; they use outcome or output performance measures; performance measures act as market proxies; and customer service is used to model organisational behaviour. The Best Value Framework introduced as part of The Local Government in Scotland Act 2003 was designed to do exactly that.

Another element of the 2003 Act was the establishment of Community Planning Partnerships (CPPs), which obliged councils to involve a range of bodies including police, health and regeneration bodies as well as community groups and of course the private sector. More recently, under the SNP, there is the single outcome agreements, yet another measure which challenges local authorities' role in local politics. The point is, only councillors have a democratic mandate, but councils are bound by legislation to these CPPs.

Other partnerships have also undermined local authority control of public assets. For example, the Private Finance Initiative (PFI) Public-Private Partnerships (PPP) and now under the SNP the Non-Profit Distributing Model (NPD). This last model was supposedly going to provide less rich pickings for the private sector, but this has been challenged.[4]

Leaving aside the question of profit, these 'partnerships' are examples of the shrinkage of democratic control. This loss of democratic control is intensified by other forms of outsourcing such as the extensively used Limited Liability Partnerships (LLPs) or ALEOs. Labour-controlled Glasgow City has around ten, employing around 12,000 staff. What is clear is that in the balance of power between local democracy and private companies power has swung away from councils. Examples of what that means include Glasgow City Council being forced to subsidise community use of school sports facilities after prices rose to unaffordable levels following their takeover by 3ED Consortium in a £1.2bn PPP deal. Glasgow's ICT and property management systems are provided by a public-private joint venture, Glasgow Access LLP, which has a complex structure including a Partnership Board which 'meets quarterly and is responsible for setting the organisation's strategic direction. It is chaired by the Chief Executive of Glasgow City Council. The council leader also attends with two senior Serco executives.'[5] Furthermore, the case study also tells us:

> Six months after the creation of Access and the commencement of the contract, Glasgow's Chief Executive invited Access' CEO to sit on his Corporate Management Team where all the Directors of service departments sit. This brought the opportunity of active participation in the council's decision-making processes and contributed to the close working relationship between Access and senior officials.

Perhaps this helps put in plain sight the end of the historical process that the neo-liberal project had in mind and the role that Britain's and Scotland's leading parties have played in it. Through a series of structural changes, local authorities have been stripped of their capacity to make major economic and therefore social impacts on the localities they represent. While this was very much the Tory project, it has continued under New Labour and so far under the SNP. It involves changing the culture of local government from a service provider to citizens based on a democratic exchange, to that of a market exchange based on actual markets or proxy market mechanisms. In all of this councils have been invited not only to engage with the private sector but also to share their way of seeing the world, so that eventually, like Orwell's allegorical pigs, it will be impossible to tell human from animal.

A question of power and political will

What then, should be the labour movement's response? Trade unions in local government have tended to see councils primarily as employers and therefore adopted a defensive strategy to protect existing services, structures and powers as a way to protect their council members' jobs. They have had little to say on the role of councils in local economic planning, stimulus and intervention, wealth redistribution and empowering communities. In recent times, in Scotland as elsewhere, the left, with some exceptions, have largely ignored local government as a place to take forward socialist policies. Generally the focus for the left has been to look to the Scottish Parliament or Westminster for redistribution of power and wealth, ignoring the potential of councils to enter this field.

Of course we need progressive policies at a UK and Scottish level, but they are also required, more than ever, at a local level. Poverty and ill health are often localised and need a local response and for that we need the greater empowerment of local government.

Just as in the late 19th century when local government responded to the dreadful levels of poverty in cities, towns and rural communities, today's councils need to use their powers of 'general competency' which would allow councils to do anything that they are not expressly forbidden from doing. For example, a council could address the issue of fuel poverty and the exploitation of consumers by the 'Big 6' power companies by establishing local energy companies which could generate and distribute cheap electricity to council tenants, services and community groups.

They could, as was promoted by the Scottish Socialist Party in the early years of the Scottish Parliament, decide to address child poverty and ill health by providing free school meals and milk, breakfast and after-school clubs for children. They could generate apprenticeships for all school leavers to equip them with the skills and qualifications necessary to escape youth unemployment.

They could impose standards and rent controls on private landlords and confiscate properties where these are not adhered to. Councils could provide advice and support to workers where an employer indicates an intention to close an enterprise so that workers have an opportunity not just to oppose the closure or negotiate better terms, but to put forward alternatives to closure, including worker buy-outs.

These are just some of the measures local government could take to be more responsive to the needs of local people and their communities. However, to undertake these types of policies, the Scottish Parliament needs to give councils the power to act. So in addition to the power of general competency, councils need specific responsibilities and powers where a local strategy would be appropriate. This should not be controversial. Councils already have responsibility for planning and delivering on housing, education, social work, etc. Whereas these responsibilities have, generally, been successfully delivered over many years, there are others that could equally be devolved to council level in an overall responsibility to provide for the well-being of the community. Local government could have a greater role in public health, local skills and employment and local industrial strategies. Tourism, skills deficits and training, sharing of resources, development of local markets, supporting new businesses (including social enterprises and co-operatives) could and should all come under local strategies. Councils could then work in partnerships, but in this case the partnership would be local communities and local businesses rather than multinational companies such as Serco.

Councils already have responsibilities to promote equality within the community and use equality impact assessments to inform their own policies. This should be extended to include social and economic impacts and could be applied to all areas of development where public money is to be utilised. Grants to, and contracts with, industry, and the private and voluntary sector should be assessed against local needs, as well as nationally set targets. This would help to ensure that public money is used for the well-being of the community.

The money trick

For any of the above to happen, councils must be given the power to raise funds to pay for their priorities. Non-domestic rates and control over council tax (or replacements for either of these taxes) should be returned to local democratically accountable councils.

We have seen above the democratic deficit of using PFI/PPP models in local government, but they have also created a financial millstone for councils. National government should free councils from this by reshaping these debts and by insisting that the profits generated for the private financial interests be redirected back to public use. Future capital spend should have nothing to do with these failed models and instead be allowed to use prudential borrowing. Councils can and do make a huge contribution to the local economy by infrastructure projects and through the training and employment opportunities that are created. These could be effectively integrated into a local economic strategy.

In addition to borrowing powers, councils should be able to tap into other sources of funding such as tourist taxes, a local supermarket tax that could help generate small business growth or an off-sales tax to help fund activities for young people. In most parts of Europe, local government can raise money through a variety of taxes. Of course, we have to be aware that it could lead to well-off areas raising more and poorer areas very little. There has to be a redistribution of wealth within and between local authority areas. A more progressive form of council tax would, however, be a useful start.

Councils should also be able to insist that the projects for wind farms, private builders and supermarket chains should be developed in full partnership with the council and community organisations or better still, by developing fully public- or community-owned schemes.

A balance of power

Opinion polls show that there is a large majority in favour of more powers for the Scottish Parliament, whether it be through enhanced devolution or full independence. A strong Parliament, whatever the constitutional arrangements, needs to be counterbalanced with strong local government with the power to act locally. The alternative is an overly centralist state with power in Edinburgh increasingly distant from local communities.

There also needs to be a balance between, or at least, concerns about unregulated post code lottery, where access to services and charges vary from one council to another, and the principle of subsidiarity, where power is devolved to the lowest level possible. However where there is a consensus around the need for some services to be delivered on an equal basis with minimum standards across the country, the Scottish Government should set these standards particularly in key services - education, access to care and standards of housing. However, local government could and should be empowered to exceed these minimum standards if there is a local priority. But also subsidiarity should involve councils developing structures at a smaller, more local level, which could be responsible for identifying local need and developing responses to these. This could be seen in childcare, support for older people, environment protection and leisure. Strong and progressive local government is not only desirable but possible. It will be an essential part of creating a fairer, more equal and sustainable Scotland.

Edinburgh City Council - a case study

> But the working class cannot simply lay hold of the ready-made state machinery, and wield it for its own purposes.
> Karl Marx[6]

> To fight for the future does not mean not to avoid doing every day what must be done for the present. These two ideas must not be confused.
> Fidel Castro[7]

The Edinburgh City Council Labour Group went into the May 2012 election with a commitment to make Edinburgh a Co-operative Council. It had studied the approach of Lambeth Council in London and after considerable internal discussion took that idea out into the city.

It was road-tested with a draft manifesto which was put out for comments and input a full six months before the election. More than 1,000 replies and two drafts later the 'Moving Edinburgh Forward Manifesto' was adopted with the ambition for Edinburgh to become a Co-operative Council. This early involvement of electors may have contributed to Labour gaining an additional five elected members making it the largest political group. However, without an outright majority it formed an administration with the SNP forming the Capital Coalition.

The co-operative ethos was made an integral part of the Capital Coalition's contract with its citizens. This was taken forward with a seminar 'Co-operative Edinburgh - Thinking Outside The Box' for elected members, officers, key partners and third-sector representatives looking at the possibilities for energy, housing, childcare and social care co-operatives which resulted in the establishment of a Co-operative Development Unit. The Unit works to a framework to advance a Co-operative Capital providing advice, co-ordination, promotion and a central hub for sharing best practice. The aim is to have, by the end of the council term, a co-op in each of energy, housing, childcare and social care.

A good example of the policy in action is the setting up of an energy co-op by Balerno Village Trust. As an industrial provident trust, the aim of this initiative is to harness energy from a weir at Harlaw Reservoir and to sell it to the grid. The surplus from this will be used to meet the community plan of Balerno Village Trust. While small in scale, it does show how a different approach can be taken to create more for the common good. The further potential of community energy co-ops to combat fuel poverty and the exploitation of people by the privatised energy companies could also be taken forward to tackle the profiteering at the public's expense.

The area already has a thriving retail group of Scotmid co-op stores competing with the giant supermarket chains. The expansion of Edinburgh Bicycle Co-op from small beginnings to a successful small business, which is now in Aberdeen, Leeds, Manchester, Newcastle and Sheffield, shows that other areas of retail apart from food can provide an alternative to the behemoths. The real challenge is to move beyond retail to a point where production itself is controlled by the producers. This can be done. Whether it is co-op farms producing products for their own range of goods or even in industry following the example of Mondragon in the Basque country.

The positive example of Mondragon coupled with examples and lessons learned from recent history such as the swords into ploughshares work by Unions at Vickers Aerospace, the UCS Work-In, the Pink Panther produced by workers at Caterpillar for Nicaragua show our true potential. In reaching that potential, class confidence is also created and begins to create the conditions in which a real transformation of production can take place.

In the meantime there is still work that can be done, not least in and by councils. Despite the constraints of the Single Outcome Agreement and the council tax freeze councils still have substantial resources that can help tackle some of the problems faced by cities in Scotland. Glasgow has a budget of £1.4bn and Edinburgh a budget of £1.1bn, which combined with the budgets of Dundee, Aberdeen, Inverness, Stirling and Perth Councils, could be used towards socially useful production and for socially useful aims.

Despite the fact that the ground is circumscribed for local government, it can still deliver. But it needs financial support from Scottish Government along with a free hand to meet local circumstances rather than work to a central diktat whether from Westminster or Holyrood.

When Marx made his observation at the head of this section it was at a time when the franchise was extremely limited. The potential is there in local government to do that hardest of tasks for socialists - to build a better world - but in doing so class confidence is built and the movement strengthened. Despite low turnout for local government elections and siren calls from the self-styled far left to leave the local government field of play, this work is necessary. This is the discipline needed by socialists to which Castro refers when he exhorts us in having one eye for the future while putting our shoulder to the wheel for what needs to be done now.

Endnotes

1. Latham, P., The state and local government, London: Manifesto Press, Croydon, 2011.
2. Lapsley, I., Pallot, J. with Levy, V., From Bureaucracy to Responsive Management: A Comparative Study of Local Government Change, ICAS, Edinburgh, 2002.
3. Kamarck, E., The End of Government as We Know It: Making Public Policy Work, London, 2007.
4. Hellowell, M. and Pollock, A.M., Non-Profit Distribution: The Scottish Approach to Private Finance in Public Services, Social Policy & Society 8:3, Cambridge University Press, 2009.
5. Sotiropoulos, A. and Duckworth, S., Glasgow Access LLP Case Study, The Serco Institute, 2011. Available at: www.serco.com.
6. Marx, K., The Civil War in France, selected works, 1970.
7. Castro, F., Capitalism in Crisis. Ocean Press, 2000.

SECTION 2
Chapter 2

PUBLIC HEALTH

David I. Conway

Public health is defined as 'the science and art of promoting health and well-being, preventing ill health and prolonging life through the organised efforts of society'.[1] It takes a broad definition of health - not merely the absence of disease - but health as 'a state of complete physical, mental and social well-being'.[2] Health is viewed as a resource for everyday life, not the object of living, but a positive concept emphasising social and personal resources to achieve and adapt to reach our potential.

The approach to public health includes: i) considering the whole population, ii) emphasising collective responsibility for health, its protection and disease prevention, iii) recognising the role of the state, the role of socio-economic and wider determinants of health and disease, and iv) building partnerships with all who contribute to the health of the population. The practice of public health covers activities ranging from health improvement and tackling health inequalities to improving the quality of NHS care defined in terms of person-centred, safe, effective, efficient, timely, and, most importantly, equitable services, as well as including important health protection work in relation to infectious diseases, chemicals, radiation, environmental hazards and emergency response.

Public health is wider than a health service-led endeavour: it is also a core function of local government. This is particularly relevant in relation to public health work associated with other public services, including education, social and care services, transport, public spaces and local amenities. Such areas of work have a greater impact on community and individual health than health services.[3] If the determinants of health were ranked in order of importance (most significant first), it would show: income and income distribution, education, jobs, social support, early childhood experiences, physical environment and personal behaviour. Health services would come towards the foot of the list. We would, therefore, get far better health benefit investing more in schools than hospitals. This is a paradox all too often lost in political priorities.

Public health work (delivered across all public service sectors) has at its heart inherent values of fairness and equity, inclusiveness and empowerment of people and communities (working with them not to them), and seeking best evidence-based practice and policies. These policies should include fuller holistic and joined-up public service solutions for improving public health and concepts of preventative spend i.e. spending on prevention to save on more costly salvage treatments or care.

These principles and values of public health very much chime with those of the Labour Party as outlined in Clause IV: that through 'common endeavour we achieve more than we achieve alone', that aim for us all 'to realise our true potential', and to create 'a community in which power, wealth and opportunity are in the hands of the many, not the few', with core values of freedom, solidarity, tolerance and respect.[4] Moreover, it is not retrograde to think that Labour values acknowledge the important role of the state in creating and supporting our society, nor in reconsidering the role of nationalisation of essential public utilities or services. These values are increasingly relevant today. The NHS, after all, is the beacon of nationalisation.

For politics, society and public health services inequality remains the greatest challenge we face. Inequalities in income lead to inequalities in health. Much of the discourse on health inequalities in public health is synonymous with the social justice agenda and with social and economic inequalities. Inequalities in health are unfair and avoidable. They are determined by wealth, education level, occupation, power and prestige (or rather the lack of these).

Inequalities in health can be defined in terms of access and uptake of health services, in health behaviours (which themselves are more socially determined rather than merely lifestyle choices) as well as in health and disease outcomes. Inequalities are replicated across almost all measures of health. Their starkest manifestation is in life expectancy. The World Health Organization (to our shame) repeatedly uses this example of health inequalities: 'In Glasgow alone we can still see differences in life expectancy as extreme as 54 years in the poorest communities and 82 years in the most affluent, a near 30-year difference'.[5] Thus, depending, literally, on which side of the railway tracks a child is born will predict how long a life they will have.

These challenges almost seem too great, too intractable. But to quote George Orwell from The Road to Wigan Pier, 'Economic injustice will stop the moment we want it to stop and no sooner, and if we genuinely want it to stop the method adopted hardly matters'.[6] The first and most important requirement therefore is to find and harness the will.

There are four basic arguments that make the case to tackle inequalities, which would carry the vast majority of public opinion. Inequalities are unfair, affect everyone, are avoidable, and the means to reduce them are available and affordable. If undertaken, these steps would provide outcomes which would benefit all in health, social and economic terms. If society and politics create health inequalities then they can be solved. The means to tackle health inequalities lie primarily in addressing the fundamental structural income and social inequalities. Consensus is also emerging on the need to refocus local action away from 'downstream' behavioural lifestyle change interventions, which have had limited success and (according to the recent Audit Scotland report)[7] cost no small fortune, to more 'upstream' and 'asset-based' approaches to improving health outcomes. This recently proposed 'asset-based' approach emphasises positive aspects of communities instead of deficits, and supports communities and individuals to have more control over their own circumstances.[8] This work is not dissimilar to community development approaches, which has largely been lost from and was never fully adopted by NHS-led public health activities. However, unlike community development, asset-based approaches fall short of explicitly focusing on the investment in disadvantaged communities which would enable local people to participate in building and developing community resources. Examples of community development work - which develops local solutions for local issues - include: fresh food co-operatives, credit unions, local energy saving initiatives and environmental enhancing schemes.

Such investment in communities does not come for free - it must involve both finance and commitment and not just the latter. This Big Society-like notion that community transformation can emerge unsupported is fantasy. We are talking about the need to target those communities which are fragmented and poor in terms of financial and social capital and local support networks. Struggling communities cannot be expected to achieve change on their own. While we are in the midst of an economic recession and finances are tight, the need for financial support is even greater. Unless a redistributive approach to resources is taken towards these communities, poverty, child poverty, income inequalities and health inequalities will all increase and worsen to the detriment of all.

Therefore, there is no doubt that political commitment is essential. The solutions are in political and economic policy. Building and harnessing the will is the key challenge and is needed across society, from local and national government to non-government organisations including Health Boards. Building and developing the will for change can only come from genuine public involvement and decision-making in health care and public services.

Community and public involvement and democracy in Scottish public health

The discourse from the Scottish Government and the health sector professionals proclaims ambitions to improve public participation in health services at all levels of decision-making. The reality in practice, however, does not match these aims. Arnstein's 'Ladder of Citizen Participation'[9] provides a model of levels of participation across government, society and public life (Figure 1).

At best, the work of the health sector with communities achieves the level of

partnership, but at worst it has
an arms' length relationship that
pretends to want partnership
but in reality, retreats from
genuine partnership. Activities
of engagement usually languish
and stall at the consultation level.
Communities unsurprisingly
sense such consultations are
academic with decisions already
made. It is not clear why there
is such reluctance from public
health decision-makers to climb
Arnstein's ladder and genuinely
work with communities. Perhaps
it is fear of loss of control, lack of trust and professional collusion to maintain the
medical-managerial dominated consensus.

Figure 1: Arnstein's Ladder of Citizen Participation

COMMUNITY CONTROL/LEADERSHIP

DELEGATED CONTROL

PARTNERSHIP/CO-OPERATION

PARTICIPATION

CONSULTATION

INFORMING

PLACATED/MANIPULATED

HIERARCHY

Indeed, despite the rhetoric, ensuring genuine public involvement in decision-making,
delivering equity of care and reducing inequities in access to this care have never been
top priorities. In Scottish Government health policy there are well-written words in
policy documents about making the NHS person-centred and a 'Mutual NHS' aiming
to 'strengthen public ownership' and 'improve rights to participate'.[10] A key step to
improving the public involvement in the NHS was the commitment to piloting the
election of board members on Health Boards; the report of the evaluation of the Health
Board elections and 'alternative pilots' was recently published.[11]

Two Health Boards, Dumfries and Galloway and Fife, had elections for half of their
board members. On the whole the evaluation was positive; the elections brought
direct local democracy and accountability to Health Boards. But some concerns were
expressed, including the low turnout, the ability for elected boards to function as
corporate entities and issues related to the limited diversity of candidates. However,
these concerns do not counter the local democratic accountability that directly elected
members deliver having the power to change the way Health Boards function and to
hold NHS management to account. It is also a major step in opening up the transparency
of regulation of public health and NHS services in Scotland from what, at present, often
seem like closed decision-making, accountability and management processes.

There will be many reasons or excuses given for not rolling out these direct elections.
Chief among them is the cost (an estimated £12 million) and there will also be questions
about the unquantifiable added value of democratic accountability. This is where the
evaluation evidence can only go so far and values become important. You either believe
that public services should be locally democratically accountable, or you believe that
they should be run by political appointees and others selected for their expertise.

However, to avoid taking the decisions to ensure health services are more democratically accountable leaves the attractive idea of a 'Mutual NHS' as hollow rhetoric.

To inform this decision another debate is necessary about the future sustainability of the 14 territorial Health Boards. One Health Board (Greater Glasgow and Clyde) already provides services to nearly 25 per cent and specialist regional services to more than 50 per cent of the country's population.[12] However, any form of centralisation of the organisation of health services into regional boards will have to be balanced in terms of ensuring local accountability. Further rationalising of Health Boards should not come at the expense of or as an excuse not to democratise their decision-making processes.

Of course there is another way to make public health and Health Boards more democratically accountable. This solution is an old one and possibly even less popular, particularly among health professionals, namely, the return 'home' of public health and indeed wider primary care health services to local government.[13] It is worth remembering that the most significant public health breakthroughs in history (e.g. water and sanitation services, clean air, good-quality housing, service and town planning) happened when public health responsibility sat within local government, with joint working between health professionals and local government colleagues.

It is the elected representatives in local government who have the more inherent and natural community and public perspective that is often missing from NHS-led public health, which is largely focused on evidence-based or cost-effective principles. Currently, there are difficulties in bringing Health Boards and councils together for the purposes of a more joined-up health and social care for elderly and children's services and this highlights the need for some form of structural reorganisation. The Scottish Government's recently published consultation response on integrated care for the elderly does not support merging services or budgets. The favoured model instead seems to be a local quango made up largely of Health Board and council representatives, with limited democratic accountability.

Reorganisation for the purposes of local accountability needs to be balanced with other assurances that the services can remain fully public. On the one hand, the NHS in Scotland is securely a public service. It has been good at resisting the creep of 'any willing provider policy', which has blighted the NHS in England and enabled health services to be delivered by private providers. On the other hand, councils have readily commissioned services to arms' length organisations and companies - rather than maintaining their services embedded within council management.

A third option is the proposed creation of a 'National Care Service' for comprehensive integrated health and social care of the elderly, neither within the NHS nor in local authorities. This, however, fails to address the issue of local accountability and creates more rather than fewer organisational structures.

The devolved Scottish Parliament has protected the NHS in Scotland from the Coalition

Government's savage and dismantling reorganisation of the NHS in England. However, within these 'reforms' there is an irony that in England, some elements of the function of public health are being located back within local government. But, this chink of light is snuffed out by the non-democratic reorganisation which amounts to privatisation.

The major reorganisation of the NHS in England follows the seemingly everlasting discussions and tweaking and 'redisorganisation' of NHS structures across the UK that have occurred over the years. While the evidence from England informs us that any similar reorganisation or reform of the NHS in Scotland is to be avoided at all cost, they need not make us fear major reform per se.

The future delivery of public health services in Scotland

The Socialist Health Association in Scotland has long supported a shift, not only of the public health function of Health Boards, but a whole shift of NHS primary care and public health services into local authority control. Local authorities would ensure democratic accountability, the integration of health and care services and using the levers of local government to tackle the wider determinants affecting public health. This would enable, for example, public health to be much more than about changing people's behaviour, but be involved in changing physical and social environments. There is no doubt councils have better knowledge of, and links to, their local communities than Health Boards. Councils are inherently much more involved in people's lives and crucially have a political imperative to establish links with communities and community groups.

Such proposals get over the issue of the current lack of coterminosity of Health Board and council boundaries (where the Health Board area and local authority boundaries are not the same as in NHS Greater Glasgow and Clyde Health which overlaps with six local authorities) but involve considering major structural reorganisation, including the numbers of local authorities and Health Boards. While on the one hand, there are strong arguments to rationalise numbers of health and local authorities in Scotland, on the other hand there are lessons from Scandinavia where they are not frightened of small area local authorities and devolution of power and where primary care and community care are brought together within these authorities.[14] Outstanding issues of how hospital and specialist care is managed and organised will crucially need to be resolved but could also form part of the new public service authorities. Time in hospital is the expensive outcome if health and social care are not fully integrated.

A key cross-cutting theme of the recent 'Christie Commission report'[15] on public services in Scotland was tackling inequalities which recognised the importance of preventative spend and of getting public services out of silo working. Christie has already taken us on the important first step in the process of reviewing the delivery of public services including considering the role of all-purpose authorities. The report also pointed to plans underway in the islands to merge Health Boards and councils to create all-purpose authorities.

It is only through fully and meaningfully integrating health and social care and wider services locally, supported by much fairer and redistributive structural and fundamental social and economic policy, that health inequalities can be tackled. Such reform is not conservative; it is radical and will require serious reforming leadership. But there is great opportunity in such change. Tackling health inequalities will be the ultimate gain, realised from tackling inequalities across society.

Detailed consideration, never mind action, on reforming public service structure is largely on ice due to the independence referendum. The two recent Scottish Nationalist governments have seemed to lack the appetite for major public sector structural reform, perhaps for fear of rocking the boat in light of their all-consuming independence agenda. However, such public service reforming powers are already within the gift of the devolved Scottish Government, even though the fundamental social, economic and welfare levers to fully tackle inequalities are not. There would be a strong argument for such enhanced powers to be further devolved although it does beg the question, what are we actually doing with the powers we already have?

The response to this ought to begin with treating councils with more respect and trust and giving them more power. Their budgets and priorities are increasingly determined and controlled by the Scottish Government - epitomised by the council tax freeze, ironically, a policy which constrains local power much in the same way Nationalists argue Westminster does to Scotland. Moreover, in the interests of public health, Health Boards and local authorities need to end the power battle and work together. As Labour's first leader Keir Hardie himself once proclaimed, 'Socialism is not help from the outside in the form of state help. It is the people themselves acting through their organisations, regulating their own affairs.' Therefore, we need to continue on our journey of devolving power and shifting decision-making from the centre to communities and the public. Local common public service authorities are a way to deliver this with democratic accountability at their heart.

Endnotes

1. UK Faculty of Public Health. 2013, http://www.fph.org.uk/.
2. WHO. Constitution of the World Health Organization, 2006, http://ww.who.int/governance/eb/who_constitution_en.pdf.
3. NHS Health Scotland. Reducing health inequalities and improving health: What councillors can do to make a difference, 2013, http://www.healthscotland.com/documents/6241.aspx.
4. Clause IV Labour Party Rules Aims and Values.
5. WHO. Commission on Social Determinants of Health, 2010, http://www.who.int/social_determinants/thecommission/finalreport/en/index.html.
6. Orwell, G., The Road to Wigan Pier, Penguin, London,1937.
7. Audit Scotland, Health Inequalities in Scotland, 2012, http://www.audit-scotland.gov.uk/work/health_national.php.

8. Chief Medical Officer Annual Report 2010 Assets for Health, 2011, http://www.scotland.gov.uk/ Publications/2011/12/14120931/0.

9. Arnstein, S.A., A Ladder of Citizen Participation, Journal of the American Planning Association, 1969, 35 (4).

10. Scottish Government, Better Health, Better Care, 2007, http://www.scotland.gov.uk/ Publications/2007/12/11103453/0.

11. Greer, S.L., Wilson, I., Stewart, E. and Donnelly, P., LSE Enterprise and University of St Andrews. Evaluation of the Health Board Elections and Alternative Pilots - Research Findings, 2012, http://www. scotland.gov.uk/Publications/2012/12/1328/downloads.

12. NHS Greater Glasgow and Clyde, General facts and figures, 2013, http://www.nhsggc.org.uk/content/ default.asp?page=s1202_1.

13. Socialist Health Association, Reform of the NHS Chronology, 2013, http://www.sochealth.co.uk/national-health-service/reform-of-the-national-health-service/.

14. Bort, E., Local healthcare provision in Norway - an expression of applied democracy, Socialist Health Association Scotland, Healthier Scotland, The Journal, 2012, http://www.shascotland.org/healthier%20 scotland%20journal%20mar12.pdf.

15. The Christie Commission Scottish Government Commission on the Future Delivery of Public Services, 2012, http://www.scotland.gov.uk/About/Review/publicservicescommission.

SECTION 2
Chapter 3

DELIVERING WELFARE
Katy Clark

When further powers for the Scottish Parliament are debated, it is usual to find aspects of welfare among the top choices for greater devolution. As the impact of the Conservative-led Government's 'welfare reform' benefit cuts are felt over the coming months that call is likely to get louder.

The bedroom tax changes to disability benefits and other benefit cuts are already causing massive anger and suffering in our communities. It is estimated that about 80 per cent of the Coalition Government's cuts have still to come so as time goes on things are going to get even more difficult. Even the minimum wage is under threat. Yet, despite all of that many people are, apparently, still not convinced of the case that there is an alternative.

The main argument for devolution of welfare is the belief that Scotland would make different more compassionate choices. That may well be true. However, to offer something significantly different to the people of Scotland on welfare it will be necessary to be far more ambitious than we have been. There would have to be a political decision to spend more money on this sector rather than simply changing priorities. As many politicians are so fond of saying, the money has to come from somewhere. In my opinion as of yet there is little reason to believe that politicians at Holyrood have been willing to consider taking the radical steps which would be needed to make significantly different choices.

Those choices that have already been taken, on prescriptions, tuition fees and on free personal care, have simply been taken at the expense of other areas of social and welfare policy - the cake has been divided differently perhaps, but has not been made bigger. Indeed there has been criticism that often it has not been the poorest that have benefitted and that these particular policies may have left less money for other areas of social provision. On the left, however, we are well aware that these are false choices. Proper funding of Higher Education should not and does not have to be at the expense of Further Education and free prescriptions should not be instead of building council housing or railways. This argument has, however, not yet been won in any part of the UK.

One of the areas of dispute is whether Scotland would or would not be better off if there was devolution of taxes or independence. Does Scotland get more out of the system or pay more in? If we collect more of our own taxes can we afford to do better? The SNP highlights oil and those against independence, the City of London and the South East. For socialists you would hope that this would not be a decisive factor and should not be the basis for our case. Do we really want to do better at the expense of the Welsh or the North East? What we should be interested in is whether wealth is divided more fairly between parts of society and parts of the country. Surely this is not about whether Glasgow or Cornwall pays in or gets out more: we want both to get a fair crack of the whip. The argument for maintaining a nationwide social security system is that it facilitates the pooling of resources and risks across the economy. It allows the possibility of redistribution from wealthier parts of the country to poorer ones. Much of that of course depends on the tax and benefit rules we put in place. We know that the current regime does not even attempt to target some of those who have the greatest ability to pay, thus for many on the left the real issue is whether Westminster is capable of delivering more progressive politics.

Also there must be an argument that we cannot pick and choose the best bits to be devolved or to be reserved. Can it be right to insist that the areas where there is the possibility of a significant redistributive effect, for example that the financial sector in the South East, remains reserved so that it can be redistributed to Scotland just because we think that suits us financially.

One of the interesting points that Johann Lamont makes, which has been much overshadowed by the 'something for nothing', speech is that she believes the biggest battle which has been lost in her political lifetime has been the arguments for progressive taxation. Indeed in recent years it has been unusual to see mainstream politicians explaining why it is necessary to pay more into the system in tax to get high-quality public services and a society worth living in. In the 1970s and 1980s, however, Labour would painstakingly explain why taxation was necessary and that it was worth paying more to get better health and education.

So far in 21st-century Scotland the political debate has been about council tax freezes, having 'Irish' style corporate taxation and getting rid of business rates. We have a huge amount of work to do to put forward the arguments that we need fundamental change in our tax system. Yes we need to tackle the £120 billion of tax avoidance both with additional resources and political will. But we also need to collect and redistribute more. The last Labour Government was very unwilling to tax to the level necessary to properly fund public services in government. That must change and there needs to be a clear intimation that it intends to overhaul the tax system.

The Calman Commission, which led to the Scotland Act 2012, looked at whether welfare benefits should be devolved and was broadly of the view that the disadvantages outweighed the advantages. It saw real difficulties with apportioning, for example, the state pension paid for out of national insurance. It was also concerned about 'benefit tourism' within the UK with people moving to areas where they could claim more, but also resulting in people feeling they couldn't move from one part of the UK to another because they might lose out. The report pointed out the very complicated nature of much of the social security system with many transitional arrangements for long discontinued entitlements.

When they looked at devolving just some of the benefits, for example ones such as housing benefit or council tax benefit which were closely tied to devolved functions, they were of the view that the close integration of the benefits systems would again make this extremely complex. What is interesting in this debate is that usually it is only some aspects of welfare which are suggested for devolution. The old age pension for example does not seem to be an area where there is much popular support for different approaches north and south of the border. The Scottish Parliament, of course, already has responsibility and powers for aspects of public sector pensions although in reality seems always to mirror whatever the Westminster Government does.

There has been a more significant debate in relation to setting different levels of benefits in Northern Ireland given there is already devolution of these powers. Benefit payments however in Northern Ireland come from their Block Grant and a system of 'parity' exists with the rest of the UK. There was a political wish to do something different on benefits given the drastic effect that the benefit cuts decided by Westminster will have. However, there was also a view that given 'parity' brought a net benefit to Northern Ireland, if they increased benefits it would risk a cut to the Block Grant. The decision has therefore been made not to do things differently at least for the time being.

In the past there has been a view that Westminster would always provide resources without the need for the Scottish Parliament to raise its own funds. The powers the Parliament has had so far have not in the main been used, whether it be the power to increase or decrease the basic rate of tax which has withered away with the failure of the SNP to ask for its extension, or the political unwillingness to look at the taxation of land. The Scotland Act is providing significant new tax-raising powers and it will be interesting to see whether there is any attempt to offer a different approach in the Scottish Parliament.

The reality is that in many areas of policy the Scottish Parliament has simply 'mirrored' whatever policy decision has been taken by Westminster. Particularly in highly technical areas this sometimes may make sense. However what would be good to see is a Parliament and politicians who, rather than simply accepting things as they are and only seeing limited choices and options, are willing to challenge the status quo and what Ed Miliband has called 'vested interests'. Westminster politicians representing Scottish seats should be actively involved in this debate and creatively trying to develop policies to redistribute in Scotland. Is there any sign that either a devolved or indeed even an independent Scotland would have a more progressive taxation system or indeed be willing to seriously look at redistributing wealth? Tax competition is likely to be a significant issue either in an independent or highly devolved Scotland where the Parliament had the wide sweep of tax-raising powers and fiscal responsibility. We need to put the case now about the direction which must be taken.

Powers to tax

There are different traditions in parts of the labour and progressive movements in Scotland which do however give hope. The strength of the anti-nuclear movement in Scotland has not been matched south of the border. The Scottish Trades Union Congress (STUC) has a proud campaigning history and has been willing to get directly involved in building movements in a way which frankly the TUC never has. The 'There is a Better Way' campaign has argued consistently against austerity economics in recent years and many in the Scottish trade unions frankly relish the opportunity to put the case for progressive taxation and redistribution. In education there has been no move away from comprehensive education or for academies or free schools. While there has been huge privatisation in Scotland, there has been some protection offered by devolution in health and other sectors.

However, to do something very different we need to take on the taxation and redistribution issue. There have been strong arguments against devolution of corporate taxation because of how difficult it is to pin down corporate profits. There is also a real fear given the current political realities that the Scottish Government might simply instigate a race to the bottom. Academics and the corporate sector will again put the case that higher taxes would lead to tax tourism and that business would simply move down south if Scotland was more expensive for them. The economic collapse in Ireland shows that a strategy of attracting investment through low taxation is also not a panacea. If the economic crisis has shown anything it is the need for higher global standards. We need tough global action to tackle low tax rather than more fragmented tax jurisdictions.

Despite notable work being undertaken about exactly who owns Scotland, we definitely are not effective at taxing them. A small number of landowners have got their hands on millions of acres of land which was once held in common. It is far from clear how much more could be recovered in tax even within the current tax arrangements. Despite devolution of land and property taxes there has been no serious attempt in the Scottish Parliament to change the taxation of land in Scotland. The most significant action has been the freezing of council tax and the abolition of business rates for most small businesses - hardly a bold socialist programme.

There is no doubt that Scotland, as indeed other parts of the UK, has huge wealth. Of course much of that wealth is hidden from most people who find it difficult to accept it exists. Do we wish to see devolution of corporation tax, inheritance tax or fuel duties and what are the arguments for and against? Realistically, there is likely to be most political support for a different level of fuel duties in Scotland. Such an approach would be fraught with difficulties including major tax avoidance as people cross the border to buy their petrol and fuel.

Housing benefit is currently one of the main welfare expenses. Its costs are of course fuelled by the high cost of housing. There has, however, been little attempt among the political classes to look at why housing costs are such a high part of many people's outgoings and whether, as a matter of social policy, that is something we should be encouraging. A debate needs to take place about what percentage of people's income should be spent on housing and whether the current level is pitched at the right level. Some argue for a land value tax as exists for example in parts of Australia and say that would put a more realistic value on land.

Using powers effectively

For me what is more interesting is what powers the Scottish Parliament chose to use rather than what further powers can be devolved. My politics are not determined by the border. I know that the situation of ordinary people in Liverpool, Hackney or Penrith is very similar to that in Aberdeen, Kilwinning or Castlemilk.

It seems that many on the left support an independent Scotland for romantic and emotional reasons. What we do share collectively is a huge lack of vision and desire to take the action necessary to tackle the massive social inequalities we have around us. Of course there are reasons for that - the enormous power of the multinationals, the City and financial institutions and the fear of rocking the boat. At the moment we cannot even get the buses regulated despite the huge public support there would be for that.

It was the Labour Party that was created to lead these struggles but, in my view, the battle is within Labour. At Westminster I have been asked to abstain on the Welfare Reform Bill, Pensions Bill which has taken more than a third out of the value of public sector pensions and on the Workfare Bill, despite huge disquiet in the Parliamentary Labour Party. There is a debate going on in the Labour Party as to whether austerity is working and about what kind of public spending and welfare state we want. Meanwhile the Tories are rolling back the state.

For those on the left in Scotland we need to be honest about the balance of forces and what the real prospects are of a more ambitious approach in Scotland. If we believe that there can be a 'shining beacon' which acts as a spur to all fighting for social justice throughout these isles, then that maybe is worth fighting for. We should, however, remember that in recent years many of the most senior figures in the Labour Party at a UK level have come from Scotland. Also, the leadership of the SNP have been quick to get in bed with business. Where is the evidence that Labour or any other party is going to be more progressive on welfare in Scotland than at Westminster? In Scotland we are faced with a real risk of social conservatism and a move to the right and to stop that we need to make the case for progressive taxation, a strong welfare state and universality. We must be honest about how we react to the major economic challenges because we face the most concerted of attempts by the markets to insist that democratic governments impose neo-liberal policies. Cuts are not necessary and they are not the cure; they are the worst thing we can do in the current economic circumstances.

Fiscal devolution to Scotland does not in any way stop the UK Government undertaking significant redistribution across the UK. We have huge economic inequality of wealth within the UK with large parts of the country facing significant social and economic difficulties. The power house of the South East of England and the City are there to be challenged. The real goal would be to win over the labour movement and the Labour Party to a strategy which takes on those interests. It is a real challenge for the Labour Party to develop effective policies and a winning strategy. A redistribution of wealth throughout the UK would be a real prize. Devolution of welfare may be part of that picture.

I, like others, have a long shopping list of things I would like to see a Scottish Parliament and indeed the Westminster Government do to address the massive social problems which are so evident. Whether Scotland decides to vote yes or no in the independence referendum next year and whether the union dissolves or not there is no doubt that England will continue to have a large say over Scotland's economic future. The context of the debate has to be whether a devolved or independent Scottish Parliament has the guts to stand out against 'Austerity Europe' with public sector spending cuts and privatisations sweeping the continent. For me it is not the powers that the Scottish Parliament has or does not have which is the problem but our collective inability to make the case more effectively for a very different world.

Chapter 4

YES MINISTER - IN THE THICK OF IT:
what role for a Scottish Civil Service?
Lynn Henderson

As we move rapidly towards 18 September 2014, there are growing concerns about what kind of Scotland either the SNP-led Yes or Labour-led No campaign are actually offering, as the quality of debate coming from Better Together and Yes Scotland continues to be drearily pedestrian.

Labour remain firmly Unionist. Miliband advocates that UK cuts are irreversible; Scottish Leader, Johann Lamont, contends that the principle of universalism is unachievable, creating a 'something for nothing' society. In this context it would appear that Labour's 'British road to socialism' is currently off the map. The SNP are little different. Despite some policies being more socially progressive than Scottish Labour, they remain firmly bedded in the big business agenda exemplified by their intentions to lower corporation tax. In short, the current political landscape suggests all the main parties, including the Tories and Lib Dems, remain firmly entrenched in the failed neo-liberal consensus of the past 30 years.

The idealists of the Radical Independence movement meanwhile discuss an academic notion of a Scottish transition to socialism, while ignoring that the powers and purse strings will not be held by the radical left in the foreseeable future but by an elected Labour or SNP Government. The reality is that however Scotland votes, our future is tied into monetary, fiscal, policy, services and structural transfers with the rest of the UK. Capital will continue to be concentrated in the City of London, and the European super market and international global forces of capitalism, militarism and repression will remain intact.

Therefore, the real debate for the labour and trade union movements is not if or how we achieve a Scottish road to socialism through independence, Devo Max or by defending the status quo, but how we tackle class inequalities, poverty and exclusion within Scotland, whatever the constitutional model. How do we deliver our society and services to a more socialistic model, and in doing so, protect public services from the dominance of the market?

The Scottish trade union movement is, once again, charged to take up its historic lead to demand Home Rule in the interest of the workers, their communities, in support of those in need and in solidarity with those in struggle globally.

Scotland as a beacon

For my union, the Public and Commercial Services Union (PCS), engagement and education on the future of Scotland is part of our ongoing message 'Austerity Isn't Working'. Tax Justice, an Economic Alternative, and a Welfare Alternative are required. On pay we published 'Britain needs a pay rise'[1] not focused solely on Scotland, but a collective analysis showing the devastating implications of the decline in public sector pay across Britain and how pay freezes and pay restraint have been applied. However, if there are opportunities for Scottish public sector pay to be a 'shining beacon' of progress, let's be having them. Sadly, to date John Swinney, SNP Finance spokesperson, has slavishly followed Osborne's pay policy, with only a flimsy tartan cover over it.

PCS is engaging members in a discussion about what kind of Scotland they wish to live in. In a widespread survey of members in 2013 we asked whether they believe, from the information currently available to them, an independent Scotland will impact positively or negatively on their pay, pensions, terms and conditions and job security. The results, when published, will inform an all-Scotland conference of branches.

Beyond PCS, the whole movement must become exercised and involved in discussion on how to participate economically as citizens and in our communities; how our children should be educated as future citizens and how our dependents should be cared for by society; what kind of social security and assistance we should expect in return for our national insurance contributions when we are ill, out of work, vulnerable or elderly; how justice should be accessible, fair and restorative; how our natural and carbon environment can be protected and secured for future generations; how our transport and technology can be improved; how we rid these waters of nuclear weapons; and, on retirement from work, what sort of pensions and dignity will sustain us into old age.

Of course PCS members have an acute interest in these issues and in the development and protection of public services. Of our 30,000 members in Scotland, almost a third are within the Scottish Government sector including Scottish Courts Service, Registers of Scotland, Scottish Prison Service, Scottish Natural Heritage, the enterprise agencies, national galleries, museums, etc. A small, but growing, number of our members also deliver public services on privatised contracts mostly to large multinational corporations. However, the majority of civil servants in Scotland and almost two-thirds of PCS members work for UK departments, delivering services from within Scotland to the public throughout the UK on welfare, taxation, defence, borders, immigration, passports, transport, tribunals, equality, and health and safety regulation.

Treatment of civil servants

The debate on Scottish public service delivery corresponds with constitutional debates. Discussions over how we deliver our services emerged during the Home Rule campaign of 1978/79 and resurfaced in the Scottish Constitutional Convention in the 1990s. It was inevitable that the future status and structure of the civil service became subject to much discussion and speculation after the establishment of the Scottish Parliament in 1999 and more prominently since the election of a minority SNP administration in 2007 and their consequent majority Government elected in 2011.

In spite of the antiquated and outdated notion of public sector workers being 'servants' to the Crown, the British civil service over the two centuries of its existence has been regarded globally as the gold standard for public administration known for its independence, probity and professionalism. Yet the political classes often hold civil servants in contempt, characterised as all powerful and manipulative by the 1970s' comedy of 'Yes Minister' and currently as ineffectual and irrelevant as shown in 'The Thick of It'.

That contempt, deliberate or otherwise, was epitomised in the form of political reality, not fictitious satire when the then Chancellor Gordon Brown stood up in the House of Commons in 2005 and announced to cheers that 100,000 civil service posts would be slashed. With that staff cut came taxes uncollected, benefits delays, IT failures and long queues at airports and ports. Devolved areas have not been immune from cuts. Although the PCS-negotiated no compulsory redundancy guarantee has been held with the SNP administration since 2008, over a quarter of civil servant jobs have been lost to the sector.

Such significant cuts raise questions over the role of the civil service. Professor Roger Surfeit and Mike Ironside undertook a study in 2005[2] for PCS which considered an alternative vision of the civil service as an essential part of democratic society and an institution that could query the economic orthodoxy of privatisation and marketisation of public services means greater efficiency. While not addressing the national question that we face in Scotland today, this work is essential reading for anyone interested in how the civil service and public services must be placed in a more socialised democratic society.

PCS played a significant role in shaping the civil service we have today in devolved Scotland. Under the leadership of Pat Kelly, my predecessor as PCS Scottish Secretary, our Union was fully engaged in the Constitutional Convention and the discussion on how the Scottish Parliament would be run, and how the Home Civil Service would serve the Scottish Government.

At the time, a separate Scottish civil service distinct from the UK Home Civil Service was carefully considered. Questions included whether the civil service should be directly accountable to Scottish ministers with senior appointments such as the Permanent Secretary made by the First Minister, and whether all aspects of civil service employment, pay, redundancy protection and pensions should be brought to Edinburgh. That model was rejected for a number of reasons: it was seen as too costly and cumbersome to administer; complex, especially transferring pensions and rights under the Civil Service Compensation Scheme; the need for a separate Scottish civil service code; and tackling the mobility clause and transferability of civil servants. In the event, it was agreed that 'if it ain't broken, why fix'.

Pay, however, is devolved to Scottish ministers in the 40 bargaining areas covered by Scottish public sector pay policy. Successive devolved administrations, including the current SNP administration, have adopted the UK Treasury guidance on civil service pay, and PCS members received the same four-year pay freeze and cap imposed by John Swinney as their UK counterparts had imposed on them by George Osborne running up to the referendum in 2014. After these dark years, PCS members in the Scottish Government may be asking themselves whether the advantages of retaining that Home Civil Service status were worth it. But they would also wonder whether a Scottish civil service controlled by Scottish ministers, of whatever political colour, would actually see any improvement.

Of course there have been debates on the future public sector landscape in Scotland. The parting shot of Sir John Elvidge, the previous Permanent Secretary, was to suggest that local and central government in Scotland could be centralised under one service. Report after report point to joined-up governance, the most significant being the findings of the Christie Commission, chaired by the late Campbell Christie, a former leader of civil service unions.

What has proved impossible is to put any of this into action in a coherent and meaningful way across the silos of Scottish public sector delivery. Co-location, shared services, IT networks, workforce development, pay coherence and HR functions all remain cumbersomely out of step. Trade unions have consistently raised the need to take a long-term view on these matters, but our cries fall on deaf ears and closed: to seriously address parity would involve a project scale beyond the one-year budget round or even the five-year Scottish Government administrative term. Networks of senior civil servants, chief executives, human resource heads and leaders in health, local government and Scottish public services may come together to endlessly discuss these concepts, but it always comes down to the same barrier: 'subject to affordability'.

Northern Ireland is an interesting study when considering a Scottish civil service delivery. For historical reasons, there is a separate civil service for Northern Ireland, the Northern Ireland Civil Service (NICS). The workforce are Crown employees, but it is distinct from the UK civil service with separate NICS Commissioners. Looking across the water, the 2007 SNP manifesto sought to create a Scottish civil service on the Northern Ireland model. PCS responded by undertaking a comparative study with our sister union in Northern Ireland, NIPSA. Of course, it is impossible to discount the historical context in which the NICS has formed over time and most importantly geo-political factors, but our primary concern was what a 'Northern Ireland model' would mean if applied to Scotland.

PCS found it would certainly mean lower pay - NICS pay is lower than elsewhere in the UK civil service. A Northern Ireland model also suggests a contractual relationship with UK departments such as the Department for Work and Pensions, whose functions are carried out by NICS staff, even though the policies and decisions over benefit levels are retained by the UK Government. Reading the Scottish Government's 'Expert Panel on Welfare Interim report' of June 2013, there are a number of parallels to suggest this approach remains attractive to a post-referendum SNP Government.

Further devolved, delegated or post-independence transitional powers to Scotland will be subject to scrutiny, negotiation and may take years, and in some cases decades, to transfer. What is immediate and clear is that in the post-referendum period between 2014 and the 2016 Scottish Parliament elections, it would be the current SNP administration that would be laying down the terms of that engagement.

Post-election, SNP or Labour are likeliest to be elected to run Scotland. Concerns over Labour's withdrawal from the principle of universal provision, and the SNP's obsession with low taxation must be a concern for us all. It is therefore essential that trade unionists, not the political parties, lay down some firm principles on key industrial structures for workers that are non-negotiable, not only in the civil service but also across the public sector in Scotland.

At the forefront of the PCS agenda in the debate over the future of Scottish public services is the protection of our members, the dedicated civil and public servants who have gone through more restructuring in the last 12 years in Scotland than in the entire history of the UK civil service. However, for PCS members it is also about protecting the vital services that they deliver.

Scottish civil servants in the Department for Work and Pensions - who have faced years of job culls, job centre closures and the transfer of employability work to profit-driven companies - will be looking to see what kind of welfare system a Scottish Government, either independent or further devolved, would provide, and what their roles would be within it.

PCS members in the Home Office - Borders Agency, Passport Office and Immigration services - want to know that their services will receive proper investment, and be backed up by policies that secure our country and are fair and humane and welcoming to peoples from other parts of the world. PCS policy is to get rid of Trident; however,

Ministry of Defence civilians need certainty that their jobs are secure and for those working in Trident-related activities that Scottish policies on defence diversification and alternative work is fit for all those who have served and administered, not just engineers and serving personnel.

Staff at the Equalities and Human Rights Commission, the Health and Safety Executive, the Tribunals Services and other UK bodies in Scotland want to know that a future Scotland will invest in their expertise but will also be strong on enforcement when companies and service providers do not comply with legislation. The many professionals at the Department for International Development in East Kilbride will ask what vision of Scottish international relations will embrace their global role in supporting the poor throughout the world.

Tax workers who have once again seen their numbers depleted by job reduction, and their expertise and skills in dealing with the public replaced by 'lean management' processes, are wondering why Mr Swinney, on the creation of Revenue Scotland to administer the new revenue powers brought in by the Scotland Act, announced to the Scottish Parliament that it would be cheaper for the Scottish Government to administer than HMRC. How tax is administered is as essential to how it is enforced. We have thousands of HMRC employees in Scotland with knowledge and expertise. Taxation should not be delivered on the cheap, and to say so reflects a view that low-cost taxation is a model that may be pursued. Over many years Scotland has been a haven for tax dodging - our hillsides are still scarred with tax plantations and our land ownership is still in the hands of feudal lairds. Scotland needs to raise revenue, not cut it, and those powers need to be enforced.

So for PCS, what is essential is that there is proper consideration, detailed and open discussions with those who carry out essential public services every day. My union has started a process to ensure that whatever Scotland decides, the people who work every day delivering key public services are at the forefront of developing a model for modern Scottish public services and that crucially they are accountable to the people of Scotland.

Listening to the views of those dedicated public sector workers is a good place to start for anyone interested in a more socialised democratised ethos in Scotland today.

Endnotes

1.http://pcs.org.uk/en/news_and_events/news_centre/index.cfm/id/5E952460-5E11-4C8B-8049A74DF8EA756F.
2.Surfeit R & Ironside M, The case for civil and public services - an alternative vision, Keele University, 2005.

SECTION 3 - DEMOCRATIC OWNERSHIP
Introduction

Tommy Kane

Considering the constitutional debate from a Labour and trade union viewpoint requires consideration of whether constitutional change in Scotland will help the material interests of the vast majority of the population. By extension it is the contention of this book that to progress the interests of the vast majority of the population necessitates a progression of socialist values and principles and more broadly the advance towards socialism.

It is apparent that no matter what the result of the referendum, the battle to achieve that political direction will still have to take place, whether in a new Scottish state or in the current UK format. The political challenge discussed elsewhere in the book is clear, not least because the political discourse and subsequent policy agendas are still influenced by neo-liberal suppositions. These are all too often complemented by a fatalistic approach with too many either unable or unwilling to consider alternatives to the current neo-liberal hegemony.

A key part of this ideological penetration has been the privatisation, corporatisation and commercialisation of industry and public services. Privatisation accompanied by regulation and corporatisation accompanied by de-politicisation have eroded the democratic control and ownership of industry, utilities, transport and other public goods and services.

Moreover, we have seen a massive transfer of wealth from public to private coffers. Perversely, this has seen the active collaboration of the state and the main political parties, which have legislated to enable the unprecedented levels of private capital accumulation that go hand in hand with neo-liberalism.

The most recent cyclical failure of capitalism shows again how this is a political and economic orthodoxy in obvious need of challenge and overhaul. Andy Cumbers has written that 'there is an increasing urgency for an alternative political economy framed around social and environmental justice'.[1] The chapters in this section chime with this call made by Cumbers. In various sectors the current model is critiqued with their respective failings evidenced. However, importantly each author has developed ideas and suggested policy proposals which offer a pathway towards an alternative political economy.

Taking such an approach is vital: if we are to advance the material interests of our people then we must be armed with the knowledge of how things are and how we can renew our vision of the better society. Some of the following chapters provide ideas that will assist in the application of practice. Far too often left thinking omits to formulate this transposition, especially those concrete ideas that move us from the current failed hegemony. As Andy Cumbers puts it:

> On the left, with a few exceptions, we seem to shy away too readily from discussing an alternative political economy, stuck in resistance groove, rather than rising to Gramsci's call for a war of position. In particular, there has been a surprising silence, given recent events, about public ownership.... [2]

The chapters contained in this section cover many fundamental elements of Scottish society, although they are representative rather than comprehensive: housing, railways, energy and renewables, water and wastewater services, manufacturing and football (yes football) are all included and all provide a road map towards more collective models of ownership. These, as the chapters show, can be community-led, fully nationalised, community-owned or fan-owned models. The hybrid nature of the suggested models highlights the scope for heterogeneous, not homogenous, forms of social ownership.

Arguably, these examples, either individually or cumulatively, will not constitute a socialist revolution. But we cannot sit back and wait for a full socialist transformation; incremental steps in the here and now can be thought of and fought for as progressive steps. As Bevan once said 'there can be no immaculate conception of socialism'. The fight for socialism and socialist policies across all and individual sectors, in industry and public services, is a constant struggle and a key battleground in the battle of ideas.

This is the value of these chapters - they provide ideas in the context of our current struggles. They argue for the creation of a new political economy and within that, they call for a renewal of public ownership and reinvigorated public services that place the wider populace, the broad public interest and the workers at their heart. Whatever the outcome of the referendum next year, these chapters are valuable contributions to the advance towards the better society.

Endnotes

1. Cumbers, A., Re-imaging Public Ownership, Scottish Left Review, January 2013.
2. See note 1.

THE IMPORTANCE OF HOUSING
James Gillies

ood-quality shelter is recognised universally as a basic human need. In the 1940s, there was a widespread consensus that at last recognised something must be done to stem the squalor arising from poor housing. As one of Sir William Beveridge's 'five giant evils', the new post-war welfare state recognised it had a duty to address this 'squalor' and help break the cycle of poverty where health problems created by inadequate housing restricted people's ability to work. Yet in the last three decades we have seen social housing completely overlooked by an unnerving belief in the private market.

A steady state withdrawal from housing reflects the influence of neo-liberalism. Housing, just like other public goods and services, has been commoditised and its value calculated principally by its exchange worth. Statistics show how, since the late 1970s, the UK has become a nation of homeowners, buyers and sellers.[1] In addition, government intervention (both Conservative and New Labour) has continually favoured a model based on equity rather than efficiency. This has resulted in policies such as the Right to Buy (RTB), which has diminished social housing stock. In Scotland alone over half a million social houses were sold off under RTB between 1980 and 2005.

Put simply, in the last three decades social housing has been sold short. Investment has been minimal and it is constantly stigmatised in media circles. Within Glasgow folklore there is a saying that 'the only difference between Barlinnie prison and Castlemilk is you know that one day you will eventually get out of Barlinnie'.[2] Public discourse consistently alludes to social housing schemes as a cause of many of today's social ills with its tenants held to account on issues such as anti-social behaviour, benefit fraud, welfare dependency and even obesity.

Numerous academic studies show clearly the correlation between manifestations of multiple deprivation including poor-quality social housing, poor schooling and low attainment levels. Policymakers may cite an awareness of this, yet disinvestment within the social housing model remains. We now have an outcome whereby Beveridge's vision of good-quality social housing providing inclusive accommodation within mixed communities has literally been destroyed. In its place we have a system that sees the urban poor contained in reserved spaces, stigmatised districts of perdition and the expanding prison system to which they are preferentially linked.[3] Gradually, social housing has shifted from a 'pillar of welfare' to a 'safety net' to house those with the greatest social problems.

The links between poverty, poor housing and neighbourhood disadvantage stretch further. Social tenants living in areas of high neighbourhood disadvantage face reduced access to work, lower levels of achievement and limited access to shopping or leisure facilities. With higher numbers of social housing located in areas of multi-deprivation, housing-led regeneration policy that ensures the most disadvantaged communities are not further socially, financially and culturally excluded must be central to political debate.

The housing crisis

In Scotland today a collection of past policies and external factors such as the RTB, disinvestment in social housing and more broadly the latest crisis of capitalism (initiated by the sub-prime crisis in the USA as a result of an over-reliance of private housing and the subsequent inability of people to afford their mortgages) has led to policies of austerity and less public money. Against this backdrop, housing finds itself in a perilous situation. In the market sector, an increasing number of homeowners face eviction with most forced into private lets which are often overcrowded with poor services and maintenance.

Another dimension to the crisis is the lack of supply needed to meet demand. There are now 160,000 households on the waiting list in Scotland, a 53 per cent increase on the 2003 figure. In addition, 115,000 socially rented Scottish homes have been lost to RTB and demolition since 2003 and homelessness applications now total over 50,000 per year. Therefore, less than a decade after the much-heralded commitment to end homelessness by 2012, Scotland has rising waiting lists, fewer affordable lets and more people in temporary accommodation and private lets than ever.

Even though private letting is regulated, standards continually fail to meet those demanded in the social housing sector. For example, a recent report by Friends of the Earth and the Citizens Advice Bureaux states that in England alone, 680,000 privately rented properties are among the worst insulated homes in the UK.[4] As energy prices reach all-time highs, thousands of private rental tenants now live in fuel poverty. Changes to the benefits system will simply compound problems in housing. Many low-income households renting privately in Scotland depend on local housing allowance (LHA) to pay their rent. As part of the government reforms to housing benefits, the amount of LHA a household receives is to change. Approximately 470,000 Scottish households are currently receiving the benefit, and it is estimated that 55,000 of these will be £10-£20 a week worse off.[5] When added to the problems faced by both tenants and social landlords alike via the introduction of the so-called 'bedroom tax' (which is nothing short of a scandalous attack on the poor), third-sector organisations are already reporting an increase in the financial pressures faced by both individuals and families alike who, through embedded structural disadvantage, are already entrenched in poverty. Arrears and personal hardship will increase and, depending on the respective landlord's policy, some will ultimately face eviction.

Current Scottish policy

Following victory in the 2011 Scottish election, the SNP Government immediately published its strategic vision for Scotland's housing, Homes Fit for the 21st Century. On the face of it, the report made for positive reading. It aimed to encourage diversity of tenure, build more homes in Scotland than at any time since the early 1990s and end RTB. Since 2007/8, a number of partnership models involving different subsidy routes, private sector participation and combinations of affordable and social rent have emerged.[6] Yet the harsh reality is that aside from providing new homes for new tenants, Scotland's Registered Social Landlords (RSLs) need to build 10,000 new social houses per year for the next three years simply to meet post-devolution homelessness commitments - a policy pledge that requires additional investment of £200 million per year. Yet despite the rich rhetoric and a recent 'housing windfall' of £38m as part of last year's budget, figures show that Scottish Government investment in housing fell from £525 million in 2009/10 to £352 million in 2010/11.[7]

Homes Fit for the 21st Century acknowledged the impact of the current global financial crisis on the provision of public services. It stated how, in order to build more homes, 'we cannot rely on traditional methods of funding therefore we will implement a radically different and innovative approach'.[8] Despite suggestions that this 'innovative' approach would not go down the same route as England and introduce short-term 'affordable' mid-market rents (usually around 80 per cent of full market price), the SNP has turned to market-based initiatives such as the National Housing Trust (NHT) to boost supply.

The NHT model began in 2009/10. It was the first real output from the Scottish Futures Trust (SFT), a government body set up to oversee and manage capital projects in health, housing and education as a not-for-profit (although it is more like capped profit) alternative to Private Finance Investment (PFI).[9] The NHT was intended to help provide good-quality rented accommodation where a need had been identified, but just how that need is determined is open to question.

NHT is a complex arrangement of Limited Liability Partnerships (LLP's), which follows an agreed path of funding, borrowing and rental arrangements until eventually the properties are sold after a period usually between five and ten years. Crucially though, NHT developments are built on land which the developers already own but as a result of failure(s) in the market they are not willing to build on them. So far the NHT

model falls well short of what is required. Since its introduction, phase one of NHT has only delivered 940 homes for rent across more than a dozen sites in Scotland.[10]
NHT is highly selective in that it is geared towards mid-market renters who cannot afford the deposit to buy. Its aim is to offer the 'correct' type of housing in the 'right location' at good value to the public purse.[11] Yet the model seems to completely neglect the homeless, the low-waged not in a position to pay mid-market rents and those who generally choose not to live in the 'right locations'. It seems founded on economic rather than social return - a view, incidentally, supported by the Joseph Rowntree Foundation which suggests that 'affordable' social rents under the NHT (normally based on 80 per cent of the area's market value) could rise by as much as £1500 per year.[12]

Models such as NHT draw much needed resources away from more democratic means of provision such as mutual or co-operative housing models towards what are effectively fashionable niche tenancies designed to plug market failure. Essentially the NHT and other such initiatives mean that the Scottish Government have blurred the boundary between 'social' homes and 'affordable' homes. Hence, it seems to have been forgotten that housing all our people, no matter their socio-economic circumstances, can only be addressed by creating a housing market that meets need, is sustainable and is not prone to the volatility of the private market.

Democratisation

It has become increasingly clear that the market model of housing provision has failed. Millions of homeowners worldwide face the fact they will never truly own their home and, in the more extreme cases, a real likelihood of repossession, while private landlords are allowed to build up their portfolio of ex-council stock and subsequently charge overinflated rent, much of it subsidised by the state. Put simply, the continual promotion of market-based housing only further stigmatises social housing as a place of last resort for those in the greatest need while exacerbating inequality, diminishing democracy and producing unequal social outcomes.

Over and above the failings in SNP policymaking regarding market-led initiatives such as the NHT, it is worth recognising that, tax and welfare housing policy apart, housing's status as a devolved issue has allowed the housing sector in Scotland to progress differently from much of the UK. First- and second-stage stock transfer brought an increase in more community-based Housing Association's and there has been growing recognition that housing sustainability can only be achieved through the development of mixed communities with a diversity of tenures. Scotland still retains some of the most progressive homelessness legislation in the world (though of course the proof of success will ultimately lie when figures show how successfully the rhetoric has been transposed into reality), while the Scottish Housing Charter introduced many far-reaching measures including statutory regulation that Scottish Housing Associations must forge closer links with tenants via increased methods of participation.

One model which can progress the building of new homes, increase participation and improve the life of tenants is the co-operative or communitarian model of housing. This is possibly one of the oldest yet least used forms of housing provision in the UK despite strong co-operative and mutual housing sectors existing in various countries across the world. Of the 35,000 member organisations of the European housing body CECODHAS, 30,000 of them are co-operative. Norway, Sweden, Austria, Germany, Italy and Spain have extensive co-operative and mutual housing traditions.[13] There is a relatively strong UK co-operative and mutual sector in areas other than housing. Over 4,820 jointly owned democratically controlled businesses are owned by more than 11.3 million people. That's nearly one in five of the British population creating and sustaining more than 205,800 jobs while contributing £28.9 billion in turnover and £9.7 billion in assets to the UK economy. Yet in housing only a small co-operative and mutual housing sector exists, largely in England, with limited debate about its relevance outside the work-related sector.[14] In Scotland the figures are verging on non-existent despite the Chartered Institute of Housing (CIH Scotland) describing how co-operative and mutual models of housing not only offer greater democratisation, but they also help break down barriers, increase empowerment and allow greater tenant control over contemporary issues such as digital exclusion and fuel poverty.

Hence, the Commission on Co-operative and Mutual Housing (2009) says that while the model is used extensively in Europe it is 'Britain's best-kept secret' in that it makes up only 0.6 per cent of UK tenure. Yet well-run housing co-operatives not only offer greater democracy, they also help 'nurture' society through small-scale decentralised organisations that are proven to offer high levels of not just tenant participation, but the ability to manage their own socio-economic circumstances much better and improve the overall social welfare and fabric of communities.[15]

The UK Commission on Co-operative and Mutual housing states that co-operative and mutual housing could provide homes in three key ways:

❑   Through mutual home ownership and community land trusts for low-income households who stand little chance of getting onto a housing ladder that's been pulled beyond their reach.

❑   Through co-housing and mutual retirement housing developing mutually supportive environments for elderly people that values their ongoing contributions and provides them with respect.

❑   Through housing co-ops, tenant management organisations and community gateways offering different ways to provide housing for low-income households that helps them to help and respect themselves and to feel like they're part of society.

In the 1980s, Fairfield in Dundee was one of the most deprived areas in Europe. After years of non-investment, a well-managed, strategic approach involving the Scottish Office and local partnerships set out to improve not just the economic, but also the social and human capital of the area. A co-operative model of housing - as chosen by the community - oversaw more than 250 properties refurbished, over 100 new houses built and a positive sense of identity return to the community. Residents were given a say in individually customising their homes and new low-cost social housing for people with disabilities helped add to the successful social mix. Now over 70 per cent of Fairfield's residents are employed, education levels have improved and life expectancy has improved. Importantly, poor housing has been eradicated and community cohesion increased.[16]

The impact of the constitutional debate

Irrespective of the outcome of the independence referendum in 2014 it is vital that the political decision-making process in place is capable of confronting the 'perfect storm' of disinvestment in social housing, the legacy of RTB and the global economic crisis. Whoever is in power has to develop ways in which we can invest in housing and circumvent the failed market model. After all, housing remains a pillar of all progressive societies wishing to better themselves in much the same way as work, health and education. Yes, all governments are currently operating in challenging times - cutting waiting lists, ending the reliance on temporary accommodation and building social houses takes money; however, housing is so important to the wider well-being and social fabric of our society that it simply has to be done. There are innovative and creative ways that it can be achieved, not least the co-operative model. Indeed along with market failure there comes the opportunity to explore such options.

The current approach of the Scottish Government to develop different forms of tenure is on the right lines, but it has to be broader in scope and meet the needs of all. Moreover it has to increase, not decrease investment and in so doing stimulate the economy as well as meet a social need. For instance it has to be in areas, both rural and urban, that take the most vulnerable individuals and multiply deprived communities into consideration and not just the 'squeezed', middle-class, first-time buyer trying to get onto the housing ladder.

The Scottish Government places great store on building 'affordable' homes. Affordable should always be an understanding that a house is more than a commodity to buy and sell. Affordable social housing should be more than just developing 'mid-market' rentals for those not yet ready to buy. Affordable should be power handed back to communities to help them build better places to live. Affordable should be well-thought-out developments that can help turn the stigmatisation of social housing on its head through the building of attractive, well-designed, well-managed houses that tackle present-day issues of fuel poverty, digital exclusion and an overall lack of esteem. Poor and insufficient housing produces a range of negative impacts such as ill health, poorly educated children, alcoholism, depression and crime. Providing homes that are sustainable, secure and truly affordable will embed democratic structures in everyday life that people will want to participate in and moreover begin to help address our present-day shame of poverty and social exclusion that still far too many of our citizens endure.

Endnotes

1. Lund, B., Understanding Housing Policy, Polity Press, 2011.
2. Shelter Client (2007) cited by Crawford (2012).
3. Wacquant, L., Urban Outcasts: A Comparative Sociology of Advanced Marginality, Cambridge, UK: Polity, Press 2008.
4. Minimum energy efficiency standard for private rented homes, 2011.
5. Berry, K., Housing Benefit Changes - Implications for Scotland, 2011.
6. JRF Report, Innovative financing of affordable housing, 2013.
7. Gibb, K. and Leishman, C., Delivering affordable housing in troubled times, 2011.
8. The Scottish Government, Homes Fit for the 21st Century: The Scottish Government's Strategy and Action Plan for Housing in the Next Decade 2011-2020, 2011.
9. Maclennan, D., Gibb, K. and Stephens, M., Innovative Financing of Affordable Housing: International and UK Perspectives, Joseph Rowntree Foundation, 2013.
10. See note 9.
11. Scottish Futures Trust (2011) National Housing Trust.
12. See note 6.
13. Bringing Democracy Home, Commission on Cooperative and Mutual Housing report, 2009.
14. See note 13.
15. Birchall, J., Building Communities the Co-operative Way, London: Routledge, 1988.
16. Regenerating Our Communities: A Snapshot in Time, CIH, 2013.

Chapter 2

A RAILWAY FOR PEOPLE AND PASSENGERS
Kevin Lindsay

P eople in Scotland and from across the UK want their railways to be reliable, affordable and punctual and also to be integrated so that connecting trains or buses are timetabled to coincide with their arrival. Those aware of environmental issues want to maximise rail freight, and the socially aware want increased passenger and staff involvement in rail services. The public's view was expressed in a public opinion survey carried out by Gfk NOP on behalf of the train drivers' union, ASLEF in October 2012.[1] Asked specifically 'Do you think UK rail should be returned to public ownership?' a whopping 70 per cent said yes, with 28 per cent disagreeing and only 2 per cent having no opinion.

Public service is a system for supplying a public need such as transport, communications or utilities. On the social side, rail enables people to travel, explore and enrich their lives in the least polluting way. In economic terms, it allows business to be flexible and expansive and it enables goods to be carried swiftly and reliably. This makes rail, by definition, a public service. So what is the best way to organise and finance our railways?

Public services should be accountable to and controlled by the people who rely on them, those who provide them and the communities that they affect. This approach has been rejected by the self-interested railway franchisers/owners and by the party that represents them. Their objective, as we know, is private ownership, where the profits are private and accountability and democratisation minimal or non-existent.

Current management of rail services is by government-issued franchises to Train Operating Companies (TOCs) and licences to Freight Operating Companies (FOCs). This system was born in the 1990s because of John Major's belief that 'private is good, public is bad'. Even Thatcher felt that privatising the railways was 'a step too far'. Major, however, was determined.

All the professional advice was that railways could not be effective if they were broken up. Planning needed to be integrated on a national basis. After all, one line leads to another and cannot be treated in isolation. This isn't a dogmatic or partisan view, as confirmed recently by Sir Roy McNulty in his 2011 report for the Government, 'Rail Value for Money'[2] where he states, 'Among the principal barriers to efficiency are fragmentation of structures and interfaces'.

However, John Major's dogmatic zeal for privatisation paid no regard to the impact on railway efficiency. He wanted the railway sold, and finding no single buyer for this huge national asset, he split up and sold off the railway network in pieces. It was an act of dogma-driven foolish irresponsibility that needs to be reversed.

It would be understandable though if there is a reluctance to simply renationalise. British Rail was not the Golden Age of myth. It had become an underfunded, neglected scapegoat paying low wages in exchange for secure employment. If that style of nationalisation was repeated there would be cuts across the board, wages would be frozen as they are for other public servants and investment in the industry would stop. So how can the railways achieve long-term investment and develop a sense of ownership from users of the service? How can we achieve these objectives without going back to the unsuccessful British Rail model?

Long-term investment

Rail planning is not something that can be switched on and off like a tap. Planning for the French high-speed rail network (TGV) began over a decade before the first train ran. Crossrail in London began work in 2012, having first been proposed in 1941! HS2 was approved in 2012, and work on phase 1 will start in 2017 and open in 2026: the phase 2 route announced in 2013 has a planned completion date of 2032. The lesson is that rail needs a long-term vision which will not come from private investors who are looking for a quick profit. Speculators may make short-term investment in a TOC with a ten-year franchise, but their interest is profit, not rail. Only government can develop a long-term strategy. The logical conclusion is that rail needs to be a public service.

Franchising prevents the integration of services. A single franchise holder on a major route may be reliable and punctual, but they have no concern about linked or connecting services. That is something that requires a broader national view that can only be provided centrally. Remember that rail privatisation and franchising were justified because they would attract private capital into the railway, but this has also failed. The rail regulator, the Office for Rail Regulation (ORR), has shown that private investment in the UK was £81 million between April to June 2012 compared with £103 million, £113 million and £158 million in the previous three quarters.

What is more, when things are not going well for private operators they abandon the franchise. National Express walked away from its Edinburgh to London routes. The company simply handed the keys back because it was not going to make sufficient profits, claiming that traffic had fallen short of its projections. The formula is that a franchise will return to public hands 'should an existing franchise not be able to complete its full term'. National Express could but it simply chose not to because its profits predictions didn't look good. This is gambling where you can't lose: win-win capitalism.

Privatisation was supposed to bring in 'risk capital' - brave take-a-chance entrepreneurs. The fact is that there is no risk capital in the UK railway. There is no risk for investors in franchises. If they perceive that their profit levels will not be high enough, they simply give the keys back and walk away.

Returning profits to the industry - for free

As in any business, investors in the railways want returns. Profit taking from franchises means money flooding out of the railway industry which could and should be used to deliver an improved railway: more track, increased capacity on trains and improved facilities at stations. It is ludicrous to bemoan a lack of available money to finance rail at the same time as supporting a system that drains money from the industry. It is an obvious contradiction.

There is a perception that every proposal to take an industry into public hands costs money. This is wrong. Actually taking rail into public hands costs nothing and is the only noticeable advantage of the franchising system. You just wait until the franchise ends and you don't renew it. Renationalising the railways is free. But, many pro-privateers still argue the now discredited mantra that private is good and public is bad; well actually the evidence is clear that nationalisation leads to greater efficiency.

Currently the East Coast Main Line, which runs from Edinburgh to London, is publicly operated. Directly Operated Railways (DOR) was established by the UK Government's Department of Transport in July 2009 when National Express walked away from the franchise. Under its not-for-profit publicly owned model, the East Coast Main Line has become one of Britain's most profitable TOCs. By the end of its financial year on 31 March 2013, it had returned £640m in premium payments to the government since it started operations in November 2009.[3]

If nationalisation was introduced across the board there would be massive scope to reinvest in the service. Surpluses could be used to tackle some of the main complaints about railways in Scotland. This could include: investing in new signalling to make lines safer (we still have semaphore signals in Scotland that are more appropriate to York's Railway Museum than Scotland's network); lowering fares; making improvements to stations; employing more station and on-board staff; improving punctuality; preparing for bad weather; lengthening trains to minimise overcrowding especially between Glasgow and Edinburgh; improving carriages; and extending electrification. Or, conversely, we could lose profits to the industry by paying out dividends to shareholders. Which do you think the public would prefer? Seeing the rich get richer, or tackling a service where, according to the ORR, less than half the rail passengers in Scotland are 'satisfied with value for money'.

Ownership by users

It can hardly be disputed that if you own something, you have control over it. Equally, if you sell something, you lose control over it. So it is with the railways. The public no longer owns it, and, economics aside, the services suffers as a result. So how do we manage to involve users and taxpayers in their railway service?

My union, ASLEF, set out a few years ago to make a bid to run the East Coast Main Line. Our objective was to see how easy it would be to establish a mutual rail company. We could hardly fail to be encouraged after the Tory manifesto said it wanted 'workers to gain ownership of the services they deliver through co-operative models' and Labour said it would 'welcome rail franchise bids from not-for-profit, mutual or co-operative enterprises'. Nice words, but in practice the franchising system presents near insurmountable hurdles to anything except a capitalist large-enterprise bid.
Bidders must:

❑ prove they have 'substantial experience of running passenger transport operations'. (We would argue that staff have a lot more 'passenger transport experience' than any desk-bound number-crunching accountant - but this isn't what the Department for Transport had in mind. They actually meant 'experience of owning a railway').
❑ have 'health and safety standing'- and in their terms, the union doesn't!
❑ provide detailed information of their balance sheets. And while this seems vaguely reasonable, how is it that huge companies like GNER and National Express have both defaulted on their franchise obligations?

❑ show 'a proven track record of service delivery and financial management' which amounts to between 70 per cent and 80 per cent of the bidding score.

❑ show three years' results of 'targets, trends, comparators and causes with sufficient scope to demonstrate capabilities'.

The message was clear: new companies (or innovative organisations like co-operatives and mutuals) need not apply. In case we were slow getting the message, we found we would also have to put up some £18 million for a performance bond facility and a season ticket bond.

Our vision is for a mutual or co-operative approach to rail combining national oversight with local organisations responsible to their communities. Recent research looking at Merseyrail and London Overground concludes that local management and accountability can improve local rail services and increase passenger numbers, reliability and accessibility. But we want to go further, and involve everyone with a stake in adequate rail services, including not only local politicians, but passengers, pressure groups, environmentalists, business people and everyone else with an interest in a reliable rail service.

A model for involvement

Scotland could be a model for such a change. ScotRail provides 95 per cent of all passenger rail services within Scotland and has services to Carlisle and Newcastle. It also operates the overnight Caledonian Sleeper services between London and Glasgow, Edinburgh, Inverness, Aberdeen and Fort William. It has the advantage of being a single entity in a specific area.

The union believes a 'not-for-profit' train operating company with a not-for-dividend structure can deliver genuine improvements to services by retaining profits and surpluses and investing them in Scottish railways. Such a model could attain much greater public accountability with active rail union and passenger involvement. I envision this model having a three-tier structure incorporating: a Scottish Rail board which would undertake day-to-day operations; a National Stakeholder Forum which would supervise the board; and a number of 'area stakeholder boards' (ASBs). The latter two would involve unions representing employees, local managers, local authorities, passenger groups, community rail partnerships, Network Rail and other relevant rail industry bodies.

The 'national' stakeholder forum would be charged with overseeing the whole network and could include representatives from the Scottish Government, Network Rail, local authorities (including some relevant ones from over the border), passenger groups, community rail partnerships, the business community and individual experts acceptable to the forum. To ensure its policies are implemented, it would nominate members to the Scottish Rail board. The ASBs would have a strong say in service delivery in its area and part of its brief would be to involve local communities. It would ensure the board delivered on its obligations and insist on the procurement of goods and services from local providers. This would not, we accept, be a full co-operative, but it would enshrine the 'not-for-profit' service ethos and seek to involve users and employees in the industry's direction. All profits, or surpluses, would be required to be reinvested into the railway.

I appreciate this would require the necessary political willingness to make the change and amendment to the 1993 Railways Act to end franchising. How much willingness exists is a moot point but what is certain is its viability and potential.

Given the current debate over Scotland's future it is imperative that we consider what constitutional arrangement would be best to achieve that change. At its 2013 annual conference, ASLEF became the first trade union to back the 'No' campaign in next year's Scottish independence vote. Delegates in Edinburgh unanimously agreed to campaign for a 'No' vote and to affiliate to the 'Better Together' campaign. Not one ASLEF branch in Scotland is in favour of taking Scotland out of the United Kingdom. This arose from the core belief that it is never helpful to erect borders, because borders divide people - and this is of even more concern to those involved in transport. We have seen above how fragmentation is the antithesis of a public rail system. Rail services in our view need to be planned, funded and designed in the broadest terms if cross-subsidy is to work.

Freight and the future

The future of the rail freight sector is less prominent in most Scots' minds, but in environmental, commercial and social terms it is massively important. Rail freight has a key role to play in the low-carbon economy to which Scotland is pledged on ethical and practical grounds. At the most basic level, it's difficult to attract tourism to the fresh-aired Highlands if the holiday-maker has to drive behind a row of articulated lorries. The benefits of moving freight by rail in Scotland are unquestionable. Rail produces 70 per cent less carbon dioxide emissions than the equivalent road journey and a gallon of diesel will carry a tonne of freight 246 miles by rail as opposed to 88 miles by road.[4]

We need policies in Scotland which will encourage rail freight, as opposed to the current system where there are no subsidies and often very little encouragement. Freight has to pay for track access (that is, to run trains) and decisions on the level of those payments are crucial. Currently the charges are set by the ORR. Earlier this year it introduced an additional charge of £4.04 per tonne of coal being used for electricity generation from 2016. This could increase the cost of transporting coal from Scotland to English power stations by up to 40 per cent. The Freight Trade Association (FTA) estimates this could lead to the loss of 4,000 Scottish jobs, some 150,000 more coal lorries being forced onto Scotland's roads, increased road congestion and accidents and increased pollution. 'How does that fit with Government's environmental agenda?' the FTA asks.

But freight has implications beyond tourism and the environment. An additional threat is that exporting coal to England could become uneconomic, which would put at risk over 4,000 jobs in rural parts of Ayrshire, Lanarkshire, Fife and Dumfries & Galloway. Opencast mining in Scotland still accounts for 1,500 jobs, supports a further 3,000 jobs and is worth more than £450 million to the Scottish economy. Transport Scotland, which speaks for the Scottish Government, said it is 'disappointed' with the ORR decision to increase track access charges. Clearly there is an urgent need for a body in Scotland which is prepared to do more than be disappointed.

A policy of full support and encouragement for rail freight, and the consideration of incentives to industry to use it, would be a positive step in the right direction and further emphasises the need to have an integrated railway which includes freight as an equal partner to passenger transport.

An opportunity to be seized

ScotRail is in a unique position as it services a discrete geographic area, even if its necessary forays across the border confirm the basic need for integration of rail into the wider area. Its profits in 2010 amounted to £14,401,000. That, for a start, is £14 million that could be used to improve Scotland's railways.

It is also a fact that rail is a public service, but it is not run as such, and that is where so many difficulties arise. As a service that is provided for the benefit of passengers and potentially the tax-payer and because its employees invest their lives in it, these are the interest groups that should be setting its direction, assessing its performance and benefitting from its successes. Our job is to organise a framework to achieve this.

Rail usage statistics published by the ORR in February 2013 show that over 385 million passenger journeys took place on Great Britain's railways in the three months between October and December 2012 - 14 million more than the same period in the previous year. In Scotland, the number of passengers ScotRail carried totalled 78.3 million in 2010/11- an increase of 1.85 million from the previous year, and a 22 per cent rise since 2004/05.

We have a success story in terms of popularity. Our task now is to make a public service that works under public control. In January 1970 the ASLEF Locomotive Journal carried an article by Ted Graham, who was then General Secretary of the Co-operative Party. He began his article by declaring that the 'basis of the labour movement rests on a trinity of the Labour Party, Trade Unions and the Co-operative Movement'. That formula could well be the instrument used to solve a different question: 'How best can rail work for Scotland and its people?'

Endnotes

1. http://www.aslef.org.uk/files/133891/FileName/Oct12journal.pdf.
2. McNulty, R. Realising the Potential of GB Rail, Report of the Rail Value for Money Study, Department of Transport and the Office of Rail Regulation, May 2011.
3. House of Commons Hansard, 20 June 2013, East Coast Main Line Franchise.
4. http://www.freightonrail.org.uk/FactsFigures.htm.

SECTION 3
Chapter 3

POWERING SCOTLAND
Dave Watson

In this chapter I will outline the importance of energy generation policy to the Scottish Government's current and post-independence economic, energy and jobs strategy. This will include the focus on renewable energy in contrast to a more balanced UK Government strategy, which they claim is supported by market reform in the Energy Bill. I will then examine the SNP's proposals to stick with the UK energy market post-independence - a remarkable example of 'indy-lite'. Finally, I will make the case for devolving energy powers and what a different energy strategy could look like.

Background

Scotland is an energy-rich nation and its energy industry is a key national resource. Eighteen per cent of the UK power sector workforce is based in Scotland and four of the six major power firms in the UK have major operations here. Although only Scottish & Southern Energy (SSE) can properly be described as a Scottish-based company, even they have major operations elsewhere in the UK. Energy is a major Scottish export, provides high-quality employment and contributes significantly to the Scottish economy. It is also an industry that has huge potential, particularly in the renewables sector. However, the industry faces a number of challenges in the so-called energy market, including cost increases, infrastructure investment and workforce skills.

There is a major challenge for existing and any future governments at UK and Scottish levels, under whatever constitutional arrangements, in combating climate change, eliminating fuel poverty and, most importantly, ensuring security of energy supply. Most of Scotland's existing generating capacity will close in the next 15 years. Without credible replacement plans, Scotland could be exposed to an energy crisis or reliance on insecure supplies. The Scottish Government's response[1] has been to use the current devolved powers to promote renewable energy, with some success, and set challenging targets for generating the equivalent of 100 per cent of electricity from renewable sources by 2020 while also rejecting nuclear power. The UK Government's energy strategy recognises the contribution Scottish renewables can make to the UK's energy needs, but aims at a more diverse range of generation, including nuclear power.

Both Governments support a market-led solution that is about to be overhauled in the Energy Bill with a complex mix of support payments that is causing considerable uncertainty in the industry and slowing investment. Something like £120bn investment is required, a hugely ambitious target in the current financial climate. In this context, Ofgem and SSE have warned that the UK Government is 'significantly underestimating' the scale of capacity crunch facing the UK.[2]

Scotland is a net exporter of electricity, exporting 26.1 per cent of total generation in 2011.[3] Nuclear output provides 33.0 per cent, coal accounted for 21.0 per cent and gas 15.7 per cent. The contribution of renewables to total electricity generation in Scotland is the biggest change in recent years, increasing from 19.2 per cent in 2010 to 26.8 per cent in 2011. As elsewhere in the UK, this energy mix is about to change. Hunterston nuclear power station should close in 2016. Longannet appears doomed by 2018/20 due to the UK Government failing to support Carbon Capture and Storage (CCS) at the site. The CCS project at Peterhead has been selected as a possible demonstrator project, which would still offer transferable technology to a coal plant, but even that has been delayed. Cockenzie has closed and will, subject to planning permission and market certainty, be rebuilt as a gas plant. The life expectancy of the remaining nuclear and fossil fuel capacity is unlikely to stretch much into the next decade.

Increasing demand means that the capacity of electricity transmission networks will have to grow from 75 GW to 110 GW by 2020. National Grid is planning £22bn of investment across the UK to 2021 with 92 projects (17 GW) in Scotland. These include the Beauly-Denny link, links to the islands, South West Scotland reinforcement and High Voltage Direct Current links to England on the West and East coasts. The recent Ofgem announcement on network investment will support many of these plans. Energy efficiency and microgeneration is another method of addressing security of supply.

Planning assumptions at UK level assume that Scotland's annual electricity consumption will increase significantly to 2030. Others argue that this assumption could be seen as unduly pessimistic because both Scottish and UK energy policies aim for a significant reduction in electricity demand. The Scottish Climate Change Act also puts Scotland's energy efficiency action plan on a statutory footing. However, given the history of increasing demand for power, it would be unwise to rely on energy efficiency alone.

For many people in Scotland, fuel poverty is an everyday reality. Older people, those with disabilities or long-term illnesses and those on low incomes are all especially at risk. The consequences are misery, discomfort, ill health and debt. Around 900,000 households in Scotland - more than one in three - are estimated to be in fuel poverty, which means they are unable to afford adequate warmth in the home. The causes are a combination of poor energy efficiency of the dwelling, low disposable household income and the high price of domestic fuel, while it is also safe to assume that welfare cuts will exacerbate fuel poverty in Scotland. Energy price rises have been the main driver in the last year.[4] For every five per cent increase in energy prices, as many as two per cent of households in Scotland are pushed into fuel poverty. Government energy policies are financed by the consumer and now account for £112 (nine per cent) of the average household bill. The UK Government is proposing measures to simplify energy tariffs while consumer groups and trade unions point to mis-selling and big pay increases for the bosses of major energy companies.[5] Others point to how energy markets are 'gamed' by the energy companies to increase prices. Welfare cuts will also exacerbate fuel poverty in Scotland.

Independence

The Scottish Government's position on energy policy post-independence is, perhaps surprisingly, to remain within the UK electricity market and not to repatriate control over subsidy levels. A Scottish Government spokesman has said:

> To ensure stable prices for customers and to promote investor confidence, we propose continuing with the proposed new energy market arrangements under constitutional reform, and do not envisage establishing a separate regime in an independent Scotland. This will be of mutual benefit to all GB customers and is consistent with the increasingly integrated European energy markets. Under these arrangements, Scotland would have a voice in the market governance. We have always recognised the importance of working jointly and collaboratively with the UK Government to secure the best outcome for Scotland.[6]

This effectively means handing over the key levers of energy policy to another country, taking independence 'lite' to new levels. As I said in the Sunday Herald at the time this was announced, I remain unconvinced that this will work: 'There's nothing that says the UK has to use renewables to meet the emissions targets - or, more importantly, Scottish renewables. There are all sorts of alternatives, such as rigging the market to favour English nuclear stations.'[7] The UK Energy Secretary, Ed Davey, has made a similar point: 'If it was an independent state, we would have to consider energy imports from Scotland in the way we would from any other country. If I wasn't Secretary of State for Energy and Climate Change with responsibility in Scotland, then that wouldn't be my first priority - constitutionally.'[8]

The key issue is funding to pay for new generation and the associated infrastructure. Currently, renewables are not viable against electricity revenue with the wholesale electricity price at roughly £50 Mwh as against onshore wind at £94 Mwh, or offshore wind at £140-180 Mwh. This means support to the renewable industry has risen from £232m in 2002 to £2.2bn this year.[9] The existing subsidy arrangements benefit Scotland because it receives a higher share of the payments made by all UK consumers. If

Scotland were independent there is a big question mark as to whether the rest of the UK would be prepared to subsidise renewables in Scotland, particularly the higher cost projects like offshore wind and marine technologies. On the other hand, there may be some EU countries that have a shortfall under the Renewables Directive that Scotland could compensate for.

EU energy policy is developing with the aim of a single European market through the Target Model.[10] The Scottish Government sees this as ensuring that Scottish renewables are not discriminated against if Scotland votes for independence. There certainly are models for a single market operated by different states. The Single Electricity Market (SEM) in Ireland could be such a model for Scotland and the rest of the UK as it works reasonably well. Of course there was strong political support following the Good Friday Agreement and there was a specific economic problem with a dominant supplier. SEM has also had difficulties when one party changes its policy, as the UK Government did with the carbon floor price policy. This was only resolved by Northern Ireland being exempted from the policy. Haley Hutson at IPA makes a similar point: 'The structure is in place to work, but it is dependent on some sort of co-operation in the same way as Ireland'.[11] Given Ed Davey's comments, there must be a big question mark over this level of co-operation.

The Scottish Government Energy Minister Fergus Ewing responded to this by arguing that UK ministers would end up accepting a continuation of the current single energy market across the UK after independence, on the grounds that, without Scottish energy feeding into the national grid, the 'lights would go out' in England. To put it mildly, this is a pretty bold claim with not much evidence to support it. Professor Gordon Hughes from Edinburgh University responded to this claim by stating that England doesn't need Scottish renewable energy.[12] He pointed to their use of biomass and I would add the Chancellor's 'dash for gas' through fracking. England also has access to the continent's power supplies through interconnectors.

Developments in interconnector access are another blow to Fergus Ewing's argument. The Scotland-Norway interconnector is running into difficulty after SSE pulled out and the Norwegian state grid operator appears more interested in a link to England. National Grid's submission to the Commons Energy and Climate Change Committee said England and Wales could meet their renewable and carbon emissions targets without any contribution from Scotland.[13] Scotland's narrower choice of energy technologies means that cross-border transfers are more important. A balanced energy policy would be a better bet for a small country.

Ed Davey sums up the energy benefits for Scotland being part of the UK in his Scotsman article:[14] 'The Scottish energy industry is clearly a success story - but also a forceful case for a flourishing Scotland in a united kingdom that is stronger together. The reason lies in the economics of energy. A united kingdom offers Scotland a single market - millions more homes in demand of Scottish generation, millions more homes to spread the costs of energy infrastructure.' He subsequently claimed it is logical to assume that energy bills will rise 'significantly' for Scottish families after independence if the burden of paying for the country's renewable sector falls upon consumers in Scotland.

In summary, it is perfectly possible for an independent Scotland to continue to develop its distinctly different energy policy. However, the SNP strategy recognises that this policy needs the UK energy market. While the rest of the UK post-independence may be willing to create an Irish style single market, it is doubtful if they would do so on the current favourable terms. I am struck by the similarity to the SNP's currency position that I have addressed in another chapter of this book. Handing over energy policy to another country is a strange form of independence and could leave Scotland with less influence over energy policy than we currently have within the UK.

Devolution

At present, energy policy is split between Holyrood and Westminster. While the UK Government drives generation policy, the Scottish Government has been able to use planning powers to stop new nuclear plants and develop a growing renewables industry.

Denmark is another small country with a strong renewable energy strategy. They are largely self-sufficient in energy with an impressive ability to develop new sources of generation. A good case study is the island of Samso featured in a recent Nordic Horizons seminar.[15] Denmark is also a model for energy devolution as Greenland and the Faroe Islands both have devolved energy powers.[16] UNISON has argued[17] that this approach could be followed in Scotland, removing the confusion over roles and enabling the Scottish Government to pursue a different energy strategy, while retaining the benefits of access to, and political influence over, the UK market.

Towards a new energy strategy

Scotland's energy trade unions have long argued for a planned energy policy that provides safe, secure and sustainable generation, which contributes to the economic future of Scotland and eliminates fuel poverty.[18] While supporting the development of renewable energy, trade unions argue for a more balanced energy policy that will ensure that Scotland is not reliant on a few energy sources.

A different strategy might also follow aspects of the Danish approach, most notably a more diverse generation ownership model. In Scotland, renewables are dominated by big business, whereas in Denmark small-scale operators play a much bigger role. Some key features we might adopt include:

❏   A strong political vision over the long term, with commensurate policy and planning provisions.
❏   Favourable feed-in tariffs to create the incentive for new generation using different

business models.
- ☐ A state-owned grid that will usually connect up communities. The cost is repaid through a public service obligation payment in energy bills.
- ☐ A clear focus on energy efficiency with measures to tackle hard-to-heat homes.
- ☐ Strengthening the ability and willingness of local government to get involved - a utilities culture largely lost in the UK. Smaller local authorities to support real communities of place might also help.

This strategy also has a key role for common ownership as an antidote to what Andrew Cumber in his new book, Reclaiming Public Ownership: Making Space for Economic Democracy,[19] calls the 'globalised privatisation regime' that has concentrated economic assets and decision-making into fewer and fewer hands. Questioning the rationale of private ownership does not mean replacing it with monolithic state enterprises. There is a role for such models, as in the Danish and Norwegian grid companies, and the Norwegian state oil company has been an undoubted success. However, where this model makes sense it must be balanced by strong democratic accountability.

Cumber uses the Danish example to illustrate how new forms of common ownership might develop. He says:

> Denmark is interesting for the way in which a diverse range of collectively owned institutions from state-owned energy producers, local wind co-operatives which account for 80 per cent of the sector and municipally owned electricity distribution companies ensure a degree and diversity of public participation and engagement in economic decision-making unparalleled elsewhere. The Danish success story, in producing one of the world's leading renewable energy sectors, is compelling in illustrating the potential for harnessing older rural traditions of mutualism, associationalism and collective practice with contemporary progressive concerns in combating climate change. There are examples of considerable public sector innovation at the local scale, notably the municipal-co-operative model of ownership piloted in the Copenhagen Mittelgrunden offshore wind development.

Denmark's example also highlights the challenges caused by the EU's liberalised energy market. Like many other market solutions, in practice it favours established large companies. There has been some resistance to the EU agenda from other countries based on the principle of national subsidiarity and flexibility. Localised ownership is undoubtedly helped by it being the main source of growth in the German renewable industry.

There are other initiatives, including Trade Unions for Energy Democracy[20] and not-for-profit supply companies like Ebico, which offer an alternative approach to the energy market. However, there needs to be some recognition that the artificial energy market has failed both the economy and the consumer. Ofgem has always been behind the game and its free market ideology has failed to tackle the 'Big 6' companies. Ironically, from a Conservative-led Government, the reforms in the Energy Bill constitute the biggest state intervention in energy for a generation. But they are still tinkering at the edges of what the retired MP Alan Simpson described as the 'grubby little energy market we have constructed in Britain'.[21]

I would argue that it is not too late to pursue a different approach in Scotland's energy industry, but it requires the political will to break away from the big business model that is concentrating the wealth of Scotland and the UK into the hands of foreign corporations. A UK public opinion poll for YGov showed 61 per cent in favour of common ownership of energy and only 26 per cent against. This shows the public are way ahead of the policymakers.

Conclusion

Why is energy so significant to the constitutional debate? Because energy is not only a vital service that we all rely on, but it is an essential element of the Scottish Government's industrial and economic strategy. That is why energy is a key issue for supporters of independence and extended devolution alike.

As with other policy areas covered in this book, it is possible to pursue a different energy policy under independence or extended devolution. The primary requirement as ever is political will. However, the proximity of almost the only energy trading partner creates real challenges for those advocating independence and they will need to do much better than 'the lights will go out in England' if they are going to convince us of the merits of their case. A balanced energy strategy that ensures security of supply, builds a more diverse industry and eliminates fuel poverty would be a start.

Endnotes

1. Cowall, R. et al., Promoting Renewable Energy in the UK: What Difference has Devolution Made? http://cplan.subsite.cf.ac.uk/cplan/sites/default/files/PromotingRenewableEnergyUK.pdf.
2. Utilities Scotland, Energy generation capacity even tighter, 22 March 2013 http://utilitiesscotland.com/.
3. For an overview of Scottish energy statistics see Energy in Scotland, http://www.scotland.gov.uk/Resource/0041/00415880.pdf.
4. http://utilitiesscotland.com/2013/01/16/energy-bills-keep-inflation-high/
5. http://utilitiesscotland.com/2013/04/03/not-a-good-week-for-energy-companies/
6. Vass, S., UK to control green subsidies in an independent Scotland, Sunday Herald, 27 January 2013.
7. See note 6.
8. Evans, N., Just where does the SNP stand on Energy, Holyrood Magazine, 25 March 2013.
9. Carstairs, J., Scotland's Future - Energy and Constitutional Change, DUP 2013.
10. EU Single Market for Gas and Electricity, http://ec.europa.eu/energy/gas_electricity/consultations/20120229_market_coupling_en.htm .
11. Tshibangu, A., North/South Divide, Utility Week, 22 March 2013.
12. Scotsman, Power of Scotland conference, http://scotsmanconferences.com/viewconference.aspx?id=25.

13. http://utilitiesscotland.com/2013/03/18/norway-interconnector-problems-dent-independence-claims/
14. Davey, E., Common goals make most of Scotland's energy, Scotsman, 9 December 2012.
15. Great Green Danes, 16 January 2013, http://unisondave.blogspot.co.uk/2013/01/great-green-danes.html.
16. Ronne, A., Energy policy and constitutional change, University of Strathclyde, 18 January 2013, http://www.scottishconstitutionalfutures.org/Default.aspx?tabid=1712&articleType=ArticleView&articleId=268.
17. UNISON Scotland, Fairer Scotland - Devolution, http://www.unison-scotland.org.uk/scotlandsfuture/FairerScotlandDevoPaperFeb2013.pdf .
18. UNISON Scotland, Scotland's Energy - Scotland's Future, http://www.unison-scotland.org.uk/energy/ScotlandsEnergyScotlandsFuture_Feb2012.pdf.
19. Cumber, A., Reclaiming Public Ownership: Making Space for Economic Democracy, Zed Books, 2012.
20. Utilities Scotland, Energy democracy - the search for non-market solutions, 18 March 2013.
21. Simpson, A., The great energy stitch-up, Morning Star, 22 February 2013.

SECTION 3
Chapter 4

WATER
Tommy Kane

How we govern and operate Water and Wastewater Services (WWS) in Scotland today marks a fundamental change from the earlier municipal socialism model which historically played a vital role in driving social progress across Scotland. Our WWS are increasingly being seen in commercialised, economic terms and in driving economic progress. An alternative to this orthodoxy, in WWS and other vital public goods and services, is needed with an approach which re-socialises and re-democratises our WWS in a way that resembles the former municipal socialist model rather than the present commercialised ethos and direction.

A bona fide, but often unheralded, triumph of neo-liberalism is its application inside the public sector. The recent transformation of the operations and governance of WWS in Scotland, arguably, epitomises the marketisation of public services, given how this new structure still resides within the public sector.

Indeed, the changes to WWS in Scotland demonstrate how the Scottish Parliament has neither encouraged nor consolidated public ownership. It has been political choices underpinned by the dominant ideology of neo-liberalism not constitutions that have led to the changes in Scotland's WWS sector.

Historical development

Providing a safe, secure and sustainable water supply with excellent sanitation services is vital for the health and well-being of any country. Scotland realised this in the 19th century though it was not until the 20th century that an adequate and near universal service was provided. Beforehand, Scotland's WWS sector resembled those that exist in the Third World today with all the associated disease, squalor and death.

Only a few generations ago, Scottish people were dying in their thousands as a consequence of poor WWS. In Glasgow in 1832, 'Cholera made its first appearance killing nearly 3,000 people mainly in the parts of the city still dependent on polluted wells - High Street, Saltmarket, Gallowgate and Trongate. A further outbreak in 1848 killed 4,000 victims, but this time it extended into more well-to-do districts.'[1] In Greenock one person in every six died from typhoid in 1819. In 1832 cholera killed 2,000, while in the same year smallpox claimed 600 victims. In 1864 thousands died from a typhus epidemic.[2]

This disease-ridden Scotland was supplied WWS by private operators who cherry-picked investments that resulted in 'pipes only being laid in parts of the city where it was thought only a financial return could be made'.[3] The scale of disease and death created 'a slow realisation that society as a whole had a collective responsibility to take remedial action…the difficulties encountered in attempting to raise finance for various private water projects led also to a similar recognition that a sustainable water supply could only be supplied using public funds'[4], which as Gow says, this led to private water companies being taken over by local authorities.[5]

Throughout the 20th century and prior to the creation of the water authorities in the mid-1990s WWS in Scotland was still influenced by the principles of municipal socialism, which enjoyed wide public and political support. Illustrating the high value the Scottish people placed on a satisfactory and publicly run WWS was the result of the now famous Strathclyde referendum on the proposals to privatise WWS in Scotland. The results were unequivocal. Seventy-one per cent of the eligible electorate voted (1.2 million ballots) and of those 97 per cent rejected water privatisation.[6]

Privatisation by attrition?

Canadian Marxist academic, Gary Teeple, wrote in 2000 that 'Where the process is politically problematic, the preferred route has been privatisation by attrition and the gradual reduction of services'.[7] He did not have Scotland's WWS in mind when making that remark but he might well have. Since the Strathclyde referendum the abundance of legislation passed in Scotland's WWS sector has resembled a privatisation by attrition type process. Yet given the scale of public opinion and awareness, as expressed in 1994, the subsequent changes to the operations and governance of Scotland's WWS have gone on largely unnoticed.

The Strathclyde referendum has undoubtedly affected the behaviour of policymakers since. This significant barometer of public expression has obviously restricted policymakers and governments for fear of electoral backlash. Thus, rather than push overtly for privatisation, the change has been deliberately incremental. The result has been significant, resulting in a utility that is, while classified as a public corporation, behaving as if it is a private business. Admittedly with one crucial difference: the sizeable surpluses that Scottish Water makes are still reinvested in the utility, although sizeable surpluses are still being lost to private operators who are currently thriving in Scotland's WWS sector.

Since the referendum, various tranches of legislation have resulted in a commercialised/ corporatised framework in the Scottish sector with the exceptions of the 1994 Local Government Act, which legislated to allow Private Finance Initiatives (PFIs), while the 1999 Water Industry Act created an 'advisory' economic regulator, then known as the Water Industry Commissioner (WIC). All the legislation that has transformed WWS in Scotland since has emerged from the Scottish Parliament. It is the Scottish Parliament not Westminster that has passed a plethora of legislation leading to the corporatisation of Scottish Water and the subsequent de-democratisation, de-politicisation, commercialisation and outsourcing of the WWS sector in Scotland.

Scottish Water is, as a consequence, seen by its management as first and foremost a business. The previous Chief Executive of Scottish Water, the late Richard Ackroyd, said that their ambition as a public company was to become 'Scotland's most trusted and valued business'.[8] Alan Sutherland, Chief Executive of the Water Industry Commission for Scotland, said that WWS in Scotland, prior to its corporatisation and tight financial discipline, was a 'financial basket case'.[9]

This betrays the thinking now at the heart of this most vital service. The economic regulator, the WIC, has fostered a so-called 'hard budget constraint' approach. But although investment has increased and assets improved, this has often resulted in a utilitarian style strategy, which often puts the balance sheet before universal needs. It has meant changes to terms and conditions for workers and delays and diversions when dealing with operational problems which affect individuals and communities throughout Scotland.

Providing a satisfactory service needs a trained and well-resourced workforce. When Scottish Water was formed it drastically cut its workforce between 2002 and 2005.[10] The cull of staff at Scottish Water was a central plank of the 'Spend to Save' programme initiated in 2002. Part of the business transformation fund, Scottish Water spent £83.1 million on staff severance payments out of an overall 'Spend to Save' budget of £200m.[11] Yet, corresponding with this reduction in Scottish Water staff was an increase in the use of private contractors and agency staff.

The cuts to staff also correspond with changes to employment conditions and an ethos of having workers deliver more for less. Trade union branch officials in Scottish Water, in an interview for this research early in 2013, suggest that this has created an increase in stress levels among staff.[12] Public Service International Research Unit (PSIRU) has analysed whether doing more for less is productive. David Hall and Emmanuelle Lobina from PSIRU state how:

> Many banks and analysts assume that the less workers, the better, and so use a standard measure of employees per thousand connections - the lower the number, the better the performance. This measure is technically weak -

if a water operator carries out its own construction, it will appear to employ far more workers per connection than another operator which outsources the work to contractors, even at a greater cost. But it also fails to recognise that extending services and providing better services often requires extra workers.[13]

As noted, Scottish Water has entered into partnerships with the private sector. Scottish Water Solutions is a joint venture with the private sector and carries out the bulk of the capital investment programme. There are also 21 Waste Water Treatment Works operated under the PFI.

The total Scottish Water budget during the period 2002-2011 was £8.870bn from customer charges and £1.020bn from Scottish Executive/Scottish Government loans. Of that total of £9.890bn nearly 60 per cent, £5.865bn, was spent on capital investment, carried out mainly by the private sector and PFI.[14] In other words Scotland's WWS sector represents lucrative pickings for the list of private companies now involved in providing WWS in Scotland. It is little wonder that there is a 'secondary market' in the PFI sector where private equity firms and venture capitalists trade PFI contracts.

It is also unsurprising that multinational companies like Veolia have significant financial interests in the provision of wastewater treatment and capital investment in Scotland. The fact that it is not motivated by notions of municipal socialism was confirmed by its Chief Financial Officer Thomas Piquemal when he told investors that 'The only growth we are interested in is growth in profits [...] we have tremendous potential to improve our profitability'.[15]

A major indication of the changes to WWS and its subsequent de-democratisation is the establishment of an economic regulator in the form of the Water Industry Commission for Scotland (WICS). The 2005 Water Services (Scotland) Act gave it the power, circumventing any elected institutions, to set both charges and budgets. As befitting an economic regulator with strong links to neo-liberal think tanks, the WICS is comfortable with gratuitously inflated salaries and bonuses paid to senior management, while at the same time attacking the terms and conditions of workers and sanctioning job losses. The WICS are also cheerleaders for the introduction of competition in the non-domestic sector, hailing its introduction with the reminder that this is a world first, with Scotland leading the way and suggesting that it could/should be rolled out to also include domestic customers.[16]

Policy development

In 2007 the WICS commissioned consultants LECG to outline an advanced plan and timetable for the legislative programme needed to change the ownership structure of Scottish Water. The final document planned in some detail a transfer from the old Scottish Water to a new model that was a company limited by guarantee.[17] Interestingly, LECG's preliminary document also suggested that privatisation had 'significant advantages' but would probably be politically controversial and that 'with careful explanation and presentation a company limited by guarantee is likely to be more publicly acceptable than either the full privatisation or concession option'.[18]

LECG epitomise how corporate consultants, financial advisers, etc. have been setting the agenda for policies from which they could benefit. For example, evidence shows how the LECG invoice to the WICS included a charge of £17,606 for external advice from Neil Summerton.[19] Mr Summerton was a non-executive director at Folkestone and Dover Water Services (now Veolia South East) from 1998 to 2009 and likewise at Three Valleys Water (now Veolia Central) from 2000 to 2009.[20] This type of arrangement leaves itself open to research being influenced by potential beneficiaries.

Scottish Government intervention

In 2010 the Scottish Government and partner agencies initiated a study of the future of Scottish Water from the Scottish Futures Trust (SFT). The SFT in turn commissioned the external consultancy firm KPMG. KPMG found that 'SW represents a core UK corporate account which should attract significant market appetite across a range of core leading and debt capital market banks'. They also asserted that 'Scottish Water will be considered a core regulated utility with ongoing funding requirements which will attract appetite from a range of banks'.[21] The SFT suggested that Scottish Water could be transformed into a Public Interest Company, a model which replicates the company limited by guarantee as recommended by the LECG in 2007.

Around the same time the Scottish Government commissioned an Independent Budget Review. This review had a broader remit than the SFT report, but also contributed to debates over the future model of Scottish Water. They also recommended that Scottish Water be changed into a company limited by guarantee style Public Interest Company.

Hydro-Nation

Despite these (government-appointed) bodies recommending a change of ownership, the SNP have, up until now, not countenanced any sale of Scottish Water. Perhaps this is out of electoral concerns against the backdrop of the current constitutional debates. Indeed it could be suggested that the current Scottish Government position is a result of two referendums, the Strathclyde referendum of 1994 and the independence referendum of 2014. They may have calculated that proposing a change to the status to Scottish Water is too risky this side of the independence referendum given the result of the Strathclyde Water referendum in 1994. Or it might be they have temporarily retreated until they know who would receive the capital receipts from any sale of Scottish Water; there is apparently some ambiguity over whether the Scottish Parliament or the UK Treasury would receive the monies from any sale.

Whatever the reason, the Government came up with the Hydro-Nation agenda which did not propose a change of ownership and retains Scottish Water under a public framework.[22] However, what constitutes 'public' appears to be open to debate. The SFT for example argued that a Public Interest Company would still be a form of public ownership. A more circumspect LECG acknowledged that such a model would still be a 'form of privatisation'.[23] Nevertheless, while not suggesting a change of ownership the Hydro-Nation strategy does reveal an intensification of the neo-liberal strand that has so influenced the direction of the WWS in Scotland over recent times.

The Hydro-Nation agenda seems to be stimulated by the Scottish Government, in a water-scarce world, seeking to exploit our water resources for monetary gain. Undoubtedly influenced by Alex Bell, adviser to the First Minister and author of Peak Water[24], the vision of the Scottish Government appears to be that Scotland could, in a water-scarce world with multiple water crises, export water, expertise and technical know-how and attract inward investment all as a result of its plentiful water supplies.

This vision entrenches the commercialisation of Scottish Water and indeed cements the commodification of both the public service and resource. Supporters argue that it would make the commercial side of Scottish Water financially viable enough to remain in the public sector. On the other hand, sceptics argue that the Hydro-Nation agenda makes Scottish Water even more of a target for the predatory markets, as confirmed by KPMG, who have a continual eye on new businesses such as water companies, like Scottish Water, that offer guaranteed returns.

A new democratised model

The current model in Scotland is a 'public' replication of the privatised model in England. Jon Hargreaves, first Chief Executive of Scottish Water, said as much to a Parliamentary Committee in 2006, stating 'What you have created in Scotland is unique - privatised regulation is not applied exactly in the same way to a public body anywhere else. That is the change in Scotland.'[25] This raises questions over the nature of public services and what constitutes the intrinsic characteristics of a public service/ public corporation. More broadly it also sheds light on the policy direction in the WWS since the recreation of the Scottish Parliament in 1999 and the common philosophy underpinning that policy.

In developing the WWS policy, in particular the legislation in 2002, the Scottish Executive looked to England for an example. But, it didn't need to; the Scottish Parliament could have looked beyond the UK and followed the lead of more progressive and socially responsive models elsewhere. Take the providers of WWS in both Paris and Amsterdam. These municipally led models recognise the fundamental importance of water and its accompanying services, not just in their own cities but also by offering services to other parts of the world that lack the means and capabilities to provide their own effective service.

For instance Waternet of Amsterdam has formed an international arm to its operations called 'World Waternet'. 'World Waternet' is paid for by asking customers to pay an additional one per cent to their overall tariff to be allocated to their international activity and donated to a recipient utility/country. There is no reason why Scottish Water could not do the same. Instead Scottish Water has created Scottish Water International. This venture has no altruistic motives or notions of international solidarity. As the then Minister Alex Neil said at its launch:

> Scotland's water is one of our prize natural resources. That is why this new legislation will draw together Scottish expertise to build an international profile of Scotland as a leading player in the water sector......It [Scottish Water International] will build on Scottish Water's success as a public sector organisation ensuring it makes best use of its assets for commercial purposes[26].

WWS are too important to be left to market devices. One eye across the world and another looking at our not so distant past tells us that without clean water and a satisfactory sanitation service, societies can, and do, break down. Conditions in 21st-century Scotland, needless to say, are not those of the 19th century, nevertheless if we embrace and accelerate marketisation and/or privatisation or a form of it, then we head down a slippery road.

We didn't have to take this path and we don't need to continue along it. To prevent such scenarios we could re-democratise, re-municipalise and socialise our WWS. We should for a start make the board of Scottish Water a robust and democratic board with a fair cross-representation of members that accurately reflects Scottish society. Prices should be set with input from elected officials, albeit still with advice from experts. Priorities should respond to need and not balance sheet needs. We should buy out the unsatisfactory PFI contracts, upgrade the skills base and increase the staff of Scottish Water and reduce the reliance on the private sector, thus investing the money lost to the private sector in the staff and infrastructure.

All of this of course could be done now under the present constitutional arrangements as this is not about borders and constitutions. Rather it is about politics, political choices and the underpinning philosophy that informs those political choices. Democratising Scotland's WWS and returning to the principles of municipal socialism that saw WWS as a public good and not a commercial vehicle is a political choice that could, but most importantly, should be made.

Endnotes
1. Notes taken from Loch Katrine Exhibition, Mitchell Library, Glasgow, December 2009.
2. Cumming, J.W., The Greenock Cut and the Story of Greenock's Water Supply, Strathclyde Regional Council, Leisure and Recreation Department, Glasgow, 1980.
3. Notes taken from Loch Katrine Exhibition, Mitchell Library, Glasgow, December 2009.
4. Notes taken from Loch Katrine Exhibition, Mitchell Library, Glasgow, December 2009.

5. Gow, B., The Swirl of the Pipes. A History of Water and Sewerage in Strathclyde, Glasgow: Strathclyde Regional Council, 1996.

6. Anderson Crooks, K., (1996) Water Warfare in Scotland: A Case Study in Issues Management, in Cooper et al., Scottish Water The drift to privatisation and how democratisation could improve efficiency and lower costs, Public Interest Research Network, Glasgow, 2006.

7. Teeple. G., Globalization and the decline of social reform, P95 Garamond Press, Aurora, 2000.

8. Kane, Conference Report from Managing Scotland's Water: Balancing the Challenges, Holyrood Magazine, Edinburgh, October 2009.

9. See note 8.

10. Stedman, L., The Good and not so good of Scotland's Road to Reform, Water Utility Management, December 2005.

11. Scottish Water, Spend to Save Annual Report, Obtained through Freedom of Information, 2004/5.

12. Interview with S. Scott and A. Nisbet, UNISON Branch Officials Scottish Water.

13. Hall, D. and Lobina, E. Water as a Public Service, PSIRU, December 2006.

14. SPICE Figures, Calculated from Scottish Water Annual Reports, 2011.

15. Veolia Slashes Investments To Boost Profits, Global Water Intelligence, March 2009.

16. Sutherland in Hobson, Alan Sutherland Gives a Progress Report on Water Competition in Scotland, Utility Week, September 2008.

17. Lisle, J., Downie, G. and Smith, G., Organisation of the Water Industry in Scotland, LECG, Shepperd and Wedderburn & ING Barings, Research Commissioned by the WICS, information obtained through Freedom of Information, May 2007.

18. Lisle, et al., Project Checkers, Survey of Options, LECG, information obtained through Freedom of Information, March 2007.

19. Water Industry Commission, Breakdown of Expenses as per FOI 09 23, information obtained from Freedom of Information, May 2009.

20. Debrets, Profile of Dr Neil Summerton: (http://www.debretts.com/people/biographies/browse/s/4206/Neil+William.aspx).

21. Stewart, J. and Noble, R., Scottish Futures Trust; Option Development: Alternative Structures and Funding Options for Scottish Water, KPMG, November 2009.

22. The Hydro-Nation policy agenda became legislation in 2013 and is known as the Water Resources (Scotland) Act 2013.

23. Lisle, et al., Project Checkers, Survey of Options, LECG, information obtained through Freedom of Information, March 2007.

24. Bell, A., Peak Water, Luath Press, Edinburgh, 2009.

25. Hargreaves, J., Evidence given to Audit Committee Scottish Parliament, Col 1411, January 2006, (http://archive.scottish.parliament.uk/business/committees/audit/or-06/au06-0102.htm|).

26. Neil, A., Making Scotland a World Leading Hydro Nation, Scottish Government News, June 2012 (http://www.scotland.gov.uk/News/Releases/2012/06/scotland-water28062012).

MANUFACTURING IN SCOTLAND
Stephen Boyd

After decades of no interest and complacency, the global financial crisis provoked politicians at Scottish and UK level to start taking manufacturing seriously again. Yet the future of manufacturing has been curiously absent from the independence debate.

Maybe there's just nothing of substance national governments can do in the age of globalisation to grow a larger manufacturing sector? This paper seeks to address this very question while examining ways in which constitutional change may help support manufacturing growth in Scotland.

Why is manufacturing important?

Despite the decline in manufacturing employment through the latter part of the last century and the first decade of the current, manufacturing remains an important employer in Scotland (194,000 people as of December 2012) and there is a widespread view that the way employment statistics are currently compiled underestimates the number of jobs which depend on the sector.[1]

Wages also tend to be higher. In 2010 in Scotland, labour costs per employee were 50 per cent higher in manufacturing than in services (although this partially reflects more part-time working in services). Manufacturing supports and sustains key strategic skills and, by providing many middle-income, middle-status, skilled jobs, manufacturing is a force for social cohesion in a way that services are not.

The spill-over effects for the wider economy are significant; manufacturing firms account for the vast majority of private research and development (R&D) spend in Scotland. The multiplier for research spend undertaken by advanced manufacturing is significantly higher than for other sectors.

Manufacturing accounts for over two-thirds of Scottish exports and the export of manufactured goods helps facilitate the export of business and financial services, a lesson the Germans have learned very well but one that is almost completely overlooked in the UK and Scottish policy discourse.

The benefits of manufacturing are not just economic. Harvard economist Dani Rodrik argues that 'without a vibrant manufacturing base, societies tend to divide between rich and poor - those who have access to steady, well-paying jobs, and those whose jobs are less secure and lives more precarious. Manufacturing may ultimately be central to the vigor of a nation's democracy'.[2]

Why has manufacturing declined more in Scotland and the UK than elsewhere?

Scotland tends not to feature as a separate entity in international comparative literature. But with manufacturing accounting for only a slightly greater share of all economic activity (around 12 per cent) in Scotland compared to the UK as a whole (around 10 per cent), UK data can be considered a decent if imperfect proxy for Scotland.

With this caveat in mind, the data[3] do tend to confirm that decline in the UK has been more rapid and severe than in other advanced economies although this can be exaggerated. In 2010 the UK ranked 9th in terms of manufacturing output (value added) behind China, USA, Japan, Germany, Italy, Brazil, South Korea and France. The UK had been 5th on this list as recently as 2000.

In 2010, the UK was 33rd in terms of manufacturing output per head (around $3700) behind most major developed countries and 108th in terms of manufacturing output as a share of gross value added (11 per cent), marginally ahead of France but, again, behind most major developed countries (Figure 1).

Figure 1. Manufacturing - % total value added

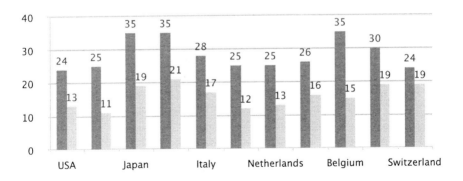

The UK accounts for around 2.3 per cent of global manufacturing output. In the early 1970s, the UK and China each accounted for around 4 per cent of global manufacturing output, whereas in 2010, China accounted for 18.9 per cent, more than the USA.

Figure 2. Manufacturing output as % of world total
(gross value added in $US at market exchange rate)

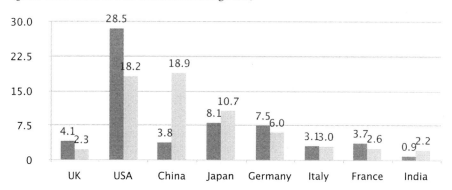

Figure 3

Country	Population (millions)	Persons Employed (100s)	Average Personnel Costs (£1000 per employee)	Value Added (€million)
UK	62	2581	34.3	143494
Germany	82	6670	47.2	381547
France	64	3054	48.1	180452
Italy	60	4169	35.8	180257
Sweden	9	676	48.3	39113
Finland	5	392	44.4	22714
Czech Rep	10	1210	14.0	15140
Poland	30	2438	9.5	21089

Source: Eurostat

Germany has fallen from 7.5 per cent in 1970 to 6 per cent now (Figure 2).

Germany is an interesting example of what can be achieved. While it has to be acknowledged that membership of the euro has hugely benefitted the competitiveness of German manufacturers, the statistics are nonetheless stark: it is, by a distance, the EU's largest manufacturer, accounting for 27.3 per cent of all EU manufacturing value added and it has the highest share of value added in 18 of the 24 manufacturing sub-sectors analysed by Eurostat. The UK tops not a single category (Figure 3).

The table below reflects two important facts. The UK remains competitive in some 'low value' manufacturing sectors particularly food and drink. And other nations with higher wage costs than Scotland have been more successful in retaining a greater share for manufacturing: Germany, Sweden, Finland and Belgium are probably the best examples.

So, if unit wage costs are higher in other more successful nations, what is it about the UK economic model that's so hostile to manufacturing? The following factors surely apply:

❑ Lack of political support: the UK political class has been hugely complacent about the decline of manufacturing and ability of services to sustain growth and create decent jobs. Industrial policy has been inconsistent and erratic. Indeed, for years prior to the financial crisis, simply using the term risked the ridicule of senior policymakers. Monetary policy has tended to be set to benefit the City and at times - the early 1980s in particular - has simply been disastrous for manufacturing.

❑ Short-termism: the short-term nature of the UK financial system disadvantages manufacturing firms who are unable to access the patient, committed capital necessary to sustain crucial investment in R&D, capital equipment and people.

❑ What Robert Skidelsky describes as the 'imperial overhang': UK firms, used to exploiting captive markets, were wholly unprepared for, and unable to deal with, globalisation.

❑ Ownership and control: among advanced nations, the UK is quite unique in its relaxed attitude to ownership. Recent Scottish Trades Union Congress (STUC) analysis[4] shows that other nations identified by the current Chancellor as more competitive operate regimes less accommodating of foreign purchases of indigenous firms. Migration of ownership leads to loss of control and decision-making and key functions such as R&D. It also leaves workers more vulnerable to redundancy as it's much more difficult for owners to close domestic workplaces.

Other nations have been much more successful in building models that support long-term investment: workers have direct input into decision-making, finance is more knowledgeable and supportive, political commitment is strong and enduring. Other EU member states retain much higher proportions of procurement spend domestically and give more to manufacturing in state aid.

What might constitutional change achieve?

The first thing to stress is that there are no quick fixes under any constitutional scenario. The factors explaining Scotland's relatively steep decline in manufacturing are systemic, with deeply embedded economic, institutional, historical and cultural roots. At risk of stating the obvious, it is how additional powers are patiently applied to overcome these problems that will determine manufacturing's long-term future in Scotland.

It's not credible to assume that constitutional change in and of itself will boost manufacturing output and jobs. Global economic forces have acted to reduce manufacturing's share in all advanced economies. These forces, particularly the rate of productivity growth due to technological and process innovation, will continue to constrain jobs growth whether Scotland is independent or not. Bad domestic policy may help explain Scotland's and the UK's relative performance but it's very far from the whole story.

Models of independence or enhanced devolution which seek to retain or replicate essential elements of the current system (e.g. predominant role of finance) are very unlikely to deliver manufacturing growth. It's interesting that one of the few clear policy priorities of the Scottish Government - cutting corporation tax - is likely to prove actively detrimental by further embedding short-termism and pressurising the investment subsidies which benefit manufacturing over finance.

If the long-term future of manufacturing in Scotland is to be assured, a change in economic and industrial strategy is required, not simply a transfer of powers.

Macroeconomic powers

As debate rages over a macroeconomic framework for an independent Scotland, it's worth considering what the main options might mean for manufacturing. The currency union model proposed by the Scottish Government's Fiscal Commission, if it can be successfully negotiated with the rest of the UK, is unlikely to worry manufacturers unduly; again, it will be the policies enacted under the framework that matter and it will be interesting to test out the extent of policy flexibility that will ultimately be available in this regard. For instance, will any fiscal agreement provide sufficient flexibility to enact the various tax mechanisms proposed later in this paper?

Significant sections of the Yes campaign, including the Scottish Green Party, support a new Scottish currency which they believe, probably correctly though it's not without risks, would provide much greater policy flexibility. However, moving to a new currency is likely to raise some alarm within manufacturing and not just for the exchange rate risk it necessarily entails.

If, as at least some on the Yes Scotland campaign appear to believe, the Scottish economy diverges sharply from the UK on the basis of rising prices and strong output from the North Sea, there is a danger that currency appreciation could endanger the international competitiveness of Scottish manufacturing, the problem known in economics as the 'Dutch Disease' after the loss of competitiveness which afflicted manufacturing in the 1960s and 1970s following the Netherlands' discovery and exploitation of North Sea gas. However, the potential impact of a currency rising on the back of exploitation of natural resources is now better understood and the Scottish Government's stated commitment to establishing an oil fund - should circumstances allow, which is highly uncertain - which will invest overseas should help mitigate the impact on Scottish manufacturing.

The euro no longer seems viable politically but it's not so long ago that manufacturing's strongest advocates (certainly at UK level) were supportive of the single currency. But Scotland's exports to the EU are currently worth £7.6bn compared to £11.6bn to the rest of the UK.[5] In these circumstances, it's difficult to see how joining the euro would boost manufacturing as a whole although there would be clear advantages for those firms who trade mainly with Europe.

It's probably worth noting that the future of manufacturing has not rated a mention in the prolonged and not very enlightening debate over macroeconomic powers, despite its key role in supporting the balance of payments of an independent nation.

Day one impact of independence

The day one impact on Scottish manufacturing of a Yes vote in the independence referendum - i.e. the immediate closure/migration of workplaces and loss/shifting of jobs - is likely to be limited. Skills and agglomeration effects in many sub-sectors will make employers wary of rash action. It's difficult to see why firms in, for instance vehicle manufacturing, chemicals or textiles, would immediately up sticks on the basis of a Yes vote if they're satisfied that the business environment will remain just as accommodating as it is at present. Nevertheless, there is a potentially severe impact on the defence manufacturing sector where many jobs are reliant on contracts directly procured by the UK Government and its supply chains.

The majority of defence contracts are exempted from EU Internal Market rules. Obvious sensitivities around ownership of advanced military technologies and, to be blunt, pork barrel politics, will ensure that defence manufacturers in Scotland will be at a serious disadvantage when bidding for UK contracts. The extent of the impact - which wouldn't occur under forms of enhanced devolution - on the supply chain and wider economy could be considerable. Indeed, the economic damage resulting from a reduction in the scale of Scotland's defence sector was an area of agreement between the four main parties in the Scottish Parliament when they came together to pre-empt the possible outcomes of the Defence Review of 2010.[6]

Whether or not the Government in a newly independent Scotland chooses to use the so-called 'defence dividend' to directly support new industrial development remains to be seen. To repeat, industrial strategy has hardly featured in the debate thus far.

Microeconomic powers

This is the most interesting area and one that could, given the right decisions on policy, deliver better outcomes for Scottish manufacturing. First, two points must be stressed:

❑   Under current devolved powers, the Scottish Government already possesses the ability to support the long-term future of manufacturing in vital areas such as skills (where it holds full powers, which is why the issue is not addressed in this paper), public procurement (powers limited only by EU Directives) and finance (powers are available as the establishment of the Scottish Investment Bank testifies, but it can be reasonably argued that budget constraints seriously limit effective action).

❑ Industrial policy is an important and legitimate function of government. Despite the new manufacturing consensus, policy remains tentative and weak and the old refrain 'picking winners' is used to delegitimise arguments for intervention. But as the economist Ha-Joon Chang argues persuasively, a government picking winners against market signals can improve national economic performance, especially if it's done in close (but not too close) collaboration with the private sector. In the same way that the success stories do not allow us to support governments picking winners under all circumstances, the failures, however many there are, do not invalidate all government attempts to pick winners.

So, what new powers may assist the stabilisation and eventual growth of manufacturing in Scotland?

Finance: the inability of the financial sector to support the Scottish manufacturing industry with the type of committed capital available to manufacturers elsewhere is a long-standing source of frustration to trade unions and, we suspect, many employers. As argued by Will Hutton and others for at least a couple of decades, it is this lack of supportive capital that explains the UK's and Scotland's poor record on investing in capital stock, R&D and human capital.

The share of domestic lending going to (UK) manufacturing fell from 5.2 per cent in 1999 to 2.3 per cent in 2007 while the share going to other financial intermediaries rose from 25 per cent to 31 per cent. Today patient investment in the companies of the future is an increasingly fringe activity compared with speculating on share prices, interest rates and currency movements. The financialised economy undermines the manufacturing industry.

Therefore serious structural and regulatory reform is necessary to ensure that the financial system starts to fulfil its primary function of allocating capital efficiently. A detailed discussion on how this might be achieved under various forms of constitutional change is beyond the scope of this chapter. However, there is a serious question as to the powers available to the Government of an independent Scotland in this regard if the currency union model is pursued. Simply put, would it have control over the structure and regulation of banking and finance in Scotland?

The Scottish Government's recently established Scottish Investment Bank is a move in the right direction but Scotland really needs an intervention on the scale of the German KfW or French Strategic Investment Fund although funding such new institutions is likely to demand very hard choices of Scottish administrations under enhanced devolution or independence. The creation and funding of a major new industrial development intervention should perhaps take priority over an oil fund in the early years of independence (if indeed any surplus is actually available to invest in this way).

Tax: it's possible to be both highly sceptical about the Scottish Government's view of tax as playing the central role in economic development and believe that the tax system could be better designed to benefit manufacturing. The headline reductions in corporation tax introduced by the coalition and proposed by the SNP under independence only provide a relative benefit to manufacturing over finance if not funded by reductions in allowances which disproportionately benefit manufacturers. In any case, as discussed above, it's very unclear whether savings on tax would be very helpful in helping Scottish firms address the productivity deficit vis-à-vis European competitors.

If policymakers are serious about rebalancing then targeted reductions in manufacturers' corporate tax rate for increasing Scottish generated value added (not value generated by overseas subsidiaries or subcontractors) output is a much better policy. Other tax instruments could include an enhanced depreciation allowance or targeted national insurance relief. It is extremely disappointing that no debate is taking place about the creative ways in which tax policy might be used to support specific policy priorities.

Economic Development Policy: as things stand, the main opportunity to grow Scottish manufacturing appears to be the renewable energy sector. It is essential that developers privileged to exploit Scotland's natural resources are tied to using as much local content as possible. In France, it has been stipulated that any offshore developer must use at least 25 per cent and this has been justified on environmental grounds. Similar if not more ambitious strategies should be adopted in Scotland.

Ownership and control: the regulatory landscape could be tweaked to make foreign takeovers more difficult. Any such proposal will inevitably be met with the cry of 'protectionism', one of economics' great debate-killing tropes. As other European countries demonstrate, it is entirely possible to play a full role in the global economy while not making it as easy as the British do to purchase indigenous firms. It isn't serious to pledge support for manufacturing while in practice demonstrate abject complacency over ownership. It's unlikely that enhanced devolution would provide additional powers in this respect and it's an issue on which the advocates of independence have been silent.

Culture change: Maybe the greatest opportunity is constitutional change precipitating radical change in Scotland's business culture. Freed from the dead hand of the City, it's possible to see a new manufacturing and innovation eco-system developing in which firms can grow organically with committed - public and private - funding partners. As investment horizons widen, management and policymakers may start to see the benefits in an approach which works for employees, communities, suppliers and customers as well as shareholders. Manufacturing may even benefit from new forms of co-operative and public ownership.

Achieving this culture change will not be easy. Building a new, successful and resilient manufacturing and innovation eco-system will require transformation of banking and financial markets, corporate governance and areas of regulation. New public interventions will have to be designed and funded appropriately. Indeed, it has to be asked whether it is even feasible under the forms of enhanced devolution and independence currently on offer. Will the policy flexibility even exist under 'Devo Plus' or currency union independence? Will Scotland be able to build upon weak and supine banking reforms at UK level?

Endnotes

1. An extended discussion over the economic benefits provided by manufacturing can be found in the STUC's 2011 paper, the Future of Manufacturing in Scotland, www.stuc.org.uk/files/congress
2. Rodrik, D., The Manufacturing Imperative, Project Syndicate, August 2011.
3. Data in this section drawn from international comparisons of manufacturing output, House of Commons Library, January 2012.
4. The Wrong Plan for Growth - Budget 2011, the Global Competitiveness Report and the dangers of formulating policy on a false premise, STUC, April 2011.
5. Global Connections Survey, Scottish Government, January 2013.
6. The UK Strategic Defence and Security Review - cross-party submission, September 2010.

Chapter 6

COMMUNITY OWNERSHIP OF FOOTBALL
David Shaw

In December 2012, PricewaterhouseCooper's (PwC) annual financial review of Scottish Premier League (SPL) clubs, The Calm Before the Storm, outlined in stark terms the challenges and choices facing Scottish football:

SPL clubs can no longer match the transfer fees or the wages to lure the top talent to Scotland, nor can they remain competitive on the global stage ... What is certain is that this gap between the two leagues will continue to grow with the SPL falling further behind following the disappearance of Rangers. However should fans continue to vote with their feet, this problem is only going to intensify.[1]

The SPL cannot compete on financial terms with the English Premier League and to attempt it would be disastrous. But even were it possible, would following the English ownership model be desirable? This chapter will begin by examining the current state of the Scottish game, before undertaking a comparative analysis of the evolution of football south of the border. It will then consider whether the model of fan ownership already well-established in Germany could provide the basis for a form of community ownership that will give football fans a degree of control and influence in the way their clubs are run to ensure that they exist for the benefits of the whole community, rather than just a privileged few.

The Scottish scene

As the PwC report makes clear, SPL clubs do not have access to the broadcasting revenues that have propelled their English rivals into the financial stratosphere. This leaves them little margin for error and far more vulnerable to external factors: the recent rise in unemployment, fall in wages and general labour market instability has directly contributed to a 12 per cent drop in attendances and consequent decline in revenues.[2]

According to PwC's annual report, 75 per cent of SPL stadiums were less than 60 per cent utilised during the 2010/11 season. Yet clubs have consistently failed to reduce ticket prices to boost attendances, with the average price of a match ticket a not inconsiderable £23. Given that playing in front of a full crowd as opposed to a half-empty stadium would, in all likelihood, enhance the performance of the teams and the quality of the matches, reducing prices seems an obvious course; however, it remains one the clubs are seemingly loathe to take.[3] Instead, SPL clubs have sought to save money by spending less in the transfer market and driving down wages (already far lower than in the English Premier League (EPL)).

Even so, the clubs incurred a collective loss of £2.5 million over the course of the 2010/11 season. It would have been worse were it not for Rangers' £8 million operating profit from the Champions' League group stages. However, Rangers can no longer be relied upon to paper over the SPL's financial cracks. Like Leeds United before them, Rangers have been laid low by owners whose hubris was matched only by their incompetence. Back in 1992, Rangers' victory over Leeds in the European Cup was cited as evidence that Scottish clubs could compete with and indeed overcome their English rivals. However, 20 years after this famous victory (and about ten years after Leeds were sucked into a financial vortex of their own making) Rangers entered administration with debts of £100 million.

The end game had begun nine months earlier, when Rangers were sold to Craig Whyte for the paltry sum of £1. Whyte had promised to pay off Rangers' £18 million debt and to invest in players. However, it soon became clear that Whyte, a man with an undeclared disqualification from acting as a company director, had no intention of risking any of his own cash; instead, he raised funds by mortgaging four years' worth of season tickets with factoring company Ticketus.[4]

Former owner David Murray, the man who sold to Whyte, insists that the club was not heading for administration when he left. However, Rangers' financial problems were well documented (hence the £1 asking price) and the £18 million debt was the legacy of over ten years of concerted spending in an audacious but ultimately foolish attempt to propel Rangers into the European elite. Unable to pay their wages and in conflict with the HMRC, Rangers were liquidated and their assets sold off to businessman Charles Green, who restarted the club as a new company.[5] Expulsion from the SPL followed, as did the sale of the club's key players. Rangers started the 2012/13 season in the Scottish Third Division. That glorious night against Leeds is just a fading memory, sweet but sad.

Fifty miles to the east of Glasgow, Heart of Midlothian is enmeshed in its own financial crisis. As with Rangers and Leeds United, Heart's predicament is largely due to the misguided pretensions of their owner, Lithuanian businessman Vladimir Romanov. When he purchased Hearts in 2005, Romanov was brash and bullish. His ambition, he said, was 'To give Hearts a much bigger fan base - bigger than Rangers and Celtic. To give the manager the kind of players he wants. To develop Tynecastle if possible, otherwise to secure a quality venue better than anything in Glasgow.'[6]

Hearts enjoyed some success, finishing second in 2006 and winning the Scottish Cup in 2006 and again in 2012. But behind the scenes things unravelled. From 2011 onwards, Hearts struggled to cope with a spiralling wage bill and were penalised by the SPL for late payment of salaries. In June 2013 they entered administration with unpaid debts totalling £25 million. The debts were owed to companies formerly owned by Romanov which were themselves adjudged 'unable or unwilling to meet their financial obligations'.[7] Hearts' administrators are now engaged in a concerted period of financial retrenchment in an attempt to avoid a 'fire sale' of the club's playing staff. This is likely to result in 14 redundancies and the sale of some senior players.[8]

The travails of Rangers of Hearts illustrate the urgent need to reform in Scotland. So what other models are available?

Sky, oil and oligarchs: the English model

Along with the Spanish Primera Liga, the EPL is widely regarded as the wealthiest and most watched in world football. However, it is also the most commercialised and least compassionate, especially where the fans are concerned.

English football as we currently know it was conceived in the 1980s, when a ticket on Liverpool FC's Spion Kop cost under £4 (roughly equivalent to £7.60 in today's money). As a time of cheap tickets, the 1980s' football scene was also a time of strife and disaster, with the Bradford City fire, Heysel and Hillsborough culminating in Lord Justice Taylor's damning Hillsborough report. Taylor recommended a thorough modernisation of the game - terraces and fences were to be abandoned and all-seater stadiums embraced. Fans were to be treated as customers, not potential criminals.

This dubious renaissance was aided by football's enduring popularity: the 1990 World Cup Semi-final between England and West Germany attracted a TV audience of 22 million.

The newly sanitised game, free of its negative 1980s' image proved to be a huge commercial opportunity. In 1992, the first tranche of live TV rights for the EPL was sold to BskyB for £302 million, a considerable increase on the £44 million four-year deal struck with ITV in 1988. In anticipation of the deal, English football's top 22 clubs had engineered a breakaway from the rest of the football league, a move the FA, in a misguided attempt to maintain its authority, had obediently sanctioned.[9] Now, the top clubs take all the profit; the lower leagues, the 'grassroots' of football, are left fighting for scraps.

Once the faucet was opened, riches poured into the English game. The latest TV deal signed with BskyB, BT and overseas broadcasters exceeds £3 billion, an increase of almost 900 per cent on the 1992 deal.[10] There is, however, a problem. Football clubs are not very good at managing money; indeed, the more they have, the more they squander.

More so even than the City, English football is the playground of profligates. Figures for the financial year 2012 show that only eight out of twenty EPL clubs registered a profit before tax, with eventual champions Manchester City losing £99 million. The combined debt of EPL clubs was £2.2bn, almost extinguishing their combined revenue of £2.4bn (75 per cent of which was spent on players' wages).[11] Of the £2.2bn combined debt, Manchester City, Manchester United, Arsenal and Chelsea (the top four clubs) constituted £1.4bn.

The prodigality of Manchester City and Chelsea has been underwritten by billionaire owners, another feature of the modern game. When Russian Oligarch Roman Abramovich bought Chelsea in 2003, they were on the cusp of financial ruin with debts of £15 million. Now their debt of £878 million is little more than a mild encumbrance.[12] Abramovich's wealth, however, pales in comparison to that of Sheikh Mansour bin Zayed Al Nahyan, scion of the ruling family of Abu Dhabi, and current owner of Manchester City. Unparalleled levels of investment have catapulted City into the ranks of Europe's elite, at least in financial terms.

Manchester United, English football's most successful and best marketed club is also under foreign ownership, albeit under somewhat shadier circumstances. In 2005, amidst angry fan protests, the US-based Glazer family borrowed £525 million from banks and hedge funds to purchase United, before promptly dumping the entire debt on the club. As a consequence, United went from being the wealthiest club in England to one of the most indebted, haemorrhaging £550 million in interest and charges alone. The rage and frustration felt by the fans of Manchester United (and Liverpool, who suffered similarly at the hands of two more American dream-peddlers, Tom Hicks and George Gillett) is shared by fans throughout football.

Because, like the shining facades of Dubai and Abu Dhabi, the glitz and glamour of the Premier League has been constructed on a parched landscape of exploitation. One of the saddest manifestations of this exploitation is occurring in Liverpool, where the failure to build a new stadium, coupled with the systematic purchase and deliberate dereliction of houses in the streets in and around the club's current Anfield stadium, has condemned one of the more deprived communities on Merseyside to decades of decline. Throughout the 1990s, Liverpool, bent on increasing the stadium capacity to compete with Manchester United, purchased as many houses as possible, which it then left vacant. As the number of vacant houses grew, so did the level of crime, anti-social behaviour and general degradation.

Suddenly, the club changed their minds. They would not renovate Anfield, but build a new stadium. The club was sold to new owners - the aforementioned Gillett and Hicks - who promised 'a spade in the ground' within 60 days. Suffice to say, this did not happen. Hicks and Gillett were eventually forced out, and the new owners, the Fenway Sports Group, American investors and owners of the Boston Red Sox, resurrected the original plan to expand Anfield and the drive to force residents out has resumed.

What has most upset local residents is the scale of the club's mendacity. The stealth and subterfuge has left a sense a betrayal that will linger long in the local memory.[13] This is an extreme example of the lengths a football club will go to safeguard its own interests, but it is by no means the only one.

With wages to pay, dividends to allot and agents to satisfy, the margins between affluence and impoverishment are excruciatingly narrow. Many clubs have already plummeted into the abyss with 56 insolvencies since the birth of the Premier League.
Fans have been forced to pay the balance. A survey of match-day tickets by the BBC[14] revealed the average price for a Premier League ticket is £42.87, £1,629 across a 38-game season.

For many on low and even middle incomes, the financial demands of following a team are becoming unsustainable. Consequently, the social make-up of football matches is changing. Clubs set prices safe in the knowledge that broadcasting and corporate revenues from those who can pay will easily compensate for those who can't. In common with the rest of society, exclusion and alienation has infected the English game.

Community ownership: a radical alternative?

If it values its soul, Scottish football will eschew the English model. There, is however, an alternative.

By international standards, Scotland is an open and democratic country. Despite this, many people feel disenfranchised, not fully in control of their lives or able to make a positive impact on the lives of others. Much of this can be attributed to the exclusion of ordinary people from ownership of tangible assets, both local and national. This explains the growing number of individuals (including key figures in the Scottish Labour Party and the Scottish Government) advocating community ownership as a means of giving power back to local communities. Football clubs are ideal candidates for the community ownership model.

Community ownership is predicated on the notion of shared endeavour: people working together to achieve a common aim for the benefit of the wider community. Fans of the same club share the same objectives: affordable ticket prices, good facilities, success on the field and, more broadly, turning the club into an asset for the community as a whole.

Community ownership can be contrasted with corporate ownership: communitarianism versus individualism; public good versus personal enrichment; equality versus excess. Community ownership is about pride in oneself, one's community and one's club.

This may sound fanciful, but it isn't. Indeed, the clubs in Germany's Bundesliga, one of the biggest leagues in world football, are currently based on a similar model. With the odd exception, Bundesliga clubs are committed to the rule of '51 per cent', whereby the majority shareholding of the club is owned by members through the club association including major clubs, such as Bayern Munich, which is 82 per cent owned by 187,865 members and Borussia Dortmund by its 30,000 members.[15] This has contributed directly to sensible ticket prices: the average is £10 and a season ticket for 2013 Champions League winners Bayern Munich can be as little as £62. This approach has proved hugely successful. Despite the financial might of the English and Spanish leagues, the 2013 Champions League Final was contended by two German clubs, Borussia Dortmund and Bayern Munich.

And there are examples closer to home. It is not a coincidence that the second cheapest ticket in British football is at Stirling Albion. In 2010, the club was sold to Stirling Albion Supporters Trust for £300,000, following an international campaign which attracted the support of Andy Murray and Christiano Ronaldo.[16] Swansea City is 20 per cent owned by the Swansea City Supporters Society Limited and although ticket prices are a little steep, the club is one of the best run in the EPL, with no debt and £5 million in the bank.

In 2010, Portsmouth FC, thanks to the recklessness of successive owners, was the first Premier League club to become insolvent. In 2013 it became the largest club in the UK to be owned by its supporters after 2,000 fans pledged a total of £2 million to purchase a 51 per cent stake in the club through the Portsmouth Supporters Trust.[17]

The emotion surrounding the successful fan takeover of Portsmouth, confirmation of which was greeted with tears and singing by those involved, illustrates an important truth: a football club is an asset for the community providing entertainment and a meeting place for those of similar passions and outlook. It reflects the spirit of the community where local tradition and culture is captured in the songs and chants of the terraces and civic symbols or important local industries are emblematised on the club badge. Joy and sorrow, frustration, humour, loyalty and anger - all the most potent of human emotions are inspired by a football club. It is bequeathed from generation to generation and the day the fans stop supporting it is the day it ceases to exist. Fans already enjoy spiritual and moral ownership of their clubs; it is time they had material ownership, too.

In the midst of Hearts' darkness there is a chink of light, a beacon that may guide us into a new era of responsible ownership. Created in 2010 by local businessmen and lifelong Hearts fans, Foundation of Hearts is a not-for-profit organisation whose vision of the future is based on 'bringing Heart of Midlothian back to the people who are truly passionate about this wonderful club - the fans'.[18] They may never have a better opportunity than now. Edinburgh MP Ian Murray has confirmed the Foundation, which already has more than 5,000 cash pledges, will submit a bid for the club. According to Murray '[The Foundation's] is the only bid that…is truly transparent and that the fans can truly influence…Every single penny given to the Foundation goes back to the club. If the fans own the club, the membership decides what is the future.'[19]

Honesty, transparency and a say in the way their club is run is all the average fan can ask for. For the sake of Hearts, and for clubs up and down the country, we should hope their bid is successful. It could herald a new era and is worth fighting for. As one former Bundesliga Official stated, 'Football is considered to be a public good, and people can be truly a part of it, by being members of a club'.[20]

If this is a sentiment we all share, community ownership of football clubs should be something we all aspire to, whatever else the future has in store.

Endnotes

1. Calm Before the Storm: Scottish Premier League Football, 23rd Annual Review of Scottish Premier League Football Season 2010/11: www.pwc.co.uk/scotland.
2. See note 1.
3. See note 1.
4. http://www.guardian.co.uk/football/blog/2012/jul/12/rangers-scottish-football-league.
5. http://www.bbc.co.uk/sport/0/football/18588740.
6. http://www.telegraph.co.uk/sport/football/2392170/Romanovs-grand-plan-at-Hearts.html.
7. http://www.heraldscotland.com/sport/football/ubig-crash-could-tip-hearts-over-the-edge.21108783.
8. http://www.bbc.co.uk/sport/0/football/22979684.
9. http://www.lrb.co.uk/v34/n16/david-conn/follow-the-money.
10. http://corporate.sky.com/about_sky/timeline.
11. http://www.guardian.co.uk/football/2013/apr/18/premier-league-finances-club-by-club.
12. http://www.guardian.co.uk/football/2013/apr/18/premier-league-finances-club-by-club.
13. http://www.guardian.co.uk/football/david-conn-inside-sport-blog/2013/may/06/anfield-liverpool-david-conn.
14. http://www.bbc.co.uk/news/uk-19842397.
15. http://www.guardian.co.uk/football/blog/2013/may/22/bundesliga-premier-league-champions-league.
16. http://fcbusiness.co.uk/news/article/newsitem=443/title=stirling+albion+football+club+sold+to+supporters%92+trust.
17. http://www.guardian.co.uk/football/2013/apr/10/portsmouth-future-fratton-park-ownership.
18. http://www.foundationofhearts.org/aims/.
19. http://www.scotsman.com/sport/football/spl/foundation-of-hearts-bid-in-next-24-hours-1-2998193.
20. http://www.guardian.co.uk/football/blog/2013/may/22/bundesliga-premier-league-champions-league.

SECTION 4 - CLASS
Introduction

Jackson Cullinane

In introducing the first Red Paper on Scotland, the editor, Gordon Brown, the then Rector of Edinburgh University, described its aims as being to 'transcend that false and sterile antithesis which has been manufactured between the nationalism of the SNP and the anti-nationalism of the unionist parties'. It sought to achieve this objective by broadening the constitutional discussion, considering it from avowedly left perspectives and presenting ideas for shaping the future of Scottish society and Scotland's economy on the basis of 'co-operative, democratic and revolutionary' proposals to address 'inequality of wealth and poverty'.

For those of us becoming active on the Scottish left in the late 1970s, the book was to become standard recommended reading.

In 2005, with the Scottish Parliament in place and varied views on its effectiveness in rolling back the devastating impact on Scotland of the Thatcher years, the 2nd edition of the Red Paper began with a critical analysis of New Labour policies in areas such as welfare benefits, the economy and public sector finance and urged the adoption of a programme of radical demands upon the Scottish Parliament, principally based around the case to democratise the Scottish economy and local government. This theme was expanded upon in essays by Labour left and Green Party activists, trade unionists, peace activists and left-leaning academics, historians and journalists covering issues such as the case for redistribution of wealth, democratisation and investment in industry and public services, community action and participation, defence diversification and the expansion of public ownership and co-operative approaches in economic policy.

The new 3rd Edition of The Red Paper on Scotland, triggered by the forthcoming referendum on Scottish independence, seeks to reflect not only the style and format of its predecessors but also the objectives of ensuring that the debate on Scotland's constitutional future is not directed by the narrow and potentially divisive constraints of 'unionism versus nationalism' but is focused instead on what kind of Scotland we should seek to create. At its heart is the conviction that the pros and cons of the constitutional question should be judged primarily on the basis of what is in the best interests of the working class. Class perspectives, therefore, permeate the bulk of the chapters in this 3rd edition. However, this section is solely devoted to and focused on the class issue with chapters exploring the nature and history of class struggle in Scotland, to what degree these struggles can be defined as specifically 'Scottish' in character, how they have or have not shaped a distinct 'Scottish identity' and, above all, how working-class unity would be potentially affected by support for independence.

In the opening chapter of this section, John Foster, who contributed to both the 1st and 2nd editions of The Red Paper on Scotland, draws on his extensive knowledge of both Scottish and Irish history and his in-depth experience of applying Marxist analysis to political, cultural and national questions, to outline how the nature of Scotland has historically been shaped by differing class interests. In doing so, he contrasts the values and institutions of landowners and industrialists with those projected by workers in struggle, notably those involved in the Upper Clyde Shipbuilders (UCS) Work-In. Having explored this background, John then presents a case for working-class unity based on the need to challenge state power at British level while harnessing the radicalism of the Scottish working class.

In the second chapter in this section, Chik Collins considers the negative effects on working-class communities in Scotland of so-called 'economic regeneration' programmes, driven by the interests of developers, financiers and governments adhering to pro-privatisation and neo-liberal economic policies. Chik's chapter, in particular, points to the methods employed to draw communities into 'partnerships' with such interests and away from alliances between community and trade union activists which have proved, for example during the World War I Glasgow rent strikes and the UCS struggle, to be effective means of building working-class unity and successful action.

In the final chapter, Vince Mills and Stephen Low also refer to the UCS struggle and the subsequent effects of the Thatcher era before presenting a case for the need to develop working-class consciousness, an understanding of the common purpose across the UK of defending and advancing trade union organisation and the welfare state and a strengthened democracy featuring more powers for the Scottish Parliament. They point out that the British Social Attitudes Survey shows how close the views of Scottish workers are to those in areas of England, notably those in the North of England.

The authors reflect on the views of those of us who see merit in keeping alive and further exploring the option of enhanced devolution, despite the outcome of the Edinburgh 'deal' between Alex Salmond and David Cameron, denying this as a specific choice for those voting in the referendum. From the outset of the current debate, media polls have consistently shown majority support for such an option, as have internal polls conducted by trade unions in Scotland. In Unite Scotland, for example, such polls show over 60 per cent favouring more devolved powers, although not necessarily support for the briefly floated SNP version of 'Devo Max', with only 22 per cent supporting the devolution of everything except defence and foreign affairs.

In promoting debate and discussion around what further devolved powers could be explored, as well as consideration of how the current powers of the Scottish Parliament can be better utilised to redistribute wealth and power and tackle social injustice, the 3rd Edition of The Red Paper on Scotland stands in the tradition of a Home Rule current in the Scottish Labour movement stretching back, at least, to Keir Hardie in 1888 when he stood as a Labour & Home Rule candidate in the Mid-Lanark by-election. That tradition is reflected in the inclusion of Home Rule in the first manifesto of the Scottish Labour Party, the advocacy of Home Rule by Red Clydesiders such as John Wheatley and Jimmy Maxton and the convening of the first Scottish Assembly by the Scottish Trades Union Congress (STUC) following the successful UCS Work-In. It continued in the involvement of labour movement activists in the Campaign for a Scottish Assembly, Scotland United, the Constitutional Convention and the successful 'Yes-Yes' campaign to create the present Scottish Parliament. The driving force for advocates of Home Rule, then as now, is support for decentralisation, redistribution of power and extension of democracy as part of the wider struggle to win working-class power over the economic, political and industrial decisions affecting the lives of ordinary people.

Chapter 1

NATION AND CLASS
John Foster

Scotland has been described as a stateless nation. But throughout the last three centuries Scotland has retained the vestiges of a state. It preserved its specific legal system - notorious through the 19th century for its anti-trade union judgements. It maintained a separate education system with universities to train the guardians of the existing order, the lawyers and the ministers of the established Church. This Church in turn had very clear views on what it was to be Scottish. In 1923 its General Assembly issued a report defining national values as individual endeavour, work discipline, sobriety and the observance of the Sabbath. It claimed that these values were now being sapped by the presence of Irish Catholics and demanded limits on further immigration.

Almost exactly half a century later, Jimmy Reid addressed the hundred thousand people who were demonstrating against the closure of the shipyards on the Upper Clyde: 'Today Scotland speaks. Not the Scotland of Edward Heath, Gordon Campbell, Sir Alec Douglas-Home - of the Lairds and their lackeys. They have never represented Scotland, the real Scotland, the Scotland of the working people.' Reid's Scotland was quite different. It included all religions and none. It defied Scottish law. It was about collectivism not individualism. It spoke in the same breath about defending Scotland and the unity of the British working class.

Reid understood the power of national identity. He linked the defence of Clydeside's shipyards to the defence of a nation. But he also understood the need to redefine that nation. The same demonstration in August 1971 heard the first calls for the convening of a Scottish Assembly. This Assembly brought together trade unions, local authorities, Chambers of Commerce and all churches to discuss the crisis of Scotland's industrial economy. It did so on terms set by the Shop Stewards' movement and the Scottish Trades Union Congress (STUC). The then General Secretary of the STUC called for the re-establishment of a Scottish Parliament which, he said, would be a 'workers Parliament'. Just six years later the Labour Government in Westminster passed the first Scotland Act.

It was not, of course, the power of Reid's oratory that secured this outcome. Reid's redefinition of Scottishness was made possible by existing events. The 'real Scotland, the

Scotland of working people' was already visible and challenging the 'other' Scotland of Gordon Campbell and Sir Alec Douglas-Home. Hence also Reid's constant references to the unity of the British working class. The UCS Work-In was an act of class defiance because it was indeed seen as part of a wider movement - posed against the state power of big business at the British level. Workers in Scotland had already taken part in one-day general strikes to oppose the Conservative's anti-trade union legislation. Those attending the Scottish Assembly in February 1972 could cheer on the miners and car-workers blockading Saltley Gates in Birmingham. They were members of the same class organisations. They were opposing the same forces. Reid neatly brought them all together. As well as Gordon Campbell, the Scottish Secretary, and Sir Alec Douglas-Home, Reid included Edward Heath, the Tory Prime Minister from Broadstairs, as representing the 'other' Scotland.

Scotland's changing identity

These snapshots, 1923 and 1972, underline three things. The first is that national identities change. The 1960s and 1970s saw Scotland's public culture redefined. In theatre (7.84 and Wild Cat), literature (Alistair Gray, John Byrne, William McIlvanney, Hamish Henderson) and humour (Connolly) references shifted - to the Scotland 'of working people'. Such references had indeed been there before. But they had not been dominant or public.

The second point is that the key forces inducing change are those of relative class power. Throughout recent Scottish history the dominant force has been that of those who own Scotland's land and capital. For them institutions influencing national identity have been an essential part of their rule. Challenges have been difficult and usually brief. Once contained, the values of the dominant class have invariably reasserted themselves - though always in new forms.

The final point follows. To understand a nation's changing identity it is necessary to know its history - not in the prosaic sense of monarchs and ministers but in terms of the dominant class forces, of the changing power relations within society and of relations between one nation and another. No nation will be the same. There has to be concrete analysis to understand what is progressive and what reactionary.

This was the argument of the Scottish-born socialist James Connolly. In his Labour in Irish History he attacked the romantic (and classless) nationalism of many of his Irish contemporaries, which he saw as highly dangerous. Its victory would perpetuate the division between Ireland's two religious communities and would thereby fasten on Ireland a new political subjection based on continued external ownership and the internal power of property.

Connolly grounded his own analysis historically in Ireland's special experience of class and national expropriation. Common land ownership had survived into the 17th century.

Dispossession was the result of alien conquest. Two sets of rulers, representing both Stuart feudalism and Williamite commercial capitalism, had played their part. Together they had created the rival cultures that continued to divide Ireland. The actual victims of dispossession were Ireland's working people. And their experience of loss had continued to be made real by two centuries of struggle against landlord power. It was a struggle which of necessity involved collective action and which progressively changed its class character as the bulk of Ireland's population became transformed into semi-proletarians.

Hence Connolly's call for the 'reconquest of Ireland'. Ireland's working people had to take back collective ownership of their country - but in the new century as workers and socialists. The green flag by itself would only divide and confuse. Only when combined with the red flag, as raised by Dublin's workers in 1913, could it unite and create a national movement with the power to liberate Ireland. The cause of Ireland and the cause of labour could never be 'dis-severed'

Connolly gained his grounding in class politics in Scotland and spent the first decade of his political life as an active member of the Social Democratic Federation (SDF) and the Independent Labour Party (ILP). A close colleague of Keir Hardie, Connolly continued to write for the ILP's Forward till shortly before his death. We know he broke with the SDF over its abstention from industrial struggle. But he never seems to have questioned the ILP's support for Home Rule for Scotland. In the 1890s, Home Rule parliaments in Scotland and Wales, on a democratic franchise, were seen as a key step in securing the immediate objectives of the labour movement in terms of public control of housing, health, education and thereby contesting the power of capital. But this was not posed in terms of national separation. The objective was to strengthen the power of working people at British level.

In a later chapter Vince Mills and Stephen Low will provide an analysis of Scotland's recent class history which underlies that position. This does not need repetition but it is important to note the main features of Connolly's general approach to the issue of nationality. Connolly knew his Marx and considered himself to be on the anti-revisionist wing of the Second International. Unlike the right wing of the British Labour Party, he saw the essential conditions for socialist change as a mass working-class challenge that dismantled and replaced capital state power. He therefore followed Marx in his conviction that the working class 'must rise to be the leading class of the nation, must constitute itself the nation' and therefore be 'itself national though not in the bourgeois sense of the word' This did not mean backing nationalism. But neither did it mean minimising the significance of national identity and the national question. Connolly himself never posed class against nation. Any challenge to the state power of capitalism had to draw on national identity. But in order to do so it was necessary to understand the class forces that moulded it so that progressive and reactionary trends could be identified. The engagement had to be active, critical and transformative.[1]

Popular defiance

Hamish Henderson achieved precisely this when he put together the words of Freedom Come All Ye in the 1960s:

> Nae mair will our bonnie callants
> Merch tae war when oor braggarts crousely craw
> Nor wee weans frae pitheid an clachan
> Mourn the ships sailin doun the Broomielaw
>
> Aa thae roses an geans will turn tae blume
> An yon black boy frae yont Nyanga
> Dings the fell gallows o the burghers doun.

Freedom, in Scottish terms, would depend on ending the legacy of colonialism and conquest by 'oor braggarts', Scotland's own ruling class, and destroying their reign of internal oppression: 'Dings the fell gallows o the burgers doun'. When Henderson was writing, the 'burgers', Scotland's industrialists and bankers, were still highly visible: the Youngers, Weirs, Lithgows, Yarrows, Coats and Colvilles. Their offspring today are less visible but, as demonstrated in an earlier chapter, the nexus of financial control still stretches between Edinburgh and London. Henderson posed against them the forces of social change internationally, 'a roch wind blawin', and Scotland's own plebeian tradition: the 'bairns o Adam'.

Scotland's history as a nation is quite different from that of Ireland. Ireland itself was the site of Scotland's first colony - established by the Scottish Parliament in 1609 and a major source of revenue for Scotland's landed and commercial elite.[2] Although the population of the Scottish land mass was historically considerably smaller than that of Ireland, and one far more divided by language and ethnic origin, some form of class-based 'Scottish' state, first feudal, then capitalist, has existed since the 10th and 11th centuries. Evidence of class resistance, of some form of plebeian tradition, also goes back a long way.

John Barbour's Bruce, written for the royal court in the 14th century, celebrates the freeing of serfs during the war of independence:

> Since for to defend the city
> Servants and thralls he made free
> And made them knights eurilane
> And when they armed were, and dycht
> And stalwart karls were and wycht
> And saw that they were free alsua
> They thought that they had lauir ta
> The deed.

Barbour's epic was not itself an expression of popular culture. What it did reflect was the attempt to co-opt such a culture to create a broader 'national' alliance. The new line of kings sought to derive such a wider legitimacy from the second phase of the war against Norman control whose victorious outcome involved switching to quite non-feudal methods - guerrilla tactics very similar to those being used in the peasant revolts then spreading across continental Europe. The Declaration of Arbroath, a propaganda document written by clerics, refers to liberi (free men) and libertas not as a rhetorical gesture but because it represented a key plank in the alliance that saw one faction of feudal lords able to engineer revolt among the vassals of their rivals. At Bannockburn the peasant levies supporting Bruce included many from the feudal holdings of those on the opposite side. Once victorious, the new royal line commuted feudal duty to that of archer service, an armed peasantry. Serfdom as such was not re-imposed. The French knights arriving in Scotland in 1385 to defend the new Scottish kingdom were appalled by the insubordination of the Scottish country folk.[3]

In the 1400s, the Makars' device of 'flyting' celebrates and echoes popular ribaldry and dissent. Robert Henryson's poem from the later 15th century expresses views almost as subversive as those of John Ball in England. Contrasting the wealthy, thieving town mouse with poor country mouse he wrote:

> My moder said eftir we wer borne
> That ye and I lay baith within hir wame
> I kept the ryt and custome of my deme
> And of my ser, levand in povertie.

Recalling this tradition is not to suggest that it was ever dominant and certainly not that it remained constant or unchanged. It is, however, to stress that there did exist a culture of popular defiance and resistance founded among those who were exploited and oppressed and which those who sought to rule had to contend with and to some extent co-opt.

All these contradictory pressures were reflected in Scotland before 1707. Its small and underdeveloped economy was fully exposed to the massive cycle of expansion and contraction that ran through Europe between the 15th and late 17th centuries. Continental populations doubled, then collapsed during a long, grinding century of poverty and war that lasted till the 1690s. The result, for pre-Union Scotland, was a strange mixture of the most advanced social forms combined with the most reactionary, of destructive obscurantism combined with scientific and scholarly advance, of populist revolt side by side with the localised re-impositions of serfdom. The mid-17th century saw intense struggle between different factions, including the temporary victory of the Presbyterian lairds and peasantry, and a further half-century of intermittent civil war over the Church settlement. The 1690s brought famine, depopulation and the disastrous failure of Scotland's third colonial venture in Panama.

The 1707 Union followed - an attempt to draw some benefit from the difficulties of England's mercantile elite in face of the uncertainties of Protestant succession and continental war. The Act sought to unite all those who would defend the Hanoverian succession in return for access to colonial markets and the retention of key parts of Scotland's state structure. Its terms were crafted to incorporate the maximum number of constituencies: the landed magnates and the mercantile elite but also the ministers of the Presbyterian Church and the smaller property owners they mostly represented. The continuing elements of the Scottish state were precisely those essential for mercantile capitalism: a separate Scottish legal system that gave protection to Scottish traders combined with structures of social control that could enforce discipline in conditions of acute labour scarcity.

Over the following generation, Scotland's economy developed remarkably fast. By the 1720s and 1730s the basis had been laid for colonial trade in tobacco, sugar and slaves.[4] By the 1740s and 1750s fine printed linens were reaching international markets. The beneficiaries were the merchants and big landlords who had backed the Union together with smaller lairds and tradesmen who dominated the new areas of production. Wages, however, continued to be very much lower than in England despite the relative shortage of labour. The concentration of social control in the hands of the presbyteries, over poor relief, schools and virtually all aspects of sexual and general conduct, remained, as did the legal prohibitions on trade union organisation.

Class unity

The beneficiaries of the Union were firmly welded into the British state. Their representatives usually backed its most reactionary elements in Westminster and were rewarded with privileged access to empire. In the 19th century employers used Scottish law to suppress trade unionism long after their counterparts in England. The biggest coal and iron producers actively recruited segmented work forces of Irish Catholics and Protestants and exploited the resulting conflicts. This was the Scotland that formed the real-life background to the Church of Scotland's 1923 declaration - and to the struggles of the Scottish labour movement's early pioneers such as Keir Hardie.[5] Robert Burns drew his inspiration from a quite different tradition: the memories of working farmers and labourers who experienced this class oppression and who risked their livelihoods to resist it. Their language, even in its apparently innocent familiarity, was itself a challenge to the existing order.

There is therefore a parallel to Connolly's conclusions on Ireland - though one that can only be appreciated through an understanding of the class forces moulding Scottish history. Scotland's workers faced a ruling class that was both integrated into the British state and able to use Scotland's remaining national institutions against them. Yet to challenge that state, to act as a class in a full sense, they had to join with fellow workers in England and Wales.

In Ireland the continuing dispossession of its people was made both real and transformative by the struggle against landlord power in a country where the landless had become workers. Reconquest demanded the union of labour and the cause of Ireland. In Scotland, class oppression was experienced at the hands of Scottish employers using Scottish institutions. Victory against it, on the other hand, depended on a wider class unity against the British state - and it was therefore within this wider unity that the democratic and radical trend in Scottish culture was forged and renewed.[6] Capitalist state power had to be seen and exposed.

In Ireland Connolly repeatedly warned against classless nationalism. It would stop Labour's reconquest - and did. Today Scotland faces a nationalism that is also apparently classless, speaks in terms of social partnership and seeks to co-opt the egalitarian values embodied in the Scottish Parliament. For those who have taken part in the struggles of the past generation this nationalism is both attractive and met with an unease that remains undefined. They know there is a tradition of Scottish radicalism that is part of their lives and with which they identify. But they are uncertain whether the current nationalism is indeed part of the same tradition as that embodied by Keir Hardie or McGahey. They are repelled by a classless unionism. They are uncertain of a classless nationalism.

This is the essence of the challenge faced in 2014. It is one that will only be resolved by a movement that both seeks wider class unity to oppose British state power and draws on Scotland's radical tradition to do so. Like labour and reconquest in Ireland, Scotland's radical tradition cannot be severed from the class that gave it life on both sides of the border.

Endnotes

1. The approach which is adopted here is very different from that of much current academic writing on nationality which broadly follows the sociology of Max Weber. A theoretical critique of Weberian approaches is developed in Foster, J., Marxists, Weberians and Nationality, Historical Materialism, Vol. 12, 1, 2004.
2. By the 1670s the 50,000 Scottish colonists in the Plantation exceeded the population of Edinburgh. Scotland's second colony in Nova Scotia, 1629, was over-run by the French in 1631. The third in Panama, 1698, was destroyed by the Spanish in 1700.
3. This analysis draws on the opening chapters of T. Dickson (ed.), Scottish Capitalism, Lawrence and Wishart, 1981.
4. Rossner, P., Scottish Trade in the Wake of the Union: the Rise of the Warehouse Economy, Steiner, 2008; Whyte, I., Scotland's Society and Economy in Transition, 1500-1700, Macmillan, 1997 makes the point that the relatively rapid growth after 1707 depended on the maturing of mercantile and agrarian forms of capitalist organisation over the previous century.
5. Campbell, A., The Lanarkshire Miners, John Donald, London,1977; Foster, J, Houston, M and Madigan, C. Irish Immigrants in Scotland's shipyards and coalfields, Historical Research, 2011.
6. Gordon Pentland demonstrates this fusion in Radicalism, Reform and National Identity 1820-1833, Woodbury, 2008 and The Spirit of the Union 1815-1820, London, 2011.

SECTION 4
Chapter 2

THE STATE AND THE MOBILISATION OF WORKING CLASS COMMUNITIES
Chik Collins

The Community Voices Network

S oon after the publication of the last Red Paper, the then Scottish Executive launched a new Regeneration Policy Statement - People and Place. It was launched with a snappy slogan: 'The Scottish Executive is open for business'.[1]

This was a signal of intent. In the preceding years, as the previous Red Paper had shown, the Scottish Executive, under the influence of Scotland's financial elite, had been re-orientating economic policy towards further privatisation - particularly in education and health. This was to be the basis for growing new 'global companies', along the lines of those which had previously emerged in transport.[2]

The aim was to use regeneration policy to help get this 'firm-growing agenda' moving. Regeneration areas, including Scotland's poorest communities, were to be seen as 'development opportunities' - not just in terms of property, but also in terms of their public services. Regeneration policy aimed to ensure that they be specifically 'opened up' for the private sector.

But opposition was anticipated from public servants - what New Labour had termed 'the forces of conservatism'. And in this context the Scottish Executive sought to set up its own national community organisation to help to meet this opposition. It was to be called the Community Voices Network (CVN), and was to bring together representatives from the poorest communities across Scotland.

CVN was launched within days of People and Place. The intention was to harness the frustration and anger across Scotland's poorest communities about the failures and abuses of regeneration in the preceding decades and direct it, not at the real causes and perpetrators, but at those standing in the way of 'public sector modernisation'.[3]

This intention was never realised. However, the fact that it was thought that it could meaningfully be acted upon was, and remains, highly significant.

Scotland has a long history of community activism, including the rent strikes of WWI and the local organisations of the unemployed in the interwar years. Somewhat later, from the mid-1960s, the development of the 'community action movement' brought a fresh burgeoning of organisation. This continued through the early 1970s, as community organisations joined with trade unionists and local government in opposing the attacks of Heath's Conservative Government on industry (notably shipbuilding in Scotland), trade unions and council housing.

In all of these cases, communities mobilised, with trade unionists, against the doctrines of (neo)liberal economics and in pursuit/defence of collective social welfare. By 2006, however, the considered view within the still-recently devolved institutions of Scotland was that local communities could be mobilised against trade unionists with precisely the opposite intentions.

Demobilisation through 'partnership' and 'empowerment'

The last Red Paper sought to provide some perspective on this scenario.[4] It outlined how key community organisations had been sucked into so-called 'partnerships' by the Conservative Government from the later 1980s - particularly through the 'New Life for Urban Scotland' programme.[5]

There were four major 'pilot' interventions (called 'partnerships') under the first stage of the 'New Life' programme. They were led by central government, which set up offices within the 'partnership' areas. These interventions promised to 'regenerate' the areas and 'empower' their local communities - and in so doing establish a new 'approach' to 'regeneration' for broader application. In practice, however, these communities were required for the purposes of initiating, legitimising and managing the implementation of a new, neo-liberal agenda.

The government had, after 1987, set out in a new way to attack the prevailing socio-political culture in Scotland, which had become progressively more hostile to the Tories - the so-called 'dependency culture'. The government sought to replace this with its preferred 'enterprise culture'. Regeneration policy was central to this agenda.

In order to curry favour within Scottish society, and to gain access to 'dependent' communities for far-reaching, experimental interventions, the government affected a new-found desire to tackle poverty and deprivation. The fundamental legitimacy of these interventions required that local organisations in the four pilot areas be seen to be willing - even enthusiastic - 'partners' of the government, participating in 'shaping a better future' for their areas.

For local communities, such participation was tantamount to self-harm; it required them to support the marketisation of public services and assets, especially housing, and to support both new 'flexible' labour market initiatives and the continuing, broader undermining of local democracy. Such policies had in fact created colossal damage across Scotland's local communities in the preceding ten years. And given the propensity of local people to perceive all of this, generating and maintaining even the appearance of such 'participation' required all kinds of manipulation, intimidation and corruption - a rather systematic abuse which could only, if it were not confronted and defeated, leave a trail of destruction.

This is precisely what happened. However it did not happen without resistance. Initially those running the 'partnerships' underestimated the likely extent of such resistance. They found that the promise of 'participation' could be exploited by local organisations to challenge and delay the implementation of 'partnership' agendas.

In the later 1980s and early 1990s such challenges threatened to join up across the pilot areas and undermine the government's narrative about its wider policy agenda. Ultimately this did not happen, but opposition from community groups continued to delay and prevent 'progress' by 'partnerships' through to the mid-1990s.

Local government, 'new realities' and 'partnerships'

That there should have been resistance within the 'New Life' 'partnership' areas for so long is quite remarkable given the energy expended on trying to extinguish it. And it was not simply central government that was so intent. Local government often acted with the same intent - and was often better placed to deliver on it.

Local government, through its pursuit of community development since the mid- to late-1970s, had helped to fashion many of the organisations which were by the later 1980s being asked to participate in 'partnerships'. Such community development had initially sought to promote vocal, campaigning groups which could fight for local resources. In the early 1980s many of these had become, in a way, the 'partners' of (Labour) local government - working to offset the worst impacts of Thatcherism. But by the later 1980s local government was generally reconceptualising 'community development'. Increasingly it preferred organisations that would help to fit local communities to the 'new realities' - flexible labour markets, housing stock transfers, property development and 'pay your poll tax'.

In the four 'New Life' 'partnership' areas the pressure to convert local organisations was even more pronounced. Here the pre-history of 'partnership' with local government against central government could be harnessed to the new project of 'partnership' with government to implement the 'new realities'. Troublesome organisations lost funding. Oblivion ensued. Those that 'got on board' frequently lost local credibility, thereby finding a different pathway to oblivion.

By this point, John Major's Government was about to implement a new raft of 'partnerships' across Scotland to further disseminate the 'New Life' 'approach'. These were the Priority Partnership Areas (PPAs), created and led by the re-organised local authorities in the mid-1990s, but on the basis of competitive bidding for status and resources from central government.

The legitimacy of these new 'partnerships' required continuing claims about the centrality of local community participation to their operation. Yet the 'New Life' experience had been that even a hollow promise of 'participation' could be exploited by local communities to pose problems. And that pointed to getting a yet tighter grip on community representation in 'partnerships'.

Increasingly the practice was to reverse the theory of representation. Individuals and organisations were to represent the needs of 'partnerships' to local people - and to feel a primary responsibility to the former. This trend was intensified by the Labour Government after 1997 - which now wholeheartedly embraced the regeneration legacy of its Conservative predecessor, rebadged the latter's PPAs as Social Inclusion Partnerships (SIPs), and designated a raft of additional areas with this title.

Depleting the soil of community strength

In order to grasp the damaging effects of all of this on community organisations, one has to bear in mind everything else communities had been dealing with since 1979: the mass unemployment resulting from the deliberately induced recession and deindustrialisation of the early 1980s; the attacks on council housing through the 'right to buy' and cuts to finance which generated 'residualisation'; the attacks on benefits and pensions leading to the intentional immiseration of huge numbers concentrated in the 'residual' council housing; the ongoing attacks against local government's broader inclination to manage - never mind address - the impacts of all of this; and, amidst all of this, the acute demoralisation and despair which the Conservative strategists, who planned it all, had fully anticipated.

The soil in which vibrant community organisations had flourished had been that of a confident and organised working class in a time of near-full employment and growing equality. The Conservatives had been seeking specifically to 'sterilise' that soil - or at least very substantially to deplete it.

By the early- to mid-1990s all of this was manifesting itself in a sharp increase in mortality in Scotland from 'external causes' - alcohol and drugs, suicide, accidents and violence. Unsurprisingly these deaths were predominantly to be found in the demoralised working-class communities which government could scarcely have created with greater efficiency if it had set out to do so.

It was also manifesting itself in the loss of vitality within community organisations. Older activists with trade union experience were ageing and dying. They were generally not being replaced. Where they were replaced it was often by younger recruits who had not had the opportunity to gain trade union experience. These recruits were vulnerable to being 'sucked in' when required by 'partnerships', before being spat out when no longer useful.

Adding insult to injury was New Labour's attack on welfare recipients. Where the Tories had failed to shift the perception that unemployment and poverty were social injustices, New Labour more successfully fostered the perception that the personal failings of individuals, and of the cultures of communities, were to blame.[6] The older sense of pride in organising to address the causes of poverty was challenged by a new, and deeply pernicious, attribution of shame - which could only be alleviated by submission to the new agenda of 'employability' in the flexible labour market (frequently on wages which left households in poverty).

From demobilising as opposition to attempted remobilising as support

Thus, by the early 2000s, a great deal of damage had been done to the network of community organisations which had existed in the early 1980s - both in terms of the depletion of the soil in which they had grown, and also in the specific cultivation of many of those organisations which had hung onto life, or been newly germinated, in the soil that remained.

Within a few more years it was felt that a further step could be taken - the step from demobilising communities as a source of opposition to prevailing neo-liberal policies, to remobilising communities as a source of support for an intensified neo-liberal agenda.

This was linked to a broader re-evaluation within government of the economic and social development of Scotland from around 2003 - following the collapse of microelectronics in Silicon Glen, the continuing growth of banking and finance, the then emergent concerns about population decline, and the obvious failures of the SIPS and the associated broader agenda for 'social justice' of the first Lab-Lib Holyrood coalition.

It was at this point that the Edinburgh financial elite reoriented the Scottish Executive towards the further privatisation of public services. Regeneration policy was again part of the implementation framework. And an aspect of its implementation was to be the attempt to remobilise communities described at the beginning of this chapter.

This was a clear example of an attempt to 'astroturf' grass roots involvement. It began from a perception of the emotional vulnerability of poor communities. There was justified anger and resentment in such communities. But increasingly it lacked leadership and was potentially exploitable. If these inchoate negative feelings could be carefully legitimated and directed at 'the forces of conservatism', standing in the way of privatisation, then key spaces could be carved out for the kind of experimentation with private finance which People and Place advocated. Central government would become the allies of poor communities - helping them voice their justifiable anger at the 'producer interests' holding back 'progress'.

The SNP, the financial crisis and the fate of the Community Voices Network

In the event, the CVN failed. But it did not fail because there was a clear response from community organisations raising awareness about its nature. There was no organised boycott or picket of its founding conference. Reasonable numbers from poor communities across Scotland attended - though it is unclear what many of them represented.[7]

However, within a few months, the approach of the 2007 Scottish Parliament elections, and the SNP's adoption of the mantle of defender of public services, forced what was intended to be a temporary cooling of the Lab-Lib coalition's 'modernisation' agenda. In the event, and in part because that cooling had come too late, a minority SNP Government was returned.

This might not have delayed the 'modernisation' agenda for too long - Sir George Mathewson, the recently retired chair of the Royal Bank of Scotland, was soon appointed Chair of Salmond's Council of Economic Advisers. But within a few months the credit crunch was seriously undermining 'regeneration' initiatives and little more than a year later, with the international banking collapse, RBS had gone from driving privatisation to being effectively nationalised.

The People and Place vision of regeneration was in tatters. In some ways the CVN seemed no longer relevant. And it was not clear that there was enough left of community organisation around Scotland to give credibility to its attempt to 'astroturf' a grass roots voice. Had the broader circumstances been different, then doubtless this would have been rather more fully tested. More probably, there would have been an attempt to cultivate the required 'community voice' in a smaller number of areas. But given the broader circumstances, the CVN was disbanded within three years.

Conclusion: facing the future

The CVN may in part have failed because there was little left in the way of local organisation across Scotland's poor communities but, ironically, without this, those who set out to create the CVN could not have hoped to achieve their aims. Even ten years previously, an attempt to create a national community front to support privatisation would have been trenchantly challenged by community organisations and Labour activists. By 2006 this was no longer the case. Nor, unfortunately, has the situation improved since 2006.

This is the starting point for any realistic assessment of the future of community organisation in Scotland. Most of the older organisations have been killed off, others remaining today are generally smaller, weaker, more isolated and less rooted and independent than their forebears. Opposition to current benefit changes could potentially be translated into a revival of combative tenants' associations, but as yet there is no clear indication of this happening.

Ironically, what is needed could be described as a 'new life programme' for community organisation. Such will not, however, come from government - central or local. Nor will it come via the activity of the voluntary sector - which has itself (with exceptions) increasingly become a vehicle for privatisation and other regressive policies. Least of all, given the demoralisation of the past 30-odd years, will it emerge as some spontaneous upsurge. The only realistic hope is that it will be led - because it will have to be led - through the intervention of the trade union movement.

Such an intervention is in the interests of the great majority in Scotland. For it is by no means unimaginable that in a post-referendum Scotland, whatever the outcome, a renewed attempt will be made to exploit some of our most vulnerable communities in pursuit of the privatisation of public services. That idea was not foisted on a reluctant Scottish Parliament by Westminster, or by the English, any more than it was by the broader agenda for privatisation to which it was tied - and which had its roots within Edinburgh, strong backing from leading SNP supporters, and some enthusiasts within the Labour-led Glasgow City Council.

In terms of the intervention which is now required, there have been some useful and important developments since the last Red Paper. In 2008, the STUC, at the prompting of trades councils in Clydebank and Dundee, held a one-day conference on Communities, Regeneration and Democracy and has since more generally shown an awareness of the importance of its own kind of community engagement, most recently around austerity, and, perhaps most importantly, the desirability of supporting and renewing local trades council organisation.

From individual unions there have been initiatives on community organising, for example from Unite, with its community membership scheme. UNISON has also embraced community organising.[8] In Lanarkshire the two local government UNISON branches have played a key role in the Lanarkshire Economic and Social Justice Forum - an active body including community organisations, churches and students.

There is also case study evidence as to the relative resilience of community organisations which are connected to the trade union movement in Scotland. And as the work of rebuilding local community organisation across Scotland is conducted, the lessons of that experience should be borne in mind.[9]

Endnotes

1. Thanks to John Foster for comments and suggestions.

2. See Baird, S., Foster, J. and Leonard, R., Ownership and Control in the Scottish Economy, in Vince Mills, ed., The Red Paper on Scotland, Glasgow, Glasgow Caledonian University, 2005.

3. See Collins, C., The Scottish Executive is Open for Business, Variant, 26, 2006.

4. Collins, C., For Local Communities Responding to Community Planning, in Vince Mills, ed., see note 2.

5. New Life for Urban Scotland, Scottish Office, Edinburgh, 1988.

6. Jones, O., Chavs, London, Verso, 2011.

7. The present author managed to gain access to the conference and to lists of attendees and their affiliations.

8. Details via the websites of these unions.

9. See Collins, C., The Right to Exist: The Story of the Clydebank Independent Resource Centre, Oxfam, Glasgow, 2008.

CLASS IDENTITY AND STRUGGLE
Vince Mills and Stephen Low

T he 1970s is what the late and unlamented, at least by the left, Lady Thatcher saved us from, if we are to believe the right-wing hagiography that followed her death. Underneath that hagiography there is also a process of falsification that would make the workers of George Orwell's ministry of truth blush. Take the nationalised industries for example, many of them privatised by Thatcher. The core nationalised industries of the UK were generally, over the period of their existence, efficient and provided a decent income for many of those who worked there, as well as generating thousands of further jobs for suppliers and for small businesses in the immediate neighbourhood of shipyards, pits and steel works. According to Parker, 'the nationalised industries improved their performance dramatically in the mid-1980s and may have again performed better than the economy in general in terms of labour productivity growth'.[1]

The distortion is illustrative of the right's desire to conjure up a dismal, hopeless inefficient socialist world in black and white about to be suffused with the bright colours of unregulated market capitalism. The truth is that Britain was far from being a socialist country in the 1970s, despite significant sections of the economy being in public ownership, and in the early 1970s unemployment was beginning to creep up to the million mark.

This helps explain the necessity and the importance of the fight back that workers in Upper Clyde Shipbuilders staged as John Foster explains in his earlier chapter. The devastation that closing the yards would have caused locally at a time when unemployment was rising not only produced the legendary Work-In, but a spate of similar actions up and down the country as a still comparatively strong trade union movement grasped the significance of defending local jobs. It was one of a very few times when the Scottish movement was in the van of struggle across Britain.

It is the purpose of this chapter to consider what the conditions were in that period which helped catapult the Scottish working class into such a leading position and whether it is to the 1970s or more contemporary campaigns we should look for strategies to reverse the politics of austerity.

In 1971 the prospects of a successful attack on the trade union movement looked remote. Only a few years earlier the movement had seen off Barbara Castle's 'In Place of Strife' which abandoned voluntarism (unions taking action based on their own rule books in order to negotiate settlements with employers) in favour of, for example, compulsory strike ballots and enforced settlements.

The successful UCS Work-In took place in a period of high trade union membership and as John Foster points out considerable community and British-wide support for the campaign, including Tony Benn, John Lennon and Billy Connolly, reflecting, not only wider support but in the popularity of artists like Connolly, a rise in the wider cultural working-class influence.

In contrast to this British capital was on the back foot:

> In 1972, Penguin published as a 'Penguin Special' a rather academic text on profits in British industry written by two left-wing academics, Andrew Glyn and Bob Sutcliffe. This showed that the commonly held belief that the share of wages and profits in the overall GDP was over time a rough constant was false and that in Britain, though not apparently elsewhere, the proportion going to wages had been systematically increasing for some time. Their statistics actually finished in 1970 but subsequent work showed that this profit squeeze intensified in the early 1970s to reach a low point in 1974 when aggregate after-tax profits dropped to as low as 3.3% once stock inflation was removed.[2]

In 1974 the crisis of profitability in British capitalism was intensified by the precipitate increase in the price of oil, inflation and yet another credit bubble bursting. The response of Western capitalism to the crisis of the 1970s is well documented in a number of texts, for example, David Harvey's popular brief history of neo-liberalism[3] which charts the rise of Reaganomics and Thatcherism and its continuation on both sides of the Atlantic, most egregiously in Britain under New Labour.

The neo-liberal response

Extraordinarily, the neo-liberal politics that Thatcher ushered in - mass unemployment, the miners' strike, the deindustrialisation, the cuts to benefits, the privatisation, the cut to real wages, a politics that Blair and Brown sustained - are still with us in the main parties and policies of the EU and the UK.

The left should consider the salient features of 1971, this most recent high water mark of Scottish working-class influence, despite the fact that it was over 40 years ago and consider the strategies it needs to develop in what is admittedly a very different world from then. That requires us to do two things. Firstly briefly consider the nature of the changed conditions and secondly assess the effectiveness of the main campaigns of the left in Scotland set up to tackle neo-liberal dominance.

In his book, Economics for Everyone, Jim Stanford[4] argues that there are five key conditions that affect the capacity of unions to organise effectively. These are:

1. The legal climate. Obviously the presence or absence of key rights, for example the right to strike, and although Stamford does not mention this specifically, the right to take solidarity action, impact profoundly on unions to achieve common objectives.
2. The attitude of workers. Here Stanford is really addressing the level of what is sometimes termed militancy. The tenacity and solidarity of trade unions is a critical factor in the successful prosecution of trade union action.
3. The cost of job loss. Stanford makes the point that the combination of high unemployment and low levels of what used to be called social security in Britain make losing your job all the more dangerous for the average worker because of course poverty may be the consequence. Further this may have an impact on the emergence of shop floor activism because activism may be a factor in getting you sacked and/or blacklisted, a practice we have discovered that was only too common in Scotland and Britain.
4. Productivity. Stanford regards this as positive for the unions if it is on the rise and allows the workforce to negotiate increases from an employer who is not feeling the pinch. On the other hand it is problematic if it is being achieved through work intensification and here the employer will certainly fight to defend profitability.
5. Finally Stanford considers competition. Here he argues that the more intense the competition between companies the harder they will defend their current cost base including wages; consequently the union strategy needs to be sector wide if that is possible. Of course the move to local or plant bargaining is designed to impede such a collective approach by unions.

We could add a sixth point here in relation to the politicisation of trade union struggles and that is the issue of class consciousness and a political strategy to match that consciousness. While it may be true that in Scotland the seventies began with levels of class consciousness no better or worse than England, nevertheless the leading sections of the Scottish working class in the trade union movement, as exemplified by the leaders of the UCS, were in a strong position, as John Foster describes it:

> In Scotland the leftward move was somewhat more pronounced...This influence was reflected in the general council of the Scottish Trades Union Congress where Communist Jimmy Milne became deputy general secretary in 1966 and general secretary in 1975. At the same time, the shift in attitudes was at this point largely confined to the Trade Union movement. Politically public opinion in Scotland was no more Left than England...[5]

Table 1. Do you think it should or should not be the Government's responsibility to provide a job for everyone who wants one? definitely should be + Probably should be %.

	1985	1986	1989	1990	1991	1996	1998	2000	2002	2006	2010
Scotland	76.68	77.71	75.43	65.5	68.17	78.25	66.43	83.17	79.05	56.41	76.77
North East	64.86	70.25	80.73	74.45	75.59	78.38	75.9	87	87.06	62.98	60.94
North West	86.70	70.39	72.04	76.69	75.7	80.58	83.34	84.35	81.73	57.15	64.95
Yorkshire & Humberside	74.83	80.03	66.36	69.59	62.07	64.36	78.16	86	85.99	44.11	56.91

Table 2. How much do you agree or disagree that ordinary working people do not get their fair share of the nation's wealth (Agree + Strongly Agree %)

	1986	1987	1989	1990	1991	1993	1995	1996	1998	1999	2000	2001
Scotland	69.82	75.9	71.66	65.72	68.89	68.86	72.47	72.32	66.24	68.07	72.61	70.15
North East	73.94	72.06	72.83	79	68.88	69.94	78.86	68.35	74.09	70.33	69.91	60.77
North West	71.58	68.13	66.73	74.15	76.99	68.33	72.61	69.43	70.35	65.86	69.98	70.31
Yorkshire & Humberside	70.58	72.09	63.7	70.55	68.78	68.16	75.06	64.34	68.34	65.37	62.95	64.38

	2002	2003	2004	2005	2006	2007	2008	2009	2010	2011
Scotland	69.49	69.96	61.42	61.32	56.02	60.33	58.27	68.97	63.49	69.37
North East	74.16	69.86	58.87	54.95	65.06	61.07	59.55	63	51.46	61.53
North West	62.4	60.94	54.47	64.29	63.09	65.93	65.18	63.98	65.37	60.66
Yorkshire & Humberside	69.52	64.63	57.46	58.4	54.76	63.97	67.34	64.68	55.69	60.37

Table 3. Would you like to see more or less government spending than now on benefits for people who care for those who are sick or disabled? (more + much more %)

	1998	1999	2002	2004	2006	2008	2011
Scotland	89.51	81.66	87.55	85.82	86.44	88.07	79.12
North East	79.04	87.12	83.08	81.85	74.04	85.37	74.96
North West	83.54	83.71	83.34	85.33	89.03	87.94	77.86
Yorkshire & Humberside	82.25	84.96	82.85	80.55	84.13	86.25	78.05

This is still the case today. The British Social Attitudes Survey[6] has since 1986 been examining attitudes in the UK. It is possible to compare opinions in Scotland with those of its closest neighbours - the 15 million inhabitants of the English North East, North West, Yorkshire and Humberside. We can compare responses to questions asked on a range of issues which might indicate some level of progressive opinion, for example the role of government in tackling unemployment (Figure 1), whether working people have a fair share of the nation's wealth (Figure 2), support for carers (Figure 3) and so on. It cannot be said that on any of these issues Scotland appears significantly different or even particularly distinct from the three English regions. Rather it is the continuity with the spread of Northern English opinion which is striking. Not only will Scottish opinion usually be within a few points of the others on any given year, Scottish opinions follow the same trends as the Northern English on all of these issues.

It can of course be argued that during this time frame Scotland operated largely within the same political and economic environment as the three regions sampled so a degree of congruence is to be expected. This would be to miss the point. It is not simply that Scottish opinion was and is the same as the North of England but rather it is that in response to the same issues Scots reacted in the same way. The opinions expressed show a contradictory picture. Over the long term (1986 onwards) support for redistributive policies has declined as has sympathy for those on benefits. At the same time the view that ordinary people 'don't get a fair share' has stayed almost static, but the idea that business has too much power has gained support. What cannot be argued is that Scotland and the Scottish working class is inherently more inclined to left politics than our southern neighbours.

Developing a campaign to fight back

Indeed one of the defining features of the current period has been the left's failure in Scotland and the rest of Britain to popularise a strategy such as the alliance against monopoly capitalism that informed the leaders of the UCS struggle. Winning support for such a strategy is desperately needed in a period when the dominance of neo-liberalism in Britain, as we have noted, has been creating precisely the opposite conditions that Stanford argues are necessary for the growth of a strong trade union movement - anti-union legislation, high and sustained periods of high unemployment, less and less social security, intense competition and low productivity as a result of low investment.

Further, these factors are inter-penetrative with unemployment not only making it difficult to recruit to trade unions, but weak trade unions meaning that building a forceful political opposition to neo-liberal politics within the Labour Party and the wider society is that much more difficult. Hence the political agency, the Labour Party, that might have been expected to challenge conditions that undermined the defence of working-class interests in effect helped create them, its leadership supported in this task by the deep pockets of the backers of Progress.

This means that any strategy designed to heighten resistance has to address all of the constraining factors described above. If this were done it is possible that like the UCS episode, an opportunity may emerge that gives expression to the discontent that is evident among unemployed youngsters, families seeking a decent place to live, neglected pensioners, harassed people on disability allowance and importantly organised workers fighting to win reasonable conditions and wages. The demonstrations that exploded over the bedroom tax at least suggested a movement echoing the Poll Tax Campaign and the UCS, where the voice of the left became the voice of the people.

The need for overarching campaigns that seek to inject a level of political consciousness has not of course gone unnoticed in Scotland or the rest of Britain. The STUC developed the innovative 'There is a Better Way campaign'. It focuses on four areas: jobs, services, a living wage and fair taxes. It was launched with universal trade union support in September 2010 as a response to the Coalition Government's austerity plans of June

2010. In terms of political response, the STUC had already developed a position in support of fiscal stimulus, dismissing the Government's view that the current crisis is one of public finances, rather than, as the STUC believes, a crisis of employment and growth.

Unlike many previous campaigns *There is a Better Way* did not seek to 'run' local campaigns out of its headquarters. Instead it sought to support and to some extent resource community-based campaigns as well as undertaking its more traditional role of mobilising for large-scale events through its trade union affiliates.

The origins of the People's Charter are more complicated. It emerged in England in 2009 supported by a group of MPs and leading political activists from a wide spectrum of the left and was subsequently endorsed by most trade unions and the TUC and the STUC. The closeness of its intentions to that of the *There is a Better Way* campaign can be seen in this description by John McDonnell MP:

> By setting out a straightforward analysis of the crisis, the charter provides an alternative view of causes of the unemployment and the threat to our public services that we are facing. By setting out a common-sense set of basic policies, the charter offers a way of developing an alternative strategy to take the economy out of recession in a way that could transform the future of our society. [7]

The Scottish Organising Committee of the *People's Charter* established in 2010, unlike its English counterpart, eventually comprised the key trade unions affiliated to the Labour Party, Unite and UNISON, as well as unaffiliated unions like RMT, FBU, POAS and PCS in addition to political groups like SNP trade union group, the Campaign for Socialism and CPB Scotland. In England, trade union influence was less pronounced.

Neither campaign allowed itself to be defined in terms of the constitutional debate. The Scottish Organising Committee of the *People's Charter* explicitly accepted the need to allow the space for pro- and anti-independence positions. Nevertheless, neither campaign has confined itself to areas within the compass of the current devolved settlement (leading some supporting SNP MSPs to qualify support for only those areas of the *People's Charter* for which the Scottish Parliament has a remit) and both make demands on the UK Government, clearly predicated on the UK-wide trade union and labour movement.

It is not yet clear, but looking increasingly likely, that *The People's Assembly* already providing a platform for an alliance of all anti-austerity groups in England will also be established in Scotland.

It would seem then that the re-creation of the conditions that put the Scottish working class in the lead and made the victory of the UCS possible require a political strategy that creates jobs, reverses attacks on welfare and builds political support for the rehabilitation of trade union rights as part of a strategy that seeks to redress the balance of power in favour of the working class.

The left needs to discuss two key aspects of the nature of such a campaign. The first is whether the anti-austerity thrust of the current campaigns is sufficient. While it is necessary that austerity be tackled and defeated, is that possible without a layer of class-conscious political activists in the workplace and the community? In other words, the desire to defeat the politics of austerity is not an end in itself but only an important first step in building a political movement that understands that given the cyclical nature of capitalism another period of austerity will be with us soon enough, if we do not tackle the roots of the problem - capitalism.

Secondly we need to address the question as to whether it is possible to generate a political strategy without having a clear perspective on whether the power of capital can be effectively challenged by a Scottish working class in a secessionist Scotland, a proposition which this book has sought to challenge.

It is time for an autonomous socialist campaign. It should draw its strength from its social and political programme and it should acknowledge the deep cultural and social links most Scots have with family, friends, colleagues as well as people they do not know throughout Britain, but with whom they empathise because of a shared popular culture as well as common institutions, like the welfare state, political parties, trade unions and a common class position.

There is considerable evidence[8] that the people of Scotland would like additional powers for the Scottish Parliament. We would argue this is because they believe that it is the best way to defend themselves against austerity. Learning from the Better Way and the *People's Charter* and the historical success of the UCS, it is surely now time to launch a campaign aimed at winning key sections of the working class which unashamedly calls for a progressive and strengthened Scottish Parliament within a progressive Britain which once and for all achieves what the workers of UCS wanted: jobs, peace and security in Scotland and Britain through an irreversible shift of wealth and power in favour of the working class.

Endnotes

1. Nationalisation, Privatisation, and Agency Status Within Government: Testing For The Importance Of Ownership. Available at: www.dspace.lib.cranfield.ac.uk/bitstream/1826/572/2/SWP2392.pdf.
2. Prior, M., The Years of Lead: Politics in the 1970s, 2006. available at http://www.hegemonics.co.uk/docs/Workers-control-1970s.pdf
3 Harvey, D.A., A Brief History of Neo-Liberalism, OUP, Oxford, 2007.
4. Stanford, J., Economics for Everyone: A Short Guide to the Economics of Capitalism, Pluto, London, 2008.

5. Foster, J., Contesting the languages of control: a comparison of working class mobilisation on Clydeside in 1919 and 1971, unpublished, 2013.

6. British Attitudes Survey available at http://www.britsocat.com/Home. Also see reference 5 above.

7. McDonnell, J., The Morning Star, Friday 20 November 2009.

8. Curtice, J. and Ormston, R., Attitudes towards Scotland's Constitutional Future, 2013 available at http://www.natcen.ac.uk/media/1021490/ssa12briefing.pdf.

SECTION 5 - THE POLITICAL CHALLENGE
Introduction

Pauline Bryan

The fact that there will be a referendum on Scottish independence within the year, just 15 years after the establishment of a Scottish Parliament, has probably been as big a surprise for the SNP as for anyone else. When the Parliament was established with a mixture of first-past-the-post and PR, the supposition was that no one party, and particularly not the SNP, could win a majority. Even if they were to be the largest party, unless they gained support from another party, they could not win a vote to have a referendum.

If the SNP had a choice they probably would not have picked this particular time to hold a referendum. It is in their favour that the Tories are in power in the UK, but on the other hand there is considerable economic uncertainty.

The first few months of the campaign were taken up with the question of whether there could be a 'second question' or a 'third option' put to voters. Elements in the SNP, and Alex Salmond in particular, encouraged the idea that a Devo Max position should be on the ballot paper. It was reported in the Sunday Herald on 1 July 2012 that Salmond gave the following response to a question at a meeting in San Francisco:

> There's a view abroad in Scotland that perhaps it would be better from where we are now - where we now control about 16% of Scotland's revenue base, that rather than become an independent country, at least in the first stage, that that fiscal base should increase to something near 100%, and that's often called Devo Max or fiscal autonomy. And it's a very attractive argument, incidentally.

Why would Salmond and others within the SNP take such a position? Perhaps there was concern that a straight Yes/No was likely to end in defeat and therefore close off the issue for some time ahead, whereas a vote for Devo Max, which adopted the SNP's fiscal approach would allow independence to be raised again under what could be more favourable conditions.

No third option will be on the ballot paper, but instead we are drip by drip being presented with the image of Scotland after independence: Scotland totally committed to membership of the EU with no question of making it more democratic or less a vehicle for neo-liberal economic policies; membership of NATO with its system of 'consensus' decision-making that requires no votes; a hereditary monarchy; being part of a sterling zone that will leave important economic levers in another country. This is not, then an exciting image of a future Scotland that can create a different type of society, but rather a steady-as-we-go approach that you will hardly notice has happened. And instead of being more responsive and democratic it could actually be less.

The SNP are not fighting the referendum on a platform of radical change and the Labour Party is not defending the Union by offering the possibility of radical change - they are both in their own ways defending the status quo. As the campaigns progress, the Radical Independence Alliance will try to inject radicalism into the Yes campaign. Nicola Sturgeon is making the case that an independent Scotland will be wealthier - but also fairer. The Labour Party has recognised that the Better Together campaign has alienated much of the labour movement. It eventually realised that just saying 'no' in alliance with the coalition partners would prevent trade union and many Labour Party members from becoming involved in the campaign.

Although ahead in the polls, Labour is in danger of losing the support of the key opinion leaders among trade union and community activists. It already lost voters to the SNP in the 2011 Scottish Parliamentary elections and if this continues during referendum there must be a real doubt about whether they will regain these voters in the General Election in 2015 and particularly in the Scottish Parliamentary elections in 2016. There is a possibility that the SNP could lose the referendum, but continue in Government.

The labour movement faces some key challenges in the run-up to the referendum. Some of these challenges are being explored in the STUC's 'A Just Scotland' consultation and in the Labour Party's Devolution Commission. The Red Paper Collective has identified the following key areas that present a particular political challenge to the labour movement.

The challenge for the environment where unplanned market capitalism drives our environmental problems: how do we integrate the labour movement's traditional concerns for social justice, worthwhile employment, equality and human rights with the need to stop climate change? We know what needs to be done, but the demands of global capitalism prevent it happening. The actions of the current Scottish Government do not offer a positive picture for the future. Matthew Crighton argues that the tight grip of economic orthodoxy on both sides of the referendum campaign must be challenged.

The challenge of the EU: particularly now that the campaign for a referendum on membership of the EU has come to overlap with the referendum on Scottish independence it is even harder to untangle the issues. Rozanne Foyer points out that both Better Together and the SNP miss the point of what EU membership means. While the EU has delivered the benefits of Social Europe, she identifies the issues that give concern and asks whether at the very time workers across Europe are rejecting austerity that the independence referendum does not result in us walking blindly into an EU nightmare.

The challenge of defence policy after the SNP has taken contradictory positions of agreeing that an independent Scotland would seek membership of NATO while at the same time demanding the removal of Trident submarines: Alan Mackinnon explores the likely pressures from the EU and NATO as well as business interests that will be brought to bear on a future government. He argues that the removal of Trident should not depend on a Yes vote at the referendum, but be fought for across the UK.

The challenge for the Scottish Labour Party includes the loss of support with the bonds that existed between it and working-class voters already weakened and its breach with the trade unions making it worse: while Scottish Labour did not adopt the market-oriented policies of New Labour, it was reluctant to explain why. Eric Shaw describes how the weakened support for Labour has been emphasised in Scotland where the Party is challenged, not from the right, but by a Party which claims the mantle of social democracy.

The challenge for trade unions in Scotland has been to enable trade union members to have a clear understanding of the arguments of the Yes and the No camps and to consult their members: the STUC and many of its affiliated unions have focused the referendum debate on how to achieve social justice in Scotland. Dave Moxham, Deputy General Secretary of the STUC describes the serious challenges being made to both sides of the debate and particularly the Labour Party. He asks serious questions about how Scotland would fare in a post-Barnett formula financial settlement.

Challenging neo-liberal economic orthodoxies recognises that the SNP's approach to independence would operate within the constraints of fiscally conservative policies particularly with its plan to reduce corporation tax which will ensure the continuation of austerity policies. On the other hand, Devo Plus strategies that rest on the 'moral hazard' that occurs when a Parliament spends but does not raise revenue also adopt neo-liberal ideas of constraining the Scottish Parliament and limiting powers for redistribution. Fiscal policy, Dave Watson argues, should support the creation of a more equal society.

The final chapter challenges those who look to constitutional change rather than political change. Posing nation against class is a blind alley which will only reinforce the country's exposure to the power of multinational capitalism. If there is to be a lasting settlement for devolution, the status quo cannot be the only alternative. Along with the labour movements in other parts of the UK we should explore the best constitutional solution to enable fairer redistribution of wealth and greater democratic control of our economies.

SECTION 5
Chapter 1

JOBS, POVERTY AND CLIMATE CHANGE - TOGETHER
Matthew Crighton

The challenge of our time is to find a way for us all to live well and fairly within our shared environmental limits. The scale of global production has reached a point at which the consequences of human activity, unchecked, will be disastrous for our life support systems. This is most clear in the case of climate change. If we do not limit man-made global warming to 2 degrees C we will witness the progressive destruction of the capacity of agricultural systems to provide food for the world's growing population. We will witness the loss of large parts of our coastal land including parts of major cities. Even within that 2 degree limit there are possibilities for large-scale climate-caused disasters. For example the disruption of the Gulf Stream could bring Scotland a climate like northern Canada.

Put simply, all aspirations for a fair and better world will melt away in the face of unchecked climate change. Although, as Nicholas Stern said, 'the poorest countries and people will suffer earliest and most'[1], even a narrow vision of protecting living standards in an imperialist heartland while attempting to insulate it from the storms raging around the rest of the world will fail in the longer run.

In the short term our main challenges are likely to be different: reducing inequality, creating full employment and ensuring high-quality public services, winning the next election or the referendum. These are issues which directly affect the well-being of people in Scotland now. Notwithstanding that they would all fit within 'a way for us all to live well and fairly within our environmental limits' there is a difference in timescale.

The question is therefore, how do our traditional concerns for social justice, worthwhile employment, equality and human rights fit with the need to stop climate change and live within our planet's limits? And the good news is, it's easy!

Intellectually, the diagnosis that unplanned market capitalism is driving our environmental problems has fairly widespread support. The logical prescription accepted by many is democratic control if not actual ownership of the core elements of the economy and that equity has to be a central feature of climate change policies; the benefits and the pain have to be equally shared rather than imposed.

Practically, much of it is easy, at least technically, and would create lots of employment. The measures which we should be implementing are all based on existing technologies. When we find the money for them they will have enormous social and economic benefits - and we know how to find the money (we did that for the banks).

The difficulty is the scale and speed with which we move, and the other big thing - the political will. The scientists have alerted us about the problem and the politicians have accepted it in principle. Engineers, experts and activists have generated a range of solutions, but progress is tragically slow. If the politicians know what needs to be done but are not doing it we need to understand why not.

Having in Scotland what the World Wildlife Fund has been described as the 'best climate change act in the world', it might be expected that there would be a more positive story to tell. However, the first-year report showed that the target set for emissions reductions was missed; and the Scottish Government's second 'report on Policy and Programmes' (RPP2) was roundly criticised by environmentalists as being less specific than the previous plan and especially weak on transport and having optimistic assumptions on emissions reduction targets.[2]

Setting targets is desirable but clearly not sufficient. This is true across the range of issues measured in that way: unemployment, child poverty, fuel poverty and climate change. Without being clear how they will be achieved, linked to methods which are adequate to tackle all the barriers in the way, laudable policy goals are in danger of becoming vacuous. What we need is a proper plan.

There could be a common solution to these challenges: large-scale, government-led investment. This could create the jobs needed to transform our economy and meet emissions reduction targets. The rest of this article concerns how to put together a programme of policies and actions which will start to deal with these economic, environmental and social priorities, which can be implemented now, and which can form a key part of a platform for mobilising large numbers of people and their organisations for radical change.

There are numerous road maps for radical reductions in our greenhouse gas emissions including the report, mentioned above, by Nicholas Stern. It was commissioned by Gordon Brown and set a framework for economic analysis of climate change which showed that it is much better to stop emissions now than face much more serious costs later.[3] For more radical proposals one can look at Heat by George Monbiot - written before the climate change acts of 2008 and 2009 to show that 90 per cent cuts in greenhouse gas emissions are realistic[4] and One Million Climate Jobs which focuses on the way in which the changes will be achieved and the jobs created as well as emissions reductions themselves.[5]

All of course assume that we need to both decarbonise energy production and reduce energy consumption. However, there are significant differences concerning both the scale and speed of the emissions reductions required and the methods for achieving change. The principal question is whether to rely on the workings of markets or to turn to publicly funded and state-led mechanisms (although the narratives about consumption patterns and behaviour change also need to be addressed).

The question of methods concerns not just whether they are effective but also the distribution of the costs and benefits - the impacts in terms of equity. Recent work shows, for instance, that the approach of the current UK Government is regressive: it 'represents a triple injustice: the lowest income households pay more, benefit less from policies and are responsible for least emissions'.[6] There is, however, a broad consensus about the measures needed that can give us a start on the journey while more challenging parts of the plan are developed. Two principal areas are dealt with below.

Electricity generation

A core part of plans for emissions reduction has to be large-scale displacement of coal and gas electricity generation by renewable sources which include onshore and offshore wind, tidal and wave power, hydro-electric, geothermal sources and solar. Scotland is particularly rich in many of these (but not the last one, although even in our climate it can make a contribution).

Growth in renewable energy generation capacity, mostly in onshore wind, can account for half of this. In 2011 this equated to over one-third of Scotland's electricity consumption. The industry has plans in the pipeline for at least double that capacity, most in offshore wind. In the process, Scottish Renewables has calculated that 'the sector directly supports the equivalent of 10,227 full-time jobs in project design, development, operation and the supply chain'.[7]

Although there has been success in increasing capacity in onshore wind generation, the number of jobs created in Scotland has been far lower than it could have been. The model followed has ensured that, despite the subsidy to the industry coming from consumers through the Renewables Obligation, many of the economic benefits have flowed out of Scotland. There has been a boost to production of turbines by European companies like Siemens and Vestas but very little generation of manufacturing employment in the UK. Note also the flow of profits to foreign-owned multinational power companies like Iberdrola, which owns Scottish Power.

Community benefits have been variable across Scotland and remain at the behest of the power companies. At the same time the continued growth of onshore wind is the subject of conflict with opponents who perceive wind farms as a serious detriment to environmental amenity. In contrast Denmark has been held up as an example of an alternative in which the benefits of wind power have been retained and dispersed widely within the country. A crucial foundation of this model has been the widespread community ownership of wind farms.[8] Yet again the UK's approach, which relies on market-driven delivery of public policy objectives and concentrates power and ownership with small numbers of multinationals, has delivered a poor deal for Scotland's people and fostered antagonism from communities which see wind farms as being imposed on them rather than assets which they own.

Looking ahead, the next set of technologies which will add additional renewables generation capacity are wave and tidal. Scotland's coastal communities could reap massive benefits from these or the pattern of external ownership and growing community alienation may well be repeated. The question of property ownership here concerns rights over the shores and inland waters. These rest with the Crown Estate but as Andy Wightman has pointed out, the power to bring the management of these rights and assets is vested in the Scottish Parliament already. Land reform in this wider sense therefore has to be addressed as part of this larger programme.

Energy efficiency in homes

In terms of reducing energy consumption, it is probable that energy efficiency in homes can deliver the largest reductions in the shortest timescale. The technology and capacity already exist and can deliver both jobs and make a serious inroad in fuel poverty.

Fuel poverty is rising because of rising fuel prices and static or falling incomes; however, a thorough programme of retrofitting existing houses would mitigate this and significantly cut greenhouse gas emissions. There are serious concerns about the capacity of the UK Government's new policies, which rely on market mechanisms, to sustain even the current level of activity - the Green Deal is unlikely to work for those in fuel poverty and the UK Government now has no publicly funded energy efficiency programme.

The Scottish Government continues to commit funding to the newly designed National Retrofit Programme, now known as HEAPS, in which it has given local authorities a key implementation role. For this it is to be applauded but it is not at anything like a large enough scale. A programme rolled out at a scale to achieve rapid reductions in emissions and in fuel poverty has such obvious merits that the question should be, not whether to do it, but how to do it.

Other areas requiring immediate and ambitious action are: transport, where there should be large-scale investment to achieve greater use of public transport; shifting to electrical power and other renewable sources; and greater energy efficiency in workplaces led by green workplace representatives.

In each area the approach has to include scoping the changes which we need to make, assessing the amount of investment needed and the number of jobs which can be created and clarifying the powers needed for effective implementation in ways which bring the maximum benefits for reduction of poverty and inequality.

The scale of the programme and how to fund it

The scale and speed of investment required are undoubtedly large compared with current progress but they are quite within the powers of a bold government determined to make them happen.

For the previous UK Labour Government, the Sustainable Development Commission proposed a stimulus package of £30bn of which at least 50 per cent should be committed to 'green' measures. Nicholas Stern in 'One Million Climate Jobs' calls for a government programme of £50bn a year which equates to about 3.5 per cent of GDP [9],while estimating that the net cost to the government, taking into account reduced unemployment payments and higher tax income, would be less than half of that. Taken down to the Scottish level, assuming its economy is about 10 per cent of the UK's, these proposals suggest Scottish expenditure of an additional £2bn to £5bn.

These are substantial sums, which is right because the scale of the changes needed is large. For the purposes of comparison, the public expenditure in the UK is about £688bn pa; the budget of the Scottish Government is about £30bn.

Within an orthodox framework, which dominates government thinking and indeed that of most economics commentators, there is no scope for this. Aren't we already spending too much? Isn't debt already far too high? Others have already de-bunked these falsehoods and presented proposals for stimulus packages funded by increased tax taken from avoiders and evaders, cancellation of Trident and increased borrowing. Certainly, to move forward as proposed we will have to break out from the falsehoods of that orthodoxy.

Indeed even the Treasury can do that when it needs to - the 2008 package to bail out the banks was valued at £500bn. The value of the Bank of England's Quantitative Easing (QE) packages comes to £375bn. This involved the Bank creating money on its own ledgers and using it to purchase bonds or other assets from financial institutions. This transfer of money into the banks eases their liquidity problems and should stimulate the economy. However, perversely, it leaves the banks with the decisions on what to do with this money. At a time when the real economy remains depressed but the stock market is soaring we again have confirmation that private banks will always use their privileged role in the economy for private gain not public.

If we can do that to save the banks we can do it to save the world. That is what is behind the proposal known as Green Quantitative Easing from Caroline Lucas MP and Professor Richard Werner, which he promoted at the Just Banking conference in Edinburgh in 2012.[10] It involves the Bank of England creating the money in the same way but directing it straight into public investment, in particular into the measures described above which will reduce greenhouse gas emissions, increase employment and so reduce poverty. Having the merit of by-passing the banks, less QE would be required for the same economic impact.

As Richard Werner says, 'Money creation is a public privilege. So using it to benefit the public and environment seems only right.'[11] Until recently that has been ruled out as an unacceptable suggestion from the radical fringe. However, some establishment commentators have broken ranks, notably Adair Turner[12] and Martin Wolf who in the Financial Times on 12 February said 'in the present exceptional circumstances … the case for using the state's power to create credit and money in support of public spending is strong'.[13] If they can say this, why can't some of our politicians?

Going back to the start, where I said that it's easy, the sense in which it is indeed easy is that we know what we should be doing, we can estimate the cost of the different parts of the programme, we know that it will have to be driven forward by the public sector and we know we can finance it. Of course politically there are formidable barriers in our way because of the tight grip of economic orthodoxy, the fear of 'alarming the markets' and the power of the banking lobby. Also the subordination of the political class in the main parties in both unionist and nationalist camps to these orthodoxies, loyalty to which is elevated above the need to address the urgent economic and environmental needs of the countries of the UK.

Reviewing the legacy of Hugo Chavez recently, I have suggested that we would benefit from some of his spirit in this country. One strand of this spirit can be summarised as 'Just Do It' - he was a pragmatist and always found ways of achieving the objectives he was elected for. His most outstanding feature, however, was his willingness to challenge the undemocratic powers of the rich and the powerful in his determination to build social justice in all its many forms, including environmental justice.

It is this spirit which we need to bring to the challenge of saving the planet from environmental destruction and its people from the scourges of poverty, unemployment and inequality.

Endnotes

1. Stern, N. The Economics of Climate Change, London: H M Treasury, 2006.
2. Government, The Scottish, Low Carbon Scotland: Meeting our Emissions Reduction Targets 2013-2027 - The Draft Second Report on Proposals and Policies, Edinburgh: s.n., 2013.
3. See note 2.
4. Monbiot, G., Heat, London: Allen Lane, 2006.
5. Campaign against Climate Change trade union, One million climate jobs, London: Campaign against Climate Change, 2010.
6. Hargreaves, K., Preston, I., White, V. and Thumim, J., Distribution of Carbon Emissions in the UK, York: Joseph Rowntree Foundation, 2013.
7. http://www.scottishrenewables.com/scottish-renewable-energy-statistics-glance/.
8. Cumbers, A., Reclaiming Public Ownership, London: Zed Books, 2012.
9. See note 8.
10. www.justbanking.org.uk.
11 See note 10.
12. Turner, A., Debt money and Mephistopheles: how do we get out of this mess?, http://www.fsa.gov.uk. [Online] February 2013.
13. Wolf, M., The case for helicopter money, Financial Times, 12 February 2013.

SCOTLAND AND THE EU
Rozanne Foyer

An independent Scotland's membership of the European Union (EU) has received a great deal of media coverage, but generally this has been from the wrong angle. Membership of the EU will have a crucial impact on a future Scotland, whatever the outcome of the referendum, but here I want to particularly explore how it would impact on an independent Scotland.

I should state from the outset that I am a constitutional agnostic. I do not hold any overriding emotional, identity based or patriotic beliefs about whether Scotland should go it alone or stay in the UK. I am also agnostic about whether the UK as we know it should remain part of the EU or whether an independent Scotland should seek to be part of the EU.

The question I pose is what will work best for the majority of working people? It is not my country but my class that I am passionate about defending. So when I consider each constitutional model I am interested in its capacity for achieving positive social change.

I don't believe Scotland can live the socialist dream in isolation. To withstand the forces of global capitalism it is crucial that workers across the world get organised, stand up together and fight back together. To do this we need global strategies to close the gap between the richest and poorest, stop the race to the bottom and end the exploitation of workers by global capital and the neo-liberal institutions that run the world. In the long term our goals should include a worldwide minimum wage and living standards, an international progressive taxation strategy, as well as establishing strong trade union and employment rights.

In order to support these goals we would have to develop strong international legal frameworks and institutions that have real teeth and which are truly democratic and accessible to the citizens of the world. But even an optimist like me recognises that we are a long way from achieving such goals. The reality is that our global institutions, while portraying themselves as the drivers of democracy and freedom, represent a form of government for the rich by the rich, and the EU is such an institution.

Starting with the big picture is important, as when you are setting out on a journey you should keep one eye on your final destination. The questions facing Scotland right now about its relationship with both the UK and the EU represent the next steps in its journey which I hope will be towards becoming a more socially just country that can contribute towards a more socially just world.

Is the media asking the right questions?

We should recognise and be concerned about the current mainstream narrative on the EU. The media and the 'No' camp delight in point scoring by suggesting that Scotland may not be accepted into the EU, and if it is it may have to join the euro. The SNP meanwhile has asserted that Scotland will be able to re-join the EU with seemingly no detrimental strings attached.

It is ironic that the SNP, while passionate about the Scottish people's right to self-determination, is not suggesting that a newly independent Scotland could have a choice about membership of the EU. Too few commentators are questioning closely enough what fiscal constraints might be placed upon Scotland as a new entrant to the EU. None of our mainstream political parties appear concerned about the EU's interference in countries like Spain, Cyprus and Greece, or the implications of EU entry on fiscal policy for a newly independent Scotland and the effect this will have on its ability to implement the social justice agenda that we are seeking.

EU - the good, the bad and the ugly

Before I continue I think it's important to acknowledge the achievements of the social strand of the EU model. Workers' councils, health and safety laws, the working time directive, equalities and human rights protections, agency labour protections, temporary and part-time workers' rights, and the right for labour to move freely across the EU are all important protections that benefit workers daily and are used by unions here in the UK in the interests of our members. They are the very reason why the Con-Dem Government wants to renegotiate powers back.

However, despite these positive achievements, I have some fundamental problems with the way that the EU and its policies impact on working people and fear that these might be compounded in an independent Scotland. So as a starting point for the debate I have five big issues, which are as follows:

Issue No 1 - the neo-liberal economic consensus of the EU

Austerity is a disaster. It is a tragedy for ordinary folk that will take generations to recover from. The fiscal compact forced on countries across the eurozone effectively forbids using Keynesian style borrowing and spending to escape recession. Austerity is a manifesto for making the poorest pay for the economic collapse which was caused by the greed and the high-risk culture of the banks.

At exactly the time when we should be investing in a living wage, welfare, education, skills, public services and infrastructure, we are gutting the heart out of them. This flawed approach will not create the recovery and growth that people so desperately need. Instead it will create real misery and destabilise society as is happening in Spain, Greece, Italy, and closer to home in Ireland and the UK itself.

The Con-Dem Government needed no encouragement to pursue a course of austerity, but it is nonetheless a fact that much of the UK's cuts agenda is directly driven by the EU's economic policies. The EU has set targets for reduction in the UK's deficit, and made it clear that it favours this being done by an attack on wages and welfare benefits expenditure and by cuts to public services, rather than through increased taxation. In March 2013 the European Commission for Economic and Financial Affairs commented that the UK fiscal strategy was 'not sufficiently ambitious and needs to be significantly reinforced'.[1] It required 'additional fiscal tightening measures'.

So whether we choose to be in or out of the UK, being part of the EU means that the austerity agenda will be alive and kicking in Scotland.

Issue No 2 - the Con-Dem led re-negotiation on repatriation of powers

David Cameron has pledged to hold a referendum on EU membership after the next UK elections in 2015 and, of course, after Scotland's referendum. So when the rest of the UK could, theoretically, be democratically deciding to leave the EU, Scotland could be applying to join, with no democratic debate.

I am, however, more worried about the re-negotiation that the Conservatives want to have with the EU than the EU referendum itself. Cameron's agenda is about ridding the UK of the only remaining good bits of EU membership - the social aspects. He aims to take back powers relating to employment law, health and safety, equalities rights, etc. This will go hand in hand with the Con-Dem Government's attack on domestic trade union and employment rights and their attacks on public services and welfare.

Despite his pledge to hold a referendum, and his hopes of rolling back employment laws, Cameron is actually determined to defend Britain's membership of the EU's single market because it serves the interests of his friends in the City of London. Similar parallels could be drawn with the SNP's interest in protecting Edinburgh's status as a banking centre, which is closely tied to the City and a link that Salmond wants to keep at all costs.

Cameron's agenda is to undercut the EU by imposing the worst employment laws and the cheapest most unprotected labour in the continent. This race to the bottom will harm workers in the UK and across the rest of the EU. In fact his strategy may be privately welcomed by the EU neo-liberals as it would allow them to start rolling back all of the rights that we have fought so hard to gain on an EU-wide level.

Issue No 3 - the stranglehold of EU membership on an independent Scotland

For those who believe independence is a vehicle for achieving a more just Scotland, there is a serious concern that by joining the EU, a newly independent Scotland will be forced to sign up to the fiscal compact.

The preamble of the 2012 Treaty on Stability states that where a country has a written constitution it would be expected that the terms of maximum fiscal deficit would be written into it. The SNP has openly stated its intention to have such a constitution. The impact of this and the fiscal compact would be like having the EU's neo-liberal economic policies and severe borrowing constraints imprinted on the new Scotland's DNA and would severely limit its ability to borrow to create growth, to implement progressive social policies, or to invest in the public sector.

The House of Lord's EU subcommittee has released a letter from the President of the EU Commission, José Barroso, to Lord Tugendhat, Chair of the Lords Economic Affairs Committee. It confirms that, in his view, an independent Scotland would have to apply to the EU on the same terms as any other accession state, with all that this entails. A post-independent Scotland would be starting from square one when applying to join the EU and if that is the case, I want to know more about that process and the obligations and constraints that may be placed on us. Certainly those placed on other accession states are considerable and include the requirement to sign the fiscal compact, which promotes increased fiscal union across the EU, promotes privatisation, sets your borrowing at less than 0.5 per cent of GDP, and is effectively a neo-liberal stranglehold on any new EU country's economic policies.

Should the new Scotland join the EU under whatever package it manages to negotiate (bearing in mind that it would be a small country desperate to get in), it would take nothing less than a further referendum to extricate us from these restraints. As the UK is an existing member it has been able to refuse to sign up to the fiscal compact. So in theory, it is still possible that, by changing the government, we could radically change the UK's economic policies.

It will not be the case that Scotland could pick and choose the terms under which it will be allowed EU membership. I would be more confident about independence if the Scottish Government were more tentative about exploring what the EU might have to offer working people, and then put their deal to the people for our consideration. Instead they are rushing headlong into the EU's arms without first considering the consequences, or indeed sharing them with the country.

Issue No 4 - the lack of any real democracy that we can exercise over many EU decisions

Tony Benn recently spoke to the Scottish officers and senior lay members of my own union Unite. When asked about the EU referendum he said that he regarded himself as an internationalist, but for him it was a question of democracy and he had real concerns about democracy within the EU.

The real power in the EU lies not with the MEPs sitting in the European Parliament, but with the Council of Europe, which takes the key decisions. Its members are not subject to election by the people of Europe.

The EU needs to have far more transparency and accountability to the ordinary people over whom it wields such enormous powers. Major democratic reform is required if we are ever to have a hope of the people, not the bosses, controlling the EU's direction. We must have the freedom to transform or, if necessary, to withdraw and then renegotiate our trading relations between the states of Europe on a democratic and equal basis.

Issue No 5 - the impact of the austerity agenda is breaking down the very fabric of our society across the EU

The withdrawal of benefits and key services to the poorest in our society, poverty, pay for those in work, rising unemployment, a lack of investment and political turmoil all contribute to a very dangerous set of conditions. You only have to look at Greece to see the frightening possibilities.

Time and again the Greek people have taken to the streets in a series of general strikes to express their fury against the austerity measures that are dismantling their society. A study by Greece's largest trade union has estimated that 3.9 million of Greece's 11 million people are now living below the poverty line.[207] And, it should be noted that the line is very low at 7,200 euros per year per head.

One-third of all adults are unemployed and almost two-thirds of Greece's young adults cannot find work. In the past five years, Greeks have suffered a 35 per cent reduction in their living standards, and yet despite all of the cuts and the austerity measures, there has still been no economic growth. It is not surprising that support for the mainstream political parties is plummeting.

Again, not surprising is the growth of the far right in Greece, under the name of the Golden Dawn, with chilling similarities to the days of the Weimar Republic in the lead up to the creation of Nazi Germany. Since the last election, Golden Dawn has gained political representation in Parliament with 14 per cent of the vote and, among police officers, over 60 per cent.

Could the EU, which many believe was created to ensure that something like WW2 would never happen again, be responsible for the rise of a major fascist movement? Have those in power in the EU forgotten the reasons for the social vision of a united Europe? Do they not realise or care that social cohesion and economic stability depend on wealth being shared among the many and not the few?

So what can we do to tackle these problems? We need to raise awareness of the impact of EU membership on working people. The people of Greece are fighting back. As I write this, its party of the left, Syriza, is high in the polls and there has been continued support for general strikes. The Italian elections in February 2013 were another slap in the face for the EU austerity agenda because although indecisive, they show a major change in people's views. Spanish workers are organising in the face of a bailout package in which the EU ordered an end to their regional and national collective bargaining structures. And the whole of Europe is reeling from the enormity of what was imposed on Cyprus. People are waking up to the insanity and unsustainability of the EU's policies.

Meanwhile here in Scotland, I grow ever more frustrated that instead of fighting the Con-Dem cuts and defending our class with all our energy, we are instead consumed with the pros and cons of becoming an independent state. On the one hand I can see that this is entirely justifiable as we are facing a truly momentous decision. But changing our flag from the union jack to the saltire will not be the magic wand that reduces inequality between the richest and poorest or halts the attacks on our most vulnerable communities.

Only the raising of the red flag will effect real social change and who can say whether an independent Scotland will provide more fertile ground on which that flag can be planted. It is therefore essential that as socialists we keep challenging both the 'Yes' and the 'No' camps for real answers to the important questions about what sort of powers their models of either independence or increased devolution will deliver for us.

That is why we must ensure the right questions are being asked about issues like the impact of re-entering the EU as a newly independent Scotland. We need to encourage an in-depth and honest debate that will expose some complex but crucial issues that we could be facing should the Scottish people decide to say Yes.

Otherwise, at the very time when workers across Europe are beginning to question austerity and calling for a better way, we could be walking blindly from the UK's neo-liberal frying pan into the EU's neo-liberal fire.

Endnotes

1. http://uk.reuters.com/article/2010/03/15/uk-eu-britain-budget.
2. http://usilive.org/greece-appeasement-resistance/.

SCOTLAND, INDEPENDENCE AND DEFENCE
Alan Mackinnon

W hatever your views on independence for Scotland, you may think one thing is uncontroversial. Independence is likely to get rid of Trident and deliver us from involvement in foreign wars at the behest of the United States. But you could be dead wrong on both counts.

The European Union

The SNP policy is that Scotland should be a sovereign independent country with an independent foreign, security and defence policy which would reflect the priorities of the people.[1] But the SNP also has a policy of 'independence in Europe'. These two policies are contradictory as membership of the EU could override a Scottish independent defence policy. The Lisbon Treaty sets out clear obligations on the part of member states:

> Member states shall make civilian and military capacity available to the Union for the implementation of the Common Security and Defence Policy....Member states shall undertake progressively to improve their military capabilities.[2]

EU military capacities are being steadily increased with the creation of 13 EU Battlegroups.[3] This force is intended to complement rather than replace the North Atlantic Treaty Organisation (NATO). And a new emphasis on interoperability and integration with NATO operations will make independent policy more difficult. Since 2003 the EU has been involved in military missions in 19 countries on three continents.[4] It would be naive to believe that these activities are simply benign 'peacekeeping' or conflict prevention. They involve a spectrum of military/civilian activities ranging from military training to full-scale war. Smaller nations within the EU who have chosen not to join NATO - Ireland, Sweden, Finland and Austria - are finding it increasingly difficult to defend their neutrality and resist this militarisation process as the EU continues to integrate as an economic, political and military bloc. An independent Scotland which joined the EU would be under considerable pressure to contribute military forces to EU Battlegroups and to increase military spending.

The North Atlantic Treaty Organisation

If 'independence in Europe' could be described as a contradiction in terms, then maintaining an independent foreign policy as a member of NATO would be quite impossible. While the EU has limited capacity to fight wars (except on a very small scale) outside its own area, it is not the case for NATO. It is often described by its critics as a 'relic of the Cold War', but sadly it is far more sinister. It has grown from 16 to 28 member nations since early 1999. And that steady expansion eastwards and southwards more than 20 years after the end of the Cold War and the disbandment of the Warsaw Pact reveals its true purpose. It is a vehicle for binding member countries into support for US foreign policy and for global intervention. It recently reaffirmed the concept of nuclear 'deterrence' and the first use of nuclear weapons:

> Deterrence, based on an appropriate mix of nuclear and conventional capabilities, remains a core element of our overall strategy... As long as nuclear weapons exist, NATO will remain a nuclear alliance.[5]

But keeping nuclear weapons as the core element of NATO's strategy is not just an issue of continuity. It is actively building a new and destabilising missile defence system to cover the continent of Europe (despite the lack of any significant external threat). Having a shield and a sword will raise the stakes and force other nuclear weapons states like Russia to respond, adding a new twist to the nuclear arms race. It takes us in the wrong direction - away from nuclear disarmament.

Its member states continue to be embroiled in the war and occupation of Afghanistan with its huge and unnecessary loss of life. That is the key problem with the SNP's wish to join NATO. The SNP defence policy talks of making Scotland's multi-role brigade available for UN-sanctioned missions and support for humanitarian peacekeeping and peace-making tasks. This could have wide interpretations. The SNP supports the war in Afghanistan and supported the NATO intervention in Libya. As a member of the alliance it would be under intense pressure to supply Scottish fighting men to future NATO missions across the world, whether UN sanctioned or not. There is, therefore, a fundamental contradiction between the laudable objective of an independent Scotland which is 'outward looking... and contributing to peace, justice and equality'[6] while also advocating that Scotland should be a member of an aggressive military alliance which is dominated by US policy at all levels.

Trident

The biggest contradiction of SNP defence policy is the desire to get rid of Britain's Trident fleet and at the same time join an alliance which has nuclear weapons at its core.

Britain's Trident strike force, as we have seen, is the core part of the alliance's nuclear policy. It is true that new NATO members are not forced to host nuclear weapons on their soil. This would, however, be an entirely different issue. It would involve a newly independent part of an existing member state which happens to host the deployment sites for the alliance's strategic nuclear weapons strike force.

An independent Scotland which wanted rid of Trident could thus wipe out a 'core element' of NATO's strategic concept. Are we seriously to believe that NATO civilian and military leaders would stand by and watch that happen without using every means at their command to stop it, particularly if a Scottish Government was, at the same time, applying for membership?

The calls from three member states - Germany, Holland and Belgium - to have US tactical nuclear weapons removed from their soil have been ignored. Indeed, the US now plans to upgrade these weapons by fitting them with a new guidance system. Why should the reaction to an independent Scotland's request to join NATO but get rid of NATO's strategic nuclear strike force be any different? The truth is that membership of NATO would place new and formidable obstacles in the way of an independent Scotland divesting itself of nuclear weapons.

There is no reason to doubt the sincerity of the SNP leadership's commitment to getting rid of Trident. But it is important to understand the political and economic pressure which will be brought to bear on the fledgling independent administration. It would be involved in simultaneous negotiations on a range of difficult issues and the UK Government would bargain hard and would play for time. The MoD knows that new bases for Trident - even if a new site could be found which would meet new stringent safety regulations - would be prohibitively expensive and would take at least 15 years to build. It would be likely, therefore, to offer the Scottish Government generous inducements to retain Faslane and Coulport as bases for the Trident fleet for a limited period, in the hope that a new government would be elected which would agree to keep it long term. This could be conditional on making progress in other areas under negotiation. A report in the Telegraph on 26th January 2012 stated that MoD officials believe that after a vote for independence, ministers in London would have no choice but to strike a deal with Scottish leaders and 'pay Salmond any price to ensure we kept access to (the Clyde bases)'.[7] As Professor Malcolm Chalmers has argued, 'I don't think the SNP would have to agree to keep Trident for ever. But if they want a post-referendum agreement with the UK, then they would probably need to agree to allow London enough time to plan and build alternative facilities'.[8]

More opposition would come from the transnational companies such as BAE and the oil lobby which now dominate Scotland's externally owned and controlled economy. BAE systems owns the submarine building yard at Barrow and would exert huge pressure on a Scottish Government to shift its position on Trident - and could be supported by a UK Government which agreed to place further orders for new warships in Scottish yards[9] only if a deal was done to keep Trident in Scotland. It is the world's third largest arms manufacturer and gets most of its business from the Pentagon and has, therefore, every reason to try to keep the US Government sweet and would apply sustained pressure on the Scottish Government to that effect.

The oil lobby as well as lobbying for business-friendly policies in the North Sea sector also has a longer-term strategic interest in binding Britain (and its component parts) into a special relationship with the United States. BP and Shell depend on US military reach for the protection of their global assets. And these giant companies have the power to make or break governments. At Holyrood the power of the oil lobby over ministers, MSPs and civil servants is even greater. Industry and company lobbyists exert influence through building personal relationships, corporate lobby groups, think tanks, PR groups and corporate-government partnerships, much of it unseen and unrecorded.[10]

None of this would necessarily make it impossible for an SNP Government to carry out its pledge to get rid of Trident. But it would make it much more difficult without the backing of a powerful mass movement. The pressure from London, Brussels, Washington and Britain's biggest companies, as well as tempting offers of cash in financially straightened circumstances, would be likely to pave the way to some kind of compromise.

This is not intended to belittle the SNP defence policy. On paper it is a great deal more progressive than that of any of the main Westminster parties and a vote for independence would, at least in theory, provide new opportunities to get rid of Trident which would require a vigorous response from the peace movement. But if you thought that it would result in a Scotland with a nuclear-free, independent foreign policy which would no longer be drawn into military adventures overseas, then think again.

Keep all options open

And that brings us to the final part of this argument. Independence is not the last or only hope of ridding ourselves of these weapons. Indeed, according to opinion polls, a majority vote for independence seems unlikely. Whatever the outcome of the referendum, the ultimate decision to cancel Trident would be taken by a UK Government at Westminster. And there is new evidence that opposition to Trident is getting stronger across Britain as the recession and austerity programme begins to bite. That is why it is essential that the wider peace movement does not lose its focus on the UK Parliament and keeps all campaigning options open.

Early in 2013, three former defence secretaries - Michael Portillo, Des Browne and Tom King - all cast doubt on the wisdom and affordability of going ahead with like-for-like replacement of Trident.[11,12,13] Many senior figures in the armed forces now believe that Trident is a useless prestige symbol and, in a few years, when we are spending up to one-third of the defence procurement budget on the replacement programme, it will bring about 'unacceptable' cuts in our armed forces. For them the money could be better spent on conventional weapons. Chief Secretary to the Treasury, Danny Alexander, has reached similar conclusions and said that like-for-like replacement for Trident was 'not financially realistic'.[14] In presenting the Trident Alternatives Review in July 2013 he described Trident as the 'last, unreformed bastion of Cold War thinking' and noted two alternatives to full-scale replacement - building two or three submarines instead of four and taking the submarines off continuous at-sea patrols.[15] There is, in other words, disunity at the heart of the Coalition Government over the future of Trident.

Unfortunately neither the Review nor Danny Alexander considered the safest, cheapest and most popular alternative of all - scrapping the system altogether. And there is growing support for that within the ranks of Labour. In July 2013, former Deputy Prime Minister John Prescott writing in the Mirror, said: 'I say we scrap Trident for good, stop being the world's policeman and spend that money protecting the health of the nation'.[16] In his autobiography, even Tony Blair wrote that he clearly saw 'the force of the common sense and practical argument against Trident' and agreed that it served no possible military use.[17]

Labour's National Policy Forum document has called for a discussion on its Trident position now that the Trident Alternatives Review has reported. Any incremental step back from full-scale replacement and 'continuous at-sea deterrence' (CASD) would be welcome but if Labour MPs are unmoved by the moral case against nuclear weapons, they can hardly ignore the economics. Public support for Trident is now at its lowest point ever, especially when you mention the cost. There are signs that Labour's leaders may be beginning to lose their 30-year-old fear of being seen as soft on defence. A Labour campaign which proposed scrapping Trident and spending the money on jobs, services and renewable energy could be a big vote winner. Such a campaign would need to include a plan for a 'just transition' to ensure that few, if any, jobs were lost at Faslane, Barrow and Aldermaston in the cancellation of Trident.[18] Now that would open up a new set of options for people across Britain. I hope Johann Lamont and Ed Miliband are listening.

Endnotes

1. Resolution to SNP Conference: Foreign, Security and Defence Policy Update, 2012, http://www.scotsman.com/news/politics/top-stories/in-full-snp-resolution-on-nato-1-2414919.
2. Lisbon Treaty, Article 42, para 3., Consolidated Texts of the EU Treaties as Amended by the Treaty of Lisbon, http://www.official-documents.gov.uk/document/cm73/7310/7310.pdf.
3. EU Battle Groups, Directorate-General for External Policies of the Union- Directorate B, http://www.europarl.europa.eu/meetdocs/2004_2009/documents/dv/091006eubattlegroups_/091006eubattle groups_en.pdf.
4. Overview of the Missions and Operations of the European Union, February 2013: http://www.consilium.europa.eu/eeas/security-defence/eu-operations.
5. Active Engagement, Modern Defence: Strategic Concept for the Defence and Security of the Members of the North Atlantic Treaty Organisation, November 2010: http://www.nato.int/nato_static/assets/pdf/pdf_publications/20120214_strategic-concept-2010-eng.pdf.

6. See note 5.

7. Kirkup, J., Nuclear subs will stay in Scotland, Royal Navy chiefs decide, The Telegraph, 26 January, 2012.

8. Barnes, E., Scottish independence: Alex Salmond's NATO U-turn is right, but Trident must stay, says Liam Fox, The Scotsman, 17 October 2012.

9. Govan and Scotstoun shipyards are owned by BAE systems and work almost exclusively on orders from the MoD. They recently completed a run of Type 45 destroyers, are currently working on the two new aircraft carriers and are expected to start on a new order for up to 13 Type 26 Frigates. Between them the two shipyards employ 3,700 people.

10. Dinan, W., Who needs democracy when you've got money?, Scottish Left Review, Issue 71, July/ August 2012.

11. http://www.bbc.co.uk/news/uk-politics-20179604.

12. Browne, D. and Kearns, I., Trident is no longer the key to Britain's security, The Telegraph, 5 February, 2013.

13. http://www.bbc.co.uk/news/uk-politics-21177620.

14. Hopkins, N., Trident: no need for like-for-like replacement, says Danny Alexander, The Guardian, 22 January 2013.

15.http://www.libdems.org.uk/latest_news_detail.aspx?title=Danny_Alexander_launches_the_ Government's_Trident_Alternatives_Review&pPK=76485538-fcff-4db1-94f2-ab4ad5a4e6dc.

16. Prescott, J., It's Time to Sink Trident now, Mirror, 28th July 2013: http://www.mirror.co.uk/news/uk-news/john-prescott-its-time-sink-2096704.

17. Blair, T., A Journey, London: Arrow Books 2010.

18. Foster, J., Mackinnon, A. and Ainslie, J., Trident, Jobs and the UK Economy, Glasgow: Campaign for Nuclear Disarmament, 2010: http://www.cnduk.org/tridentjobs.

SCOTTISH LABOUR'S PREDICAMENT
Eric Shaw

In the 2011 Holyrood elections, the SNP received its highest share of the vote ever (45.4 per cent of constituency votes), whereas Labour's share slumped to its lowest level since 1918 (31.7 per cent) Although Labour's vote slipped only modestly compared to 2007 it was the culmination of a steady shrinkage of its vote since the first devolution election in 1999, as well as being far short of the 42 per cent captured in the 2010 Westminster elections. There were a range of short-term factors which help explain Labour's dismal performance, including a poor campaign, an inability to match Alex Salmond's leadership skills and appeal and a general air of disorganisation. Research indicates that the SNP led Labour on competence, image, leadership and capacity to defend Scottish interests. Compared to Labour the SNP was seen as more capable of strong government, more united, more in touch with ordinary people, better at defending Scottish interests, more likely to keep promises and more effective in managing the impact of Westminster-driven cuts.[1]

However, these problems should not mask deeper trends which have been eroding Labour's electoral base in Scotland - indeed in the UK as a whole - for some time. Traditionally, Labour's strength in Scotland has been rooted in the politics of class, community, the workplace and trade unionism. At least since the 1970s, collective class identities forged by work, neighbourhood and unions have weakened. In what is known as a process of party dealignment, allegiances have been for years slowly decomposing and the social-psychological bonds tying voters to parties have been progressively frayed. As a result, connections and identifications with the institutions of labour have languished and become more sporadic - indeed in much of the private service sector trade unionism has virtually disappeared. The outcome is a party system where many voters have only a fragile and tentative attachment to any party.

The working class in Scotland (as elsewhere) has always been divided by internal tensions, on the basis of skill, status and religious denomination. But with deindustrialisation and mass unemployment it has further fragmented and the close-knit occupational communities which were once Labour bastions have in many areas disintegrated. The days when party loyalty was handed down through the generations like a family heirloom have emphatically passed. Many voters now are the children of parents who themselves held weak party loyalties and hence did not experience any intergenerational partisan socialisation. We have entered an age of electoral volatility in which switching between parties has become common. Added to this, the class structure itself has been transformed with manual workers now composing well under 40 per cent of the labour force, professional and administrative workers constituting over 30 per cent and most of the rest in largely clerical occupations.[2] Added to this, many of those who work in private sector manual jobs do so in conditions where - in contrast to the mines, steel mills and car factories of the past - unionisation is hard and collective identities more difficult to forge.

For those who hold a simple dichotomous model of the class structure - working class and middle class - all this would seem to spell bad news for Labour. In reality the truth is far more complex and less discouraging. The middle class is composed of groups which are even more varied in terms of interests, values and lifestyles than the working class. For example, there is a major divide in political attitudes, values and voting behaviour between public and private sector white-collar workers. Similarly, within the private sector routine clerical and administrative workers share few material interests with highly paid managers, corporate executives and professionals. What unites public sector white-collar workers and clerical workers in the private sector is that both have a strong shared interest in a universal, well-funded welfare state producing high-quality services. This means that they form a large reservoir of votes for Labour.

The problem for Labour is that, in Scotland, it has a formidable competitor for the self-same voters: the SNP. In the 2011 elections the SNP won a higher percentage of the vote in all social groups, including the working class, than Labour - indeed the social profile of the two parties is broadly similar. Seeking to undermine the SNP's legitimacy by dubbing them 'Tartan Tories' simply lacks credibility. Switching between Labour and the SNP is common: around 30 per cent of voters who backed Labour in 2010 opted for the Nationalists the following year.

The fact that there is a lack of clear ideological division between Labour and the SNP has caused the former particular problems over the last two years - and these problems may persist. Election experts distinguish between 'position' and 'valence' issues. 'Position' issues refers to issues where there are major differences of values and goals, 'Valence issues' refers to where there is broad agreement over the goals and the differences between the parties over which is best equipped to achieve them. According to 'valence theory' where the latter two issues prevail then voters judge parties on the basis of comparative assessments of their capacity to deliver what both are promising, that is to say on their perceived competence, trustworthiness and the quality of their leadership.[3] As has been noted above, on all these properties voters rated the SNP more highly than Labour for, on most issues, they see the two parties as occupying broadly similar ideological territory and accept the SNP's own self-designation as an essentially left-of-centre party.

Nor should one dismiss this as self-serving. The SNP's record in government indicates that it has no more enthusiasm for market-based solutions in health and education than Scottish Labour, and on many devolved policy matters it is difficult to discern major differences of principle between the two parties. The Nationalists represent a broad coalition with both a social democratic and a more rightist pro-market wing. Rather than damning the SNP as a whole, Labour should adopt a more nuanced and sophisticated strategy exploiting the internal differences and contradictions within the present Scottish Government.

Unfortunately, Labour in Scotland has been unduly infected by the legacy of Westminster-style adversarial politics with its accent on minor point scoring, personal attacks and opposition for its own sake. Scarce communication and research resources are routinely funnelled into formulating short-term responses to SNP initiatives with tactical exigencies seeming always to trump the devising of longer-term strategy. This is not only misguided but counter-productive - it tends to alienate voters and confirm their view that politicians are small-minded, petty and endlessly 'squabbling'.

A social democratic project

At the root of Labour's strategic myopia is what we may call the presumption of entitlement: the belief that Scotland is natural Labour territory, that it in some way belongs to Labour, and that the Nationalists are little more than interlopers. This is reflected in the wrong-headed 'core vote' strategy which holds that the party should focus its campaigning energy on identifying and then seeking to mobilise its (supposedly) working-class 'core'. But the core is wasting away. Scottish Labour's leaders have failed to fully grasp that with the loosening of the social anchorage of traditional party attachments, many more votes are up for grabs - and have to be fought for. Identifying 'the Labour vote' and then wheeling it out on election day has ceased to be a viable electoral strategy, if it ever was.

This does not mean that Labour inevitably haemorrhages votes - party dealignment affects all parties adversely - but that more effort has to be put into devising coherent political strategies, of finding means to inspire, galvanise and mobilise voters. This is no easy task; at the very least it requires that the electorate has a much stronger sense of what the party stands for, what principles animate it and what type of society it is trying to create. Labour, in short, has to repair the emotional bonds that once tied it to the fabric of Scottish society. This means finding something to replace the ties of class, workplace and close-knit occupational communalities. It means laying claim to and vigorously articulating such values as equality, social justice and social solidarity which are part of a common Scottish inheritance.

We live in an age where the cult of the market is relentlessly propagated, where private is seen as best, where the pursuit of personal gain is venerated and allegedly 'old-style' public sector routinely sneered at and disparaged. Much to its credit Scottish Labour, while in government, eschewed the market-oriented policies so vigorously prosecuted by New Labour in Westminster. But it was reluctant to explain why - to critically engage with neo-liberal, market-oriented recipes. Indeed, its repudiation of market thinking was less than full-throated. It convinced itself that financially disastrous Private Finance Initiative (PFI) schemes were more efficient ways of building public infrastructure simply because they tapped into the 'expertise' and 'dynamism' of the private sector. To that extent Scottish Labour was beguiled by the myths of the age.

The fact is that Scottish Labour has for years evinced a pronounced reluctance to engage in serious ideological debate. This reflects some enduring traits, notably its essentially cautious, empirical and practical character; its disinclination to reflect on where it is going and what it is seeking to achieve. Labour needs to energise voters by offering a vision of the sort of society it wishes to establish and how it would set about building it. This requires the Party to think much harder about the ideals - of social solidarity, equality and mutual support - that inspire it and how they can be embodied in policies and institutional arrangements. These ideals, and not the misdemeanours of the present Government, should form the basis of Labour's appeal to the Scottish electorate.

Scottish Labour and the wider Party

Of course, no clear social democratic project in Scotland can be formulated without reflecting on the general problems of social democracy in a highly globalised and economically integrated world. The impact of a massive upsurge in financial flows, of deregulation and liberalisation of economic activity and the dominant role played by multinational companies in trade and production has undermined the power and autonomy of the nation state. All this underlines the crucial importance of economic policy. Economic policy - policies on tax and spending, on financial issues, on industry and the regions - to a large degree forms the overarching framework within which policy on other issues is hammered out. For the most part, it remains a reserved matter. But one paradoxical effect of devolution is that Scottish Labour seems to have lost interest in non-devolved issues, however important. Individual politicians may play influential roles (Douglas Alexander, Jim Murphy) but this is as individuals and not as representatives of the Scottish Party. Indeed, there is anecdotal evidence that attendance by Scottish Constituency Labour Parties at the British Party's annual conference has steadily dwindled and few participate in National Policy Forum activities or any other form of state-wide policy formation.

This is short-sighted. In other countries with federal or devolved structures (e.g. Germany, Spain, Canada, Belgium), regional parties play a dual role as important players in the national or federal party as well as in their own areas. They operate as autonomous power centres and sources of policy innovation over the whole spectrum of policy. There is no reason why the party in Scotland - along with the party in Wales and London - should not begin to act as a power broker within the party at large, maximising its voice on organisational, strategic and programmatic questions. More thought needs to be given to the overall structure of the UK Party.

Nor need Scottish Labour confine its interest and operations to the borders of the UK. It prides itself on being Euro-oriented. It should consider developing ties, exchanging ideas and liaising with regional party organisations in other countries with federal or devolved political structures, such as Germany and Spain. We may claim to recognise the long shadow cast by globalisation, but too often think and behave parochially.

Endnotes

1. Johns, R. et al., Why we voted that way, Scottish Election Survey: www.scottishelectionstudy.org.uk/docs/Johns_slides.pdf.
2. McCrone, D., Understanding Scotland, Routledge, 2001.
3. Sanders, D., Clarke, H.D., Stewart, M.C. and Whiteley, P., Downs, Stokes and the Dynamics of Electoral Choice, British Journal of Political Science, 41, 2011.

SEEKING A JUST SCOTLAND
Dave Moxham

In May 2013 Scottish Labour launched 'United with Labour', its distinct campaign for the Union. Earlier, at its Spring Conference in Inverness, Labour was urged by a series of delegates, particularly trade unions and specifically members of the Red Paper Collective, to put forward a distinct, positive argument for remaining in the UK. Arguably, it also completes the institutional campaigning landscape in the run-up to the September 2014 referendum. Prior to this launch, four main arms existed for the pro-independence campaign: the Scottish Government, Yes Scotland, the SNP and the collection of organisations making up the Radical Independence Conference. For No, the Westminster Coalition Government and Better Together were effectively the only two campaigns for the Union, and neither is Tory-free. Labour and its political representatives have not been absent from the debate but it has been a position defined by opposition, whether to the Scottish Government or to the Tory/Liberal coalition and this has placed the Party in a tight political spot and one in which almost unrelenting negativity had been its chosen message.

In launching 'United with Labour', Anas Sarwar who co-ordinates the campaign said: 'We are excited about putting forward our case for Scotland in the United Kingdom based on Labour values of solidarity, community, fairness, equality and social justice'. This represents something of a victory for those on the left and particularly trade unions which have argued consistently that the prism through which the referendum debate needs to be conducted is 'how we can best achieve social justice in Scotland'. This approach is reflected in the Scottish Trade Unions Congress's (STUC) 'A Just Scotland' interim report.[1] A final report will be submitted to Congress in March 2014 when Scotland will be just a few months from voting.

It has clearly come as a surprise to many that the majority of Scotland's trade unions are content for this amount of time to pass before reaching a definitive position. For many in the leadership of Scottish Labour the reaction has not just been surprise, but extreme annoyance. To some extent this is understandable. Many Scottish political commentators expected that Scottish trade unions would line up fairly quickly behind a 'No' vote, particularly unions that are affiliated to the Labour Party. Thus any apparent divergence from the expected course is presented as a negative for the pro-union campaign. 'Not Better Together say unions'[2] was the Sunday Times headline which greeted the publication of 'A Just Scotland', and the Wikipedia entry for trade unions under the 'Scottish independence referendum' states that the traditional association of trade unions in Scotland and the United Kingdom as a whole with the Labour Party, which is campaigning against Scottish independence, has not, as some expected, resulted in an outright declaration of support for the Union from leading trade unions. The Scottish Trades Union Congress refused an offer to join the Better Together campaign in 2012.'

Those who have read 'A Just Scotland' will know that the report also laid down serious challenges to the SNP and Yes Scotland, and STUC can claim some of the credit for the shift towards social justice themes among pro-independence campaigners during 2013. Indeed, Yes Scotland was noticeably quicker to recognise the importance of STUC's position and considerably lighter on its feet in fashioning an initial response. 'Yes To A Just Scotland' was a fairly thoughtful response to STUC challenges, albeit noticeably quiet in recognising the contradiction between current economic orthodoxies espoused by the SNP and the challenge of achieving a fairer society through wealth distribution. This omission should not come as a surprise. For reasons, one presumes, of electoral mathematics, it is important for the more mainstream elements of the pro-independence campaign to maintain a 'steady as she goes' approach to key issues such as currency, economic policy and tax at the same time as promoting a vision of a more progressive Scotland built on better values and based on a Scandinavian approach to public spending. Inevitably, this position continues to unravel. In one interview Cabinet Secretary for Finance, John Swinney, committed the SNP to no tax rises after independence whereas Deputy First Minister Nicola Sturgeon has repeatedly referred to a more generous welfare system and stronger public services post-independence.

Analysis by my STUC colleague Stephen Boyd[4] shows that the Scandinavian model redistributes significantly more through public spending than the UK, and one of its main levers is higher consumption taxes. Indeed, despite traditionally higher top rate tax rates in Scandinavian countries, Boyd challenges the assumption that the Scandinavian tax model is more progressive than that of the UK. Put simply, should it wish to adopt a Scandinavian style redistributive model a future Scottish Government would also need to win the case that most people at most income levels would have to pay more in tax. This is a position STUC would happily endorse under any constitutional scenario, but it is not one that most members of either the pro- or anti-independence campaigns seem happy to countenance.

The Scottish Government's Fiscal Commission[5] envisages continuing membership of sterling and supports a conservative institutional fiscal framework in Scotland. It imagines therefore that the two chief redistribution levers available to a Scottish Government under independence would be tax and welfare. While it can be plausibly argued that a Scottish Government with limited fiscal freedom and very limited say over interest rate policy and financial regulation would be in no worse a position than currently, it is not a vision which is likely to excite the left. Indeed, it is strongly arguable that within such a framework, such fiscal freedoms that did exist post-independence would encourage policy that leaned towards fiscal conservatism and tax competition. Such arguments will only be strengthened so long as the Scottish Government talk of lower corporation tax and 'business-friendly' measures continues and while business leaders such as Jim McColl are encouraged to argue for lower taxation as the main driver for independence.

In the absence of a commitment to higher post-independence taxes, the mainstream pro-independence campaigns have increasingly sought to base their promise of a more generous welfare model on arguments about Scotland's relative fiscal position compared to the rest of the UK (rUK) under the current tax regime - more of which later.

If the challenge to the pro-independence campaign is to come clean on tax and spend, the STUC's explicit challenge to the Scottish Labour Party in the 'A Just Scotland' report was to shift away from negative campaigning to promoting a vision of social justice. '"Not being the Tories" and negative messages about the SNP will not suffice and [trade union] members will require a clear steer on how economic and social justice will be achieved at all levels of government and to be convinced that the Scottish Labour Party intends to play an active and radical role in achieving this.'[6] The STUC also called on the Scottish Labour Party to develop a position on enhanced devolution.

Labour's vision

The creation of the 'United with Labour' campaign has provided the Labour Party with a vehicle with which to respond to this challenge. 'United with Labour' has, as a central theme, the presentation of a positive vision of social solidarity and of the central role of the UK in achieving it. This was the main message put forward by Gordon Brown in the inaugural Campbell Christie lecture[7] delivered in 2012 which presented a positive view of the United Kingdom as a political entity which has delivered the welfare state, National Health Service, the minimum wage and other key equalising institutions. He presented these as key achievements of the labour and trade movements united in purpose and across national boundaries.

This position was augmented by Anas Sarwar in a speech early in 2013 in which he placed a heavy emphasis on the role of the UK as a redistributor of wealth between its regions and countries based upon need. Taken together these messages constitute a potentially strong dynamic within the debate. Avoiding negative 'too poor, too wee' messaging, it implicitly accepts the possibility that a future independent Scotland might find herself in a relatively strong fiscal position but challenges us, particularly those on the left, to eschew the politics of narrow self-interest in favour of solidarity across the UK. It is an attractive argument to those in the trade union movement who espouse working-class solidarity.

Strong though this theme may be, it does not liberate Labour from a number of ongoing difficulties. In the first instance, the celebration of collective and hard-fought gains such as the creation of a welfare system and a publicly owned and universal NHS only holds sway to the extent that these key institutions continue to function to the purpose for which they were intended. With the NHS down south under assault (and, in any case, already devolved) and with the continuing ideological attack on welfare, arguments which are built on the foundations of past accomplishments should be approached with care. Labour's record in areas such as welfare is far from clean: it failed in government to promote and sustain a sufficiently broad and progressive tax system to facilitate the transfer of wealth and, perhaps most fundamentally, it failed to create an economy with sufficient good-quality employment, wage share and pay equality to reduce the reliance on the equalising institutions in the first place. Depending on these 'achievements' will not suffice.

Resting on the laurels of the existence of UK-wide equalising institutions also repeats the mistake of most of those in the pro-independence camp who, in adopting the 'safety first' approach towards independence, have almost completely ignored the role of decent pay and good-quality employment in achieving wealth redistribution. To Ed Miliband's credit he has at least made an early move towards embracing the idea of 'pre-distribution'. This seeks, according to political scientist Jacob Hacker, 'to focus on market reforms that encourage a more equal distribution of economic power and rewards even before government collects taxes or pays out benefits'.[8] Instead of equalising unfair market outcomes simply through tax-and-spend or tax-and-transfer, we engineer markets to create fairer outcomes from the beginning. Miliband has thus far failed to recognise the radical regulatory reform which is necessary if such an approach is to be adopted, and, importantly, to recognise the fundamental role that strong and free trade unions engaged in collective bargaining must have in its delivery.

The importance of fair pay and decent employment in the independence debate should not be underestimated. With an integrated economy such as exists across the UK, it is difficult to imagine significant divergence in wage share and employment conditions between Scotland and rUK, whether under independence or the status quo. Scottish Labour has the opportunity to make this matter by putting forward a clear vision of a fairer labour market within the UK and to make the case that only through reform at Westminster and in Europe can such a goal be achieved.

Funding redistribution

The second strand of the 'United with Labour' argument, as proposed by Anas Sarwar, presents a picture of the UK state acting as an effective agent for redistribution across her regions and countries. But this is open to challenge. The National Economics Foundation reproduced ONS data which starkly demonstrated the extent to which the UK fails on regional distribution of output compared to all other EU countries.[9]

The reasons for regional inequality in the United Kingdom are many, including the failure at the UK level to construct an effective regional economic policy; the creation of a London-centric financialised economy; the centralisation of fiscal levers; and the disempowerment of local government. But even if one confines oneself to considering straightforward fiscal transfers (redistribution through public spending) the picture, particularly in Scotland, is not necessarily the one which 'United with Labour' paints.

Clearly the operation of an effective welfare system should act as an agent of regional equalisation (proportionate to how progressively and actively such policies are regulated and implemented) as should the implementation of UK-wide pay policies, whether through general regulation or through public sector pay bargaining.

It is equally well recognised that the provision of public services free at the point of delivery and funded through taxation also act as an agent of regional redistribution. In the case of Scotland this funding (constituting approximately 60 per cent of all public spending in Scotland) comes through the Scottish Block Grant, honed annually through application of the Barnett Formula. Contrary to the perception of many, the Barnett Formula is an adjustment mechanism designed to achieve convergence on public spending levels rather than the basis for funding differentials across the UK, and it has no direct relationship to relative need. It is also inevitable that if Scotland votes 'No' then at some point in the foreseeable future the current funding mechanisms will be altered.

On any sensible analysis, the current arrangement is not equally redistributive. The per capita funding in Scotland afforded by the Block Grant favours Scotland over a number of English regions, Northern Ireland and Wales. The Scottish Government spends between 15 and 20 per cent more per head of population than the comparable English figure. The false perception that the Block Grant is linked to need has endured partly because throughout the first years of its operation from the late 1970s onwards, Scotland's high levels of unemployment could be added to poor health outcomes and service delivery issues linked to geography and infrastructure to 'justify' the additional spend.

While Scotland's health record and geography would continue to argue for enhanced funding levels under a needs-based formula, Scotland now performs no worse than the UK average with respect to unemployment or GDP per capita (even excluding North Sea oil).

Put simply, therefore, the geographically redistributive UK state which 'United with Labour' presents as a major persuader for rejecting independence would, if funded through a formula based on need rather than the current settlement, see a fairly hefty reduction in Scotland's Block Grant settlement.

As John Kay[10] among others has argued, the continuing level of the Scottish Block Grant can be sensibly understood not as a needs-based mechanism, but as an organically developed political fix designed to offset the political impact of Scotland's geographical entitlement to North Sea oil revenues with the case for devolution and/or independence. Comparisons between public spending in Scotland since the early 1980s and its notional fiscal position including the revenues from North Sea oil and gas[11] show a strong correlation between the average spend and the average notional GDP over that time (albeit with some year-on-year divergences consistent with oil price and supply fluctuation and differences in the economic cycle).

The apparent historical health of Scotland's fiscal position relative to the UK has been a key argument adopted by the pro-independence campaigns to justify a 'Yes' vote. There is of course a weakness in projecting how fiscally viable Scotland would be post-2016 based upon what its relative fiscal position was two or three years ago - particularly given that North Sea oil and gas is an uncertain and diminishing asset. However, this cannot entirely divert attention from consideration of the counterfactual. Put simply, following a 'No' vote a new 'needs-based' funding formula for Scotland might significantly impact the Scottish Block Grant and therefore the funding of public services - perhaps to the tune of £2 billion.

This potential loss would not of itself be avoided just by devolving additional tax powers. If oil revenues are disregarded, the Scottish tax base differs only in small part from the UK average and would therefore not liberate the level of funding required to maintain the currently higher per capita levels of public spending in Scotland. The response thus far from proponents of enhanced devolution such as Professor Alan Trench and the Devo Plus campaign has been a metaphorical shrug which amounts to the view that 'if you want to stay part of the UK, that's the price'.

Such an approach will not suffice for Scottish Labour. As analysis of the counterfactual position develops it will become clear that Scotland's current bargain with the rUK is partly based on her oil reserves and her capacity, if she so wishes, to choose independence. If Scottish Labour wishes to project a future in which Scotland's public spending capacity is protected, it must develop a model in which, either through the Block Grant or through including a geographical share of North Sea oil in its devolved tax base, an enhanced devolution settlement reflects this situation.
So Labour must, to a greater extent than it has thus far, be the party of Scotland - prepared, to fight Scotland's corner even if this suggests some degree of departure from the 'fairness across the UK' position.

Labour must also be a radical voice for redistribution between classes and Scottish Labour should, without fear, establish itself as a distinct voice within the wider labour movement, which consistently makes that case. Policies cannot be built on opinion poll responses alone, but it is nevertheless instructive to observe that people in Scotland and across the UK continue to respond positively to the idea of fairer pay through increasing the minimum wage and introducing wage maximums. People understand that multinational companies which avoid tax at the same time as undermining employment conditions should be challenged. In that context there is little appetite for a 'race to the bottom' on corporation tax which the SNP has discovered to its cost and Labour has realised as an advantage. There is also a strong understanding of the role of properly funded childcare in increasing participation and achieving equal outcomes. The European diktats limiting the use of procurement to fight inequality must be challenged anew. The lead taken by Neil Findlay MSP, Drew Smith MSP, Ian Davidson MP and others on Blacklisting is justified both in terms of natural justice and reiterating that Labour can be the party of working people and is comfortable with its trade union alliances.

Thus a Scottish Labour Party armed with a commitment to fight Scotland's corner within the UK and articulate the case for real redistribution within the UK Labour Party could strengthen its own position and contribute to a much needed improvement in the quality of the referendum debate overall.

Endnotes

1. A Just Scotland Interim Report, STUC, November 2012.
2. www.thesundaytimes.co.uk/sto/news/uk_news/scotland/article1167989.ece.
3. http://en.wikipedia.org/wiki/Scottish_independence_referendum,_2014.
4. http://stucbetterway.blogspot.co.uk/2013/04/scotland-and-nordics-part-1-tax.html.
5. www.scotland.gov.uk/Publications/2013/02/3017/0.
6. http://ajustscotland.org/files/Report/A%20Just%20Scotland%20interim%20report.pdf.
7. www.youtube.com/watch?v=k7elWz7GP30.
8. http://www.guardian.co.uk/commentisfree/2012/sep/12/ed-miliband-predistribution.
9. www.neweconomics.org/blog/entry/Breaking-free-of-London-focused-growth.
10. www.johnkay.com/2011/05/31/scotland-would-gain-few-benefits-from-going-it-alone-that-it-cannot-already-get-as-part-of-the-united-kingdom.
11. www.scottisheconomywatch.com/brian-ashcrofts-scottish/2013/04/scottish-tax-and-spend.html.

SECTION 5
Chapter 6

CHALLENGING NEO-LIBERAL ORTHODOXIES

Dave Watson

In this chapter I look at some of the economic implications of independence and extended devolution with a focus on public spending, monetary and fiscal policy. I will argue that there is a remarkable consistency in the mainstream offerings on both sides of the debate. The Yes campaign with its 'steady as you go' approach is exemplified by the Fiscal Commission report[1] and the various extended devolution offerings so far. I will then set out a different approach that challenges the neo-liberal orthodoxies that underpin these campaigns.

Independence

John Swinney MSP has set out the SNP's post-independence fiscal and monetary strategy, which includes keeping the pound within a sterling zone, including financial services (and possibly consumer) regulation. His strategy also includes a VAT cut for tourism and construction coupled with a corporation tax cut that aims to give Scotland a 'fiscal edge'. Other business-friendly policies include: cutting business rates; tax breaks for R&D and renewables; a review of competition policy; and the apparently obligatory cutting of red tape.

This approach has been expanded in the work of Crawford Beveridge and his team who have been drawn from the First Minister's Council of Economic Advisers. The first report of the Fiscal Commission Working Group[2] sets out a very similar monetary approach by keeping the pound within a sterling zone and UK co-ordination of financial supervision. Its fiscal recommendations are also similar, although it says more about the public spending implications of fiscal policy. It describes a fiscally conservative approach in the early years of independence in order to establish Scotland's credibility as an independent nation. This very much reminds me of Gordon Brown's approach as UK Chancellor in 1997.

The report recommends that, 'in addition to boosting economic growth, the Government should explore and prioritise opportunities to address inequalities and to promote intergenerational equity and environmental sustainability.'[3] That's a fine objective, but the report goes on to link fiscal policy to the UK through a, 'fiscal sustainability agreement with overall objectives for ensuring that net debt and government borrowing do not diverge significantly'.[4]

Estimates of income and expenditure allocated to Scotland are not an exact science in an integrated UK. The 'Government Expenditure and Revenue Scotland' (GERS)[5] data estimates that income, excluding North Sea revenues, is £45,177m rising to £53,128m, including North Sea revenues allocated on a geographical basis. Against this, the Total Managed Expenditure is £63,807m. However, the data also shows that Scotland would run a smaller fiscal deficit than the UK (4.4 per cent as against 6.6 per cent) although this would depend on post-independence negotiations over debt allocation and other matters. We also need to take account of other commitments, including the costs of demographic change as highlighted in the recent Scottish Parliament Finance Committee report.[6]

The Fiscal Commission report recognises that GDP per capita and disposable income is slightly lower in Scotland than the UK average. This is based on ONS data that excludes North Sea income and the SNP therefore argues that Scotland will be a much richer country on its own. The problem with this argument, as the Centre for Public Policy for Regions (CPPR) analysis[7] shows, is that much of this income ends up overseas and not in household income.

The balance of Scotland's relative strength depends heavily on revenue from the North Sea. Estimates of this revenue vary widely and are subject to worldwide price volatility. As Andrew Goudie has rightly warned, 'GERS captures the actual flows that result from economic activity in a specific year. It reflects government economic policy and the current constitutional arrangements.' He concludes, 'It, therefore, reveals little, if anything, about the state of the public accounts were a radically different constitutional arrangement to be put in place'.[8]

The Fiscal Commission recommends establishing a stabilisation fund from oil revenues that exceed current budget requirements to smooth out and future-proof financial shocks. While this is a prudent measure as part of their fiscal framework, it does limit the ability of the Scottish Government to tackle structural inequality. In fact, the framework they propose would significantly constrain the ability of the Scottish Government to adopt an alternative economic strategy such as 'A Better Way' advocated by the STUC. In essence, it foresees a fiscally conservative approach that places market credibility above almost any other considerations. In practice, this could mean austerity economics continues for Scotland, even if we are spared the underpinning ideology.

The SNP and the Fiscal Commission's approach to monetary policy also have major shortcomings. There has to be a huge question mark over the willingness of the rest of the UK (rUK) to enter into their proposed sterling zone and to share governance of the Bank of England in the way the Fiscal Commission suggests. Even if that were to be possible, and the Treasury analysis[9] questions the benefits for rUK, Scotland would at best be a junior partner with a minority say over a key lever of economic policy. Handing over monetary policy to rUK also limits the scope of fiscal policy. We only have to look at the eurozone crisis debate to see the link between monetary and fiscal policy. John Kay has expanded[10] on this point and sets out clearly the currency options for an independent Scotland. Sadly, none of them is very attractive because small countries close to their major trading partner have limited economic independence. If the key economic levers are controlled by another country, then there is less influence on monetary, and fiscal, policy than under devolution.

Dr Angus Armstrong from NIESR[11] has highlighted another challenge for the monetary union. If we had another oil price boom, Scotland's economy would be in growth while England's would slump. The same applies in reverse if the oil prices crashed. Either way, this would require very different monetary and fiscal policies that would probably end the union.

Others in the Yes campaign argue for a separate Scottish currency as Alex Salmond once put it, 'Sterling is like a millstone around Scotland's neck'. Jim Cuthbert articulates this view in his Reid Foundation paper,[12] arguing that the UK's economic performance reflects chronic long-term mismanagement, in particular, the underlying balance of trade and focus on the financial sector that was not in the interests of the wider economy. On this basis he argues that Scotland should not remain in a 'sub-optimal currency union'. The political conundrum for the SNP is that if they adopted this view and abandoned sterling, the polls show a big drop in support for independence.

My biggest difficulty is with the concept of a 'fiscal edge'. It appears that SNP policy is still wedded to the Celtic Tiger strategy. Even if desirable, you simply cannot replicate Ireland of the 1990s. Other small countries like Denmark, Norway, Sweden and Finland all have higher corporation tax and better performing economies. The UK business tax rate has already been cut and there is limited evidence that tax cuts pay for themselves. Any savings go into profit not investment and many of our companies are sitting on vast cash reserves already. There will certainly be a huge hit on public finances that is unsustainable. Even a true believer like George Osborne doesn't believe his tax cut will bring in more revenue, as the Office of Budget Responsibility forecasts for this year's budget show.[13] A better way is actually higher taxation to fund investment in people, plant, infrastructure and research.

The Laffer curve theorists that promote this low tax approach also support the flat tax approach to personal taxation. Yet there is no clear evidence of a link between different levels of taxation and economic growth. John Swinney has recently said, 'I don't envisage increases in personal taxation in an independent Scotland'.[14] That doesn't sound like a call for progressive taxation and doesn't rule out the application of Arthur Laffer's doctrine to personal taxation.

The Fiscal Commission's much vaunted flexibility under independence is looking more like a straightjacket for a future Scottish Government. It may help to make independence sound less threatening to the financial markets, but there is little for those who argue that an independent Scotland should break away from the neo-liberal orthodoxy.

Extended devolution

The Scotland Act 2012 does give the Scottish Parliament significant new fiscal powers, albeit with significant constraints. These include: a Scottish income tax to replace part of the UK income tax; the devolution of stamp duty land tax and landfill tax; the power to create or devolve other taxes to the Scottish Parliament; new borrowing powers (although only a consultation on bonds); and a Scottish cash reserve to manage fluctuations in devolved tax receipts. In addition, we already have the council tax and business rates. The UK Government uses this Act to demonstrate the flexibility of devolution. As Scotland Office Minister, David Mundell MP, put it 'The devolution settlement is capable of change when the case is made as the Scotland Act 2012 delivered by this government has shown. So it is simply wrong to characterise the referendum as a choice between change and no change. By changing and adapting the devolution settlement will continue to deliver the best of both worlds for Scotland. Independence would end it.'[15]

There are three main proposals for extended devolution other than the Red Paper. Firstly, we have Devo Max,[16] the proposition that all revenues would be raised in Scotland and the cost of reserved services would be paid to London out of these revenues. The mechanisms for this have been set out in some detail but there is limited evidence that having greater fiscal autonomy policy is beneficial to economic growth. In addition, this model in full is untested anywhere in the world and, therefore, there must be a real risk of unintended consequences. Perhaps more importantly, it has no political backers since the SNP ended its flirtation with a second referendum question.

Next we have Devo Plus.[17] This concept proposes that most revenues would be raised in Scotland to pay for devolved services, with VAT and NI retained at UK level to pay for reserved services. Again, the mechanisms have been worked out in some detail based on the concept of a 'moral hazard' when parliaments spend but don't raise revenue. This leads to their attempt to match income and expenditure at every level of government in an unnecessary and overly complex mechanism.[18] What is less clear is the purpose of this devolution. For that we need to look at the authors' (Reform Scotland) objectives that are apparently the, 'traditional Scottish principles of limited government, diversity and personal responsibility'. Translated, this means small state, privatisation and blaming the poor!

Finally, we have the new entrant on the block, Devo-More[19] from the respected think tank IPPR. Their first paper focuses on fiscal devolution and sets out similar mechanisms to those argued in the first Red Paper. The analysis rightly highlights the impact the Block

Grant approach has on different public service approaches in Scotland, rather than the 'moral hazard' case that underpins Devo Plus. However, this is only part of the story. We also need additional powers for Parliament to allow for significant redistribution of wealth within Scotland and greater control over the economy by working people.

In summary, none of the above proposals meets our key test of devolution - will it create a more equal society?

Towards a different fiscal approach

If we look at other European countries that devolve fiscal powers, taxes on income are the most popular, followed by property and then taxes on consumption. The Scotland Act 2012 already gives Scotland significant powers over income tax and many property taxes are already devolved. Consumption taxes, primarily VAT, are difficult to devolve because EU rules generally do not allow variations within nation states. Whatever taxes are devolved, there has to be some mechanism through grants or borrowing to address volatility in tax revenues.

At present, the revenue from devolved taxes in Scotland is one of the lowest in Europe at 13.8 per cent, just over £4bn. After the Scotland Act 2012 is implemented that will rise to 30.8 per cent, just over £9bn. This will put Scotland in the same league as Germany and Sweden, with one of the most devolved tax revenues in Europe. However, because a Scottish Government can't vary the rate in each band, any increase in income tax is not as progressive as we would wish. There is a growing consensus around the full devolution of income tax including the interim report of Scottish Labour's Devolution Commission.[20]

In this context, the Red Paper fiscal mechanisms might look like this:

❑   Devolve all property-based taxes. They already largely will be after the Scotland Act 2012 is implemented. I am agnostic on adding inheritance tax, given the modest amount it raises but logically this should be included.
❑   Income tax fully devolved. Partial devolution doesn't make a lot of sense. This could include NI as the link with contributory benefits, while important to retain, is becoming increasingly weak. Parliament needs to consider the full impact of changes on personal taxation and the current cap is anything but progressive.
❑   Business taxes should remain at UK level for the reasons I set out above when addressing the SNP's Laffer curve economics. Tax competition is wrong in principle and, in any case, will be constrained by tightening EU rules in this field.
❑   Consumption taxes (primarily VAT) largely at UK level because the EU rules do not allow variable rates in the same state. There is a stronger policy element to fuel duty, tobacco and alcohol taxes, but given the integrated nature of the UK, it is hard to see how these could be set differently in Scotland. Unless, the aim is to promote the sales of white vans!

Taxation is not the only power we should consider. The Scotland Act 2012 gives the Scottish Government new borrowing powers and there is a UK Government consultation on bond issuance. However, again these are very limited, both in method and amount, with the Treasury orthodoxy insisting on central government's right to control overall state finances. This is a crucial issue for Scotland and it is essential that Scotland gets wider borrowing powers. The only restriction should be prudential i.e. whether Scotland can finance the cost of borrowing from revenue. This power already exists for local government; therefore it seems absurd that devolved administrations should not have similar powers. With such flexibility, we could finally get rid of the huge cost of Public Private Partnership/Private Finance Initiative schemes by giving prudential borrowing powers to Health Boards, Non-department Public Bodies and public corporations, such as Scottish Water.

While this chapter focuses on fiscal powers, we should not ignore the devolution of other powers based on the principle of subsidiarity. The UNISON Scotland publication, Fairer Scotland and Devolution,[21] is the first to give serious consideration to this issue in the constitutional debate. There is little purpose in having fiscal powers if the other policy levers are retained unnecessarily at Westminster.

With the focus of debate on independence and extended devolution, we should not lose sight of the value of fiscal solidarity across the UK. Allocating resources on the basis of need happens in other European countries using mechanisms such as shared taxation, hypothecated spending and equalisation mechanisms. Even under greater fiscal devolution there will still need to be a balancing mechanism. Greater fiscal autonomy must still allow for resource transfer to areas of need across the UK. In particular, we need to recognise where real economic power lies on these islands and even under independence, it isn't here in Scotland. This is because Scotland operates in a global market dominated by the Washington Consensus. On tax, this means promoting falling income tax rates, low corporation tax, higher consumption taxes, low taxes on wealth, tax simplification (including flat tax) and creating tax competition with a race to the bottom for the rich. In the UK over the last 30 years, this ideology has resulted in UK income tax rates falling from 60 per cent to 45 per cent, and corporation tax from 52 per cent to 22 per cent. VAT has increased from 12.5 per cent to 20 per cent, tax havens encouraged through a 5.5 per cent tax rate and inheritance tax almost gone. We now have the lowest number of HMRC staff ever, creating a tax gap of some £130bn.

If Scotland had these fiscal powers we then need to give consideration to how we might use them differently. While this would be a chapter in itself, a key issue is recognising that we can't have Scandinavian levels of public services without higher levels of taxation. Stephen Boyd at the STUC has taken a closer look at Nordic models of taxation[22] and there are some interesting, and complex, lessons as to how aggregate tax levels can be raised. Paul Johnson from IFS[23] has also highlighted the more even income spread in Scotland that makes tax redistribution more challenging. This possibly places more emphasis on the role of wages or 'pre-distribution' as Ed Miliband describes it.

Equally important is how tax is used, not just to create a more equal society, but also to develop a more productive economy.

For all the debate around fiscal powers, we need to return to the question of what we want these powers for. Fiscal policy should support the creation of a more equal society that allocates resources to tackle poverty through progressive taxation and welfare support. The role of business is to pay taxes, provide decent jobs and social sustainability in return for state support, while the state promotes collective ownership and management of the means of production.

Many will remain sceptical, based on experience since devolution, whether further fiscal devolution will significantly improve the governance of Scotland. Political will remains more important than mechanisms. However, these proposals could provide the fiscal levers to deliver the wider ideas set out by comrades in this book as well as the funding and redistribution of wealth to create a better and more equal society.

Endnotes

1. Fiscal Commission Working Group First Report - Macroeconomic Framework, February 2013.
2. See note 1.
3. Recommendation 19 - Fiscal Commission Working Group First Repor,t 2013.
4. See note 3.
5. GERS: http://www.scotland.gov.uk/Topics/Statistics/Browse/Economy/GERS.
6. Finance Committee: Demographic change and an ageing population, February 2013.
7. CPPR, Measuring an Independent Scotland's economic performance, April 2013, http://www.gla.ac.uk/media/media_275906_en.pdf.
8. Professor Goudie, A., Scotland's Future: the economics of constitutional change, DUP, March 2013.
9. HM Treasury, Scotland analysis: Currency and monetary policy, https://www.gov.uk/government/publications/scotland-analysis-currency-and-monetary-policy.
10. Professor Kay, J. Scotland's Future: the economics of constitutional change, DUP, March 2013.
11. National Institute Economic Social Research, paper presented to Future of Scotland and UK conference, April 2013.
12. Reid Foundation, The Mismanagement of Britain: A record of the UK's declining competitiveness and its implications, April 2013.
13. Watson, D., Corporation Tax and Independence: http://unisondave.blogspot.co.uk/2013/03/corporation-tax-and-independence.html.
14. Scotsman, quoting BBC Scotland interview on 8 February 2013.
15. Launch of Scotland analysis series, Devolution and the implications of Scottish independence', February 2013.
16. Hughes Hallet and Scott, Scotland: A New Fiscal Settlement
http://www.st-andrews.ac.uk/CDMA/papers/wp1009.pdf.
17. http://www.devoplus.com/.
18. I covered this in more detail in an article in the Scotsman (Perspective, 21 December 2012), http://redpaper.net/2013/01/09/devo-plus-for-a-purpose/
19. Trench, A., Funding Devo-More: http://www.ippr.org/publication/55/10210/funding-devo-more-fiscal-options-for-strengthening-the-union.
20. Scottish Labour Devolution Commission, Powers for a purpose - strengthening devolution, April 2013.
21. UNISON Scotland, Fairer Scotland and Devolution, http://www.unison-scotland.org.uk/scotlandsfuture/FairerScotlandDevoPaperFeb2013.pdf.

22. Boyd, S. Scotland and Nordics, http://stucbetterway.blogspot.co.uk/2013/04/scotland-and-nordics-part-1-tax.html.

23. Institute of Fiscal Studies, paper presented to Future of Scotland and UK conference, April 2013, www.esrc.ac.uk/scotland.

POWERS FOR POLITICAL CHANGE
Pauline Bryan

The world, it is said, is getting smaller and that we are all part of a global village. Local cultures are being subsumed into a worldwide culture including food, fashion, communication and even speech patterns.

Peter Dicken describes those who adopt what he believes is the majority opinion as 'hyper globalists'. According to him they argue 'That we live in a borderless world in which the "national" is no longer relevant. In such a world, "globalization" is the new economic (as well as political and cultural) order. It is a world where nation-states are no longer significant actors or meaningful economic units and in which consumer tastes and cultures are homogenized and satisfied through the provision of standardized global products created by global corporations with no allegiance to place or community. Thus, the "global" is claimed to be the natural order, an inevitable state of affairs, in which time-space has been compressed, the "end of geography" has arrived and everywhere is becoming the same.'[1]

The world has, however, gained 34 new nation states in the past 22 years, most of them in Europe and there may be more to follow, perhaps even Scotland. Many of these recent states have claimed a specific national identity based on all or some of history, language, religion and ethnicity. We appear to have simultaneously a reduction in differences and an increase in demands for self-determination based on differences.

The demands for autonomy in Scotland and Catalonia while receiving most attention are not alone. In Spain there are the two other 'historic nationalities', Basque and Galician, as well as the 14 other autonomous communities. Belgium is perhaps the most divided population in Europe, where the Social Democrat parties and some of the trade unions are divided by language. At various times in Italy there has been support for increased federalism from the centre-left and for outright separation from the Northern League (Lega Nord).

These demands for greater autonomy are usually linked with the desire to stay within the European Union. Leanne Wood of Plaid Cymru stated 'The argument for staying part of the EU - certainly with steps to make it more efficient and more responsive to the diverse needs of European regions - are more clear-cut here in Wales than as seen in England. On balance we in Wales would probably prefer to stay put.'[2]

Artur Mas, President of the Generalitat of Catalonia, says 'the wealthy and influential north-eastern region gets a raw funding deal from the central government'. His centre-right Catalan nationalist coalition (CiU) argues a Catalan state would fare better as a member of the EU than a province of Spain.[3]

This demonstrates that demands for self-determination can co-exist with membership of a wider federation and in the case of the EU, one which has less democracy than national governments. In some cases, as shown in the BBC report on Artur Mas, the argument for greater autonomy includes the claim that the region/country is wealthier than other parts of the nation and that independence would enable it to keep more of its own resources. Northern Italy and Scotland share this approach. Regions in southern Spain, southern Italy and Wales have been less keen on independence and argue instead for more powers to be accompanied by guarantees of fiscal equalisation. We do not, currently, hear arguments for independence accompanied by an appeal to the population to be prepared for a reduction in living standards, because it will be worth it to gain recognition of one's national identity.

Scotland and Catalonia share something else. They are described by Keating as being involved in Second Round Reform.[4] Having achieved a degree of autonomy through devolved powers, other powers are identified as essential and meanwhile the claim for full independence continues. It does seem to be the case that the achievement of increased autonomy rarely makes demands for independence go away. Support for the SNP grew significantly after the Scottish Parliament was introduced, and even the other political parties found themselves making the case for more powers, it's fair to say they had not used the powers they already had available to them. Where the devolved Parliament or Assembly lacks fiscal autonomy in the original settlement it is likely that there would be demands for greater powers even without a nationalist movement to spur it on.

If the 2014 referendum in Scotland results in a No vote it is likely that there will be some form of 'national convention' with the Tories, Lib Dems and Labour all making a commitment to further reform. Even before the reforms of the Scotland Act 2012 come into effect we are discussing the next set of reforms, including the Scottish Labour Party's consultation around the 'Powers for a Purpose' proposal to devolve income tax. These piecemeal changes though are unlikely to result in a settlement that will draw a line under constitutional change. It seems that once the process of devolution has started it gathers momentum and the danger is that Scotland and countries in similar positions neglect the politics of vision because the politicians are bogged down in the politics of structure. They are more involved in discussing powers than using powers.

Keating says of Second Round Reform: 'This suggests that constitutional politics will not be a once-in-a-generation phenomenon leading to a period of stability but part of the political mainstream. The question of inter-territorial equity, which is not strictly a constitutional issue, is likely to become even more important but in the absence of agreed principles on how to do it, will also be dealt with by incremental adjustments and compromises.'[5]

One of the penalties of the ongoing preoccupation with the constitution is the formation of broad alliances on either side. 'They usually bring together classes and interest groups which otherwise have little in common with each other or whose aims are mutually antagonistic.'[6] In Scotland we can see that the SNP and particularly the Yes campaign is a broad alliance across the political spectrum, and the referendum has resulted in the 'Better Together' campaign which has the support of the Tories, Lib Dems and Scottish Labour. It takes the politics out of politics.

Is it possible, then, to have a resolution this side of independence? Or is it the case that once you have started along the devolution route it is inevitable that you become stuck in a cycle of demands and concessions where independence is the only escape.

Finding a settled will

STUC and Labour Party in Scotland have through most of their histories supported some form of Home Rule for Scotland. The STUC founded in 1897 first formally adopted a policy of support for a Scottish Parliament in 1914. The Independent Labour Party, which went on to help form the Labour Party, was from its inception in 1893 committed to Home Rule and played a prominent role within the Scottish Home Rule Association. The labour movement demands were for a federal arrangement rather than for independence. The Scottish Home Rule Bill, introduced in 1924, which failed due to insufficient time being allowed for its progress, proposed that the Westminster Parliament had responsibility for the post office, the military, customs, foreign affairs and tax collection. There was to be no reduction in the number of Scottish MPs in the House of Commons, but Scottish Members would abstain from voting on English matters. A joint Exchequer board would allocate finances.

The labour movement's position, unlike the nationalist one, acknowledged the bonds the British working class had forged in two centuries of political struggle and recognised shared class interests over and above the shared interest of living in Scotland. Far from wanting to separate from the English they wanted to join with working people across Britain and Ireland in creating a socialist alternative. While campaigning for the devolution of powers, the early pioneers adopted internationalism as their ideal. They wanted devolution of power so that they could tackle poverty, poor housing, inadequate public services and industrial closures and not for its own sake.

Now that we have the Scottish Parliament, Welsh and Northern Irish Assemblies we have the basis for a federal arrangement with power devolved within the UK, but with the strength of a single Parliament dealing with macroeconomic issues and international relations. This dual approach allows variations in policy within the constituent parts, but can provide the combined strength to operate within the global economy.

Can federalism win support?

In the first few decades after the Second World War, the German recovery was enhanced by its federal system:

> given the considerable diversity of the West German Länder in size, problem loads, economic prosperity and fiscal and administrative capacity, political demands and a constitutional mandate to create 'equal living conditions' were accommodated not only by a fiscal regime of shared income and turnover taxes and ever more perfectionist vertical and horizontal 'fiscal equalization' transfers, but also by the institutionalization of an elaborate system of jointly financed and jointly planned programmes...[7]

Partit del Socialistes de Catalunya (PSC) has adopted support for a federal solution to the demands for Catalonian independence. This has put it at odds with the national Partido Socialista Obrero Español (PSOE). In February 2013 the Spanish Parliament debated petitions for the Spanish Government to enter into discussions over the future of Catalonia. The PSOE remained firmly opposed to Catalonia's right to self-determination and voted against while the PCS accepted Catalonia's right to self-determination even though they oppose Catalonia's independence from Spain. After the massive 1.5 million strong demonstration in Barcelona in support of independence, the PSC General Secretary, Pere Navarro, asked the PSOE to embrace federalism and work for a reformulation of the Spanish state.

We do not have to look so far afield to find an advocate of federalism. In Scotland generally, and in the Scottish Labour Party in particular, little attention is given to what is being said in Wales. As a result we are missing some important ideas. Carwyn Jones the Leader of Scottish Labour's sister Party and First Minister of the Welsh Assembly has been considerably more thoughtful on the future of the UK than we have seen from the Labour Party leadership in Scotland.

In a speech given in Cardiff in March 2012 he stated 'We are on the brink of huge constitutional change in the UK. There is a strong case for reforming our central institutions to reflect the emerging reality of a looser UK....The UK has changed beyond recognition over the past 15 years and it is time that our constitution recognised this.'[8] Reiterating his earlier call for a Constitutional Convention he said the future of the UK should be considered in the round and not, as it has been, nation by nation in a piecemeal fashion. He described the present constitutional set-up as 'an incremental asymmetric quasi-federation' that was far from satisfactory. 'The UK has changed and the constitution needs to catch up.'[9]

He has restated Tam Dalyell's 'West Lothian Question' as 'the Bridgend Question', referring to the anomaly in which MPs from Wales and Scotland can vote on English domestic affairs, while English MPs cannot vote on those same matters in Wales and Scotland. But he also pointed out that the needs of Welsh Agriculture are represented in the EU by an English Minister for Agriculture.

However, the First Minister's 'line in the sand' is that there could be no movement on taxation to make the National Assembly more fiscally accountable until the prior issue of funding via the Block Grant was settled satisfactorily. He also recognised the devolution of corporation tax would risk a 'race to the bottom if all the devolved administrations decided to have a bidding war on lowering the rate'.[10]

Carwyn Jones acknowledged that he was unlikely to get a sympathetic hearing from the Prime Minister David Cameron or the Secretary of State Cheryl Gillan, 'But we should at least start the debate', he said, noting that Wales had developed its constitution much faster over the past decade than many people had anticipated.

> In 1999 it would have been thought unlikely that the people of Wales would have supported primary legislative power so emphatically in the referendum last year. At the moment the UK Government has its eyes turned to Scotland. But you cannot solve these problems by looking at just one part of the UK.'[11]

There is, quite rightly, concern that the future of the UK is being decided largely in Scotland when the implications will be felt much wider. John Osmond, from the think tank the Institute of Welsh Affairs, says 'In Wales there is concern that the country is being sidelined in a debate that inevitably tends to focus on an axis between Edinburgh and London.'[12]

At least when we look to Wales we can see that the Welsh Labour Party is using its powers, even though they are more limited than in Scotland, to greater effect. It was first to abolish prescription charges, it has used its powers to end the Private Finance Initiative (PFI) and to reject school league tables.

In March 2013 the First Minister of Wales announced that the Welsh Government had purchased Cardiff Airport. Edwina Hart, Minister for Economy, Science and Transport said: 'The airport is a major piece of economic infrastructure for Wales. I look forward to working in partnership with the workforce at the airport as we develop a high quality service for passengers and create a facility of which Wales can be proud.'[13]

We do not hear the Scottish Labour Party commending such bold policies from Wales, but the First Minister and Leader of the Welsh Labour Party has, however, had to deal with fall-out from Johann Lamont's comments. In the Welsh Assembly he was asked by a Conservative AM to respond to Ms Lamont's criticism of universal free prescriptions being available even to people who earn over £100,000 a year. His response was that means testing would cost more than it would save.

Carwyn Jones is seeking a UK-wide approach to devolution and has called for a Constitutional Convention for the whole of the UK. He states, '…for me, devolution is not about how each of Wales, Scotland and Northern Ireland are separately governed. Rather it is about how the UK is governed, not by one but by four administrations, and which are not in a hierarchical relationship one to another.' He also states 'representatives of all the states should come together and agree amongst themselves what limited range of powers should be conferred "upwards" on the federal authority'.[14]

What democratic federalism could deliver

What might a democratic federalist arrangement mean for Scotland? For a start it would resolve the West Lothian question. Scottish representatives would have the right to vote on issues that impacted on the UK as a whole and on Scotland in particular. They would not have the right to vote on issues that relate only to England or other parts of the UK. It would, however, safeguard the ability to redistribute wealth within the UK and allow the labour movements in the whole of the UK to collaborate in resisting attacks on working people. It would lessen the likelihood of a race to the bottom in making Scotland a low pay, low corporation tax economy that could result from independence. It would reduce the extent of the London-centric nature of the Westminster Parliament which is as damaging to Lancashire as it is to Lanarkshire.

Dave Watson in a previous Red Paper publication made the case for fiscal devolution which, unlike Devo Max and Devo Plus, allows for a progressive approach to taxation.[15] This would give a Scottish Government powers to redistribute wealth within Scotland, but also allow for redistribution within the UK. The power held by the Scottish Parliament could be used more flexibly to create a fairer tax system both nationally and locally that can improve public services and the pay and conditions of public employees and make requirements on private sector employers to pay a living wage.

We should support the extension of the capacity to borrow for capital and revenue purposes that go well beyond the limits set out in the Scotland Act 2012. This should be used to end the Scottish Parliament's dependence on Public-Private Partnership (PPP), PFI or the non-profit distributing model.

A Scottish Parliament should, in appropriate situations, have the right to take land and enterprises into public control. These rights could be used to safeguard jobs and industries or where the best interests of those dependent on the land or the enterprise are in jeopardy.

A Scottish Government should be able to create publicly owned enterprises to rebuild Scotland's industrial base on green technology, renewable and high-value manufacturing;

addressing unemployment black spots and creating a more prosperous future for the people, especially the young people, of Scotland.

The position of England in a federal arrangement would be up to those living in England to decide. I suspect the dominance of London would be felt even more keenly as more powers are exercised in Belfast, Cardiff and Edinburgh. Organisations such as the Hannah Mitchell Foundation, which is seeking 'devolution to local and regional government just like in London, Wales and Scotland', would probably gain support with the growing expectation of representation on a regional basis.[16]

Whatever the ultimate solution for the UK the answer to the real problems facing us all will not be found in constitutional change, but in political change. If we want more local powers, can we use them to create a more equal society and achieve greater democratic control of our economy? For without that we are, at best, rearranging the furniture, and at worst, leaving ourselves even more vulnerable to the grasping power of international capital.

Endnotes

1. Dicken, P. , Global Shift. Mapping the Changing Contours of the World Economy, The Guildford Press: New York, 2011.

2. http://www.huffingtonpost.co.uk/leanne-wood/eu-referendum-wales_b_2551732.html.

3. BBC Europe, 26 November 2012.

4. Keating, M., Second Round Reform. Devolution and Constitutional Reform in UK, Spain and Italy, LSE Europe in Question Discussion Paper Series, 2009.

5. See note 4.

6. Moreno, L., Ethnoterritorial Concurrences and Imperfect Federalism in Spain, Instituto de Estudios Sociales Avanzados (CSIC) Working Paper, 93-1, 1993.

7. Scharpf, F.W., No Exit from the Joint Decision Trap? Can German Federalism Reform Itself?, MPIfG Working Paper 05/8, September 2005.

8. http://www.clickonwales.org/2012/04/wales-and-the-future-of-the-united-kingdom/.

9. See note 8.

10. See note 8.

11. http://www.clickonwales.org/2012/03/carwyn-jones-calls-for-written-constitution.

12. Osmond, J., Federalism, devolution and the breech of British sovereignty, Background paper for the Changing Union Forum Federal Future for the UK, 21-22 September 2012.

13. http://wales.gov.uk/newsroom/firstminister/2013/7232836/?lang=en.

14. http://unlockdemocracy.org.uk/blog/entry/a-constitutional-convention-for-the-uk.

15. Watson, D., Fiscal Implications of Constitutional Change in People Power the Labour Movement Alternative for Radical Constitutional Change, Red Paper Collective 2012.

16. http://www.hannahmitchell.org.uk/blog/.